CIVIL WAR
Quilts

PAMELA WEEKS & DON BELD

SCHIFFER PUBLISHING

4880 Lower Valley Road • Atglen, PA 19310

Cover design by Ashley Millhouse
Type set in NewBskvll BT/Optima/Times

ISBN: 978-0-7643-5888-3
Printed in China

Published by Schiffer Publishing, Ltd.
4880 Lower Valley Road
Atglen, PA 19310
Phone: (610) 593-1777; Fax: (610) 593-2002
E-mail: Info@schifferbooks.com
Web: www.schifferbooks.com

For our complete selection of fine books on this and related subjects, please visit our website at www.schifferbooks.com. You may also write for a free catalog.

Schiffer Publishing's titles are available at special discounts for bulk purchases for sales promotions or premiums. Special editions, including personalized covers, corporate imprints, and excerpts, can be created in large quantities for special needs. For more information contact the publisher.

We are always looking for people to write books on new and related subjects. If you have an idea for a book, please contact us at proposals@schifferbooks.com

Templates printed from EQ7

To the men and women
who serve in our Armed Forces,
and to their families who serve
beside them in war and peace. —*Don Beld*

To the thousands of women who,
during the Civil War, held jobs,
held families and farms together,
held their worlds together,
and still found time to produce goods
for soldiers on the field and in hospitals. —*Pamela Weeks*

CONTENTS

CIVIL WAR QUILTS

QUILTS TO MAKE TODAY

PREFACE

Donald Beld contacted me somewhere around 2009, wanting information about potholder quilts, which are a form of quilt as you go (QAYG) and are made block by block. Several of the quilts made for Civil War soldiers are constructed this way, and Don heard I was studying these rare and unusual quilts. One of Don's passions was American Civil War quilts, and for years he visited the Lincoln Shrine in Redlands, California, to study the Vernon, Connecticut, quilt, which bears the stamp of the US Sanitary Commission. At some point he was contacted by Debbie Knapp, who owned a quilt believed to have been made for Civil War soldiers' use, and it was made in potholder style. Don wanted to pick my brain about this unusual way to make a quilt. Over a year or more we had many conversations and eventually agreed that we should combine our efforts to produce this book. I was working on the history and researching some of the soldiers' quilts, and Don was light-years ahead of me in making examples and collecting Civil War stories related to quilting.

The original intent of the book was to include only quilts made for Civil War soldiers, fleshing it out with information on quiltmaking and women's benevolent work in the nineteenth century, and to provide instructions for today's quilters to use for creating quilts inspired by the originals. We soon found other intriguing quilts and stories related to the Civil War, such as a quilt made for a specific soldier by his mother (see page 58). It represents several quilts that survived the war, treasured by the soldiers for whom they were made. Also included are the family history represented by the Pratt Family quilt and Don's study of the history of the Medal of Honor. He made a potholder quilt with a block for every recipient since the first such medal was awarded during the Civil War, so the story of the first recipient is contained here as well.

Shortly after the first edition of *Civil War Quilts* was published, I was invited by Jamie Franklin, curator of the Bennington Museum in Bennington, Vermont, to examine the Jane Stickle quilt, and to dig a little deeper into the background of the quilt and its maker. Thanks to a book written by Brenda Manges Papadakis in 1996, it is perhaps one of the most famous quilts made during the American Civil War. Her pattern book, containing some of Jane's history and Brenda's

patterns for reproducing the quilt, has sold more than 100,000 copies. Quilters all over the world continue to make quilts ranging from copies as close to the original as one can get with reproduction fabrics, to those made with bright modern batiks or an original arrangement of some of Jane's unusual block patterns. The research is an ongoing team effort, and the results of this recent work are contained in a chapter here.

Despite knowing the conditions of the battlefield and hospital, it is astonishing to consider that we currently know of fewer than twenty Northern soldiers' quilts. It is our hope that more will come out of the woodwork after this book is published, and the four-year sesquicentennial of the Civil War brings these objects to wider public attention.

We have permission to publish fifteen of these very rare quilts to illustrate the period in which they were made. These quilts tell stories about soldiers, their mothers, their sweethearts, and their wives. The stories include the organizations formed to relieve the suffering of the wounded on the battlefield, to improve hospital conditions, and to ease the soldier's trip from hospital to home. The stories are about local neighborhoods, women's groups, and individuals, all striving to assist the cause of preserving the Union, and their legacies are the quilts that survived.

We limited our stories to quilts made in the North for two reasons: first, it's where one of the authors lives, close to primary sources—visiting the towns where the quiltmakers lived, and seeing their neighborhoods and their graves, fills out the stories for us and makes them more complete. And second, it's where the majority of the surviving Civil War quilts for soldiers were made. Very few that we know of survive in the South, and the authors argued about whether to include them!

There is great interest among today's quilters to reproduce quilts from the Civil War era. Many contemporary patterns are available, but to us these modern patterns and quilts are romanticized versions of the quilts that were actually made. The quilts pictured here are utilitarian, made for everyday use in hospitals and camps. They are generally not fancy quilts; in some cases they were put together quickly but still were meant to give comfort. They share the characteristic of bearing inscriptions, with the exception of the quilt made by a soldier while recovering from his injuries.

The patterns we include are inspired by the quilts themselves. The block patterns are simple and are still in common use today. The authors did not make actual copies of the quilts but encourage you to do as they did—work from the patterns to create your own version of a Civil War soldier's quilt.

Pamela Weeks
Auburn, New Hampshire

A special thanks goes to:

Bernice Foster for her incredible appliqué and embroidery work on the Eagle Medallion and the Stars & Shield quilt

Members of Citrus Belt Quilters Guild and the dedicated quilters of the Home of the Brave Quilt Project, for their service to our nation's armed forces

Jonathan Strait, photographer at j@jonathanstrait.com, for his photography of Don Beld's quilts

The folks at the Lincoln Memorial Shrine, Redlands, California, who tolerated Don's enthusiasm for their quilt for many years

Barbara Knapp Trust (Ric Knapp, trustee), for permission to include a photograph of the Hingham Sanitary Commission quilt

Debbie Knapp, who came to Don with the Hingham Sanitary Commission quilt in 2007 and has allowed unlimited access to her information

Laura Hobby Syler, Cindy Brick, and Nancy Kirk, who supplied information about the Norridgewock Sanitary Commission quilt

Lynne Bassett, who discovered the Granville, New York, Sanitary Commission quilt just in time for inclusion in the list of Civil War Union soldiers' quilts

The New England Quilt Museum, the Vermont Historical Society, the Montana Historical Society, the Rochester (New York) Historical Society, and the Oklahoma Historical Society for their help with the quilts, the images, and information about the quilters

Doris Bowman, curator of textiles at the National Museum of American History

Grant Fairbanks, great-grandson of Caro and Luke Fairbanks, for sharing his research, images, and family history

Megan Pinette, president, Belfast (Maine) Historical Society

Jane Stickle Crosier, for sharing her research on her great-great-aunt, Jane A. Stickle.

Sherry Massey, senior registrar, Oklahoma Museum of History

Jamie Franklin, curator of collections; Callie Raspuzzi, collections manager; and Tyler Resch, librarian, Bennington Museum, Bennington, Vermont

Kathy D. Duncan, who found Jane and Walter Stickle's wedding announcement, and whose work continues to inform the treasure hunt for information about Jane Blakely Stickle's life

INTRODUCTION

Many towns and states in the North prepared their regiments for war and billed the federal government afterward. Men mustering from Claremont, New Hampshire, assembled for a special ceremony before mounting the train to Concord, and each recruit was presented with a revolver, a knife, a bound pocket Testament, and clothing, from flannel shirts to woolen socks.[1]

The need was great and immediate, and help was forthcoming from households, local provisioners, and groups that formed to provide soldiers' aid. This aid would continue during the Civil War, and by its end it was estimated that many millions of dollars were donated in cash, goods, and foodstuff. Hundreds of thousands of shirts, socks, drawers, and blankets were donated, as well as many thousands of comforters and quilts.[2]

Neither the northern United States nor the southern Confederate States were ready for a prolonged conflict at the start of the American Civil War in April 1861. The governments of both sides were not prepared for the immediate muster of tens of thousands of soldiers who needed uniforms, boots, shelter, and bedding. Men were so enthusiastic to enlist that they left home with just the clothes on their backs, expecting to be provisioned at the recruitment centers.

Historian Virginia Gunn estimates, in her seminal 1985 article in *Uncoverings*, that more than 250,000 quilts were made for soldiers' aid during the American Civil War.[3] The first section in this book includes some of those quilts made to be donated to the general relief efforts by individuals or groups. Current documentation shows that these soldiers' quilts were used in the field, in hospitals, or perhaps to raise funds to meet soldiers' needs.

Many men who enlisted in the excitement of the first few weeks of the war left home with little more on their backs than the recruit pictured here. Sketch of a Civil War soldier from *Frank Leslie's Illustrations: The Soldier in Our Civil War*.

Standard equipment for Union soldiers included a rifle with bayonet and ammunition, a haversack for food and necessities, a canteen for carrying water, a blanket, and a vulcanized-rubber blanket used as a ground cover. One soldier partnered with another, and each carried one-half of a tent, his equipment, food, and water for two to three days. If he was lucky, he had an extra shirt, footings (stockings), and drawers (underwear). Winter conditions required heavy woolen topcoats and mittens—if he could get them. Because the government often couldn't provide the soldier's needs, clothing and supplies were requested from home.

At the outset of the war, women in both the North and South responded immediately and independently by sending food, clothing, and bedding to their family members, neighbors, and townsmen in the military. Families packed up and shipped what was at hand. Shipping depots, military headquarters, and regiments were swamped with donations. Some of the supplies were needed, but a large amount was inappropriate and sometimes misdirected. Letters traveling from soldiers to home bearing requests took days to arrive, and the responses, many days more, rendering them useless. Boxes and barrels were lost, some were stolen, and many simply couldn't catch up to the mobile units. Too often, jars of preserves or meat were not packed correctly and, when they broke, spoiled the contents of the box or barrel. Tons of goods were misdirected or sent to regiments that were already well supplied.

The chaos created by this patriotic, enthusiastic outpouring to fill the soldiers' needs required direction, and there was also a need to organize the many untrained women who leaped to volunteer as nurses. In a series of informal meetings, Dr. Elizabeth Blackwell and others resolved to form an organization to meet these needs. Refused by American medical schools, Blackwell had trained in Europe and was a friend of Florence Nightingale, who revolutionized the care of wounded on the battlefield and the military hospital system in Europe during the Crimean War. Blackwell understood what was ahead for the United States military in the war.[4]

The numbers of concerned citizens grew with each meeting in New York City, and on April 25, 1861, a crowd of more than 3,000 enthusiastically voted for the formation of the Woman's Central Association for Relief (WCAR). Dr. Blackwell, with eleven other women and twelve men, was elected to the Board of Management, with many more appointed to committees to oversee the organization's goals.

Originally there were three goals for the Woman's Central Association for Relief. The leaders would coordinate the relief work of existing women's charities and organize more aid societies, they would communicate with the US Army Medical Department to meet the needs of the army, and they would register and train nurses. It was agreed that representatives should be sent to Washington, DC, to promote their ideas to the Lincoln administration.

The Rev. Henry Bellows represented the WCAR in the capitol. There he toured military camps and saw the deplorable conditions that already existed. Bellows met with Dorothea Dix and others in Washington, who eventually convinced him that an organization with a broader scope be formed, a sanitary commission mirroring that of Florence Nightingale in the Crimea in the 1850s.

The United States Sanitary Commission (USSC) was created to provide many forms of aid for soldiers on the battlefield and in camps, hospitals, and prisons, and to channel donated supplies to the areas of greatest need. It would oversee sanitary conditions in camps and hospitals, with the purpose of preventing disease

Sketch of a Civil War soldier from *Philadelphia in the Civil War*

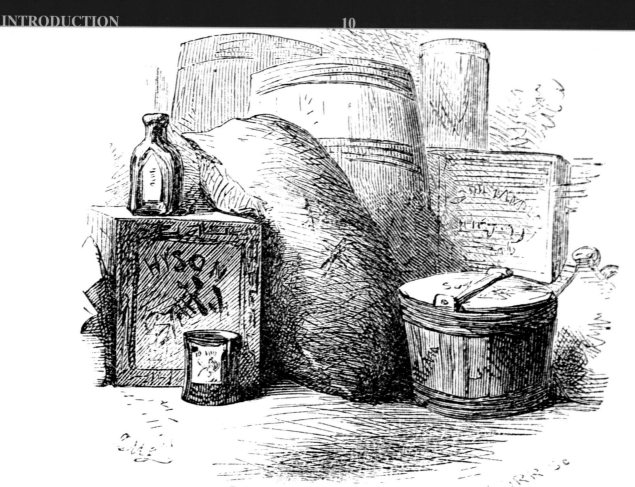

Goods for the front, waiting for shipment. From *The Tribute*

and improving transportation and care of the wounded. On June 9, 1861, the secretary of war approved the creation of a "Commission of Inquiry and Advice in the respect of the Sanitary Interests of the United States Forces."

The USSC fulfilled only one of the three original goals of the WCAR, that of communicating directly with the Army. Dorothea Dix was initially given authority to train and assign nurses, although by the autumn of 1861, that responsibility reverted to a committee of the WCAR, led by Dr. Elizabeth Blackwell.

The WCAR, with offices in New York City, was authorized to organize aid coming from cities, towns, and villages across the North. The WCAR became an auxiliary branch of the USSC, and the leading committee of the WCAR immediately arranged for a notice to go out to the public to explain what was needed for soldiers' aid, how to pack it, and where to send it. Regional offices were established in the New England states, New York, Philadelphia, and other northern cities.

An open letter appeared in thousands of newspapers, addressed to "The Loyal Women of America!" The formation of societies was encouraged, and that they

> devote themselves, for a time, to the sacred service of their country; that energetic and respectable committees be appointed to call from house to house, and store to store, to obtain contributions in materials suitable to be made up, or money for the

Description of Articles Most Wanted

- Blankets for single beds

- Quilts, of cheap material, about seven feet long by fifty inches wide

- Knit Woolen Socks

- Woolen or Cotton Flannel Bed gowns Wrappers, Undershirts, and Drawers

- Small Hair and Feather Pillows and Cushions for wounded Limbs

- Slippers

> purchase of such materials; that collections be made in churches, and schools, and factories, and shops, for the same purpose; that contribution boxes be placed in post-offices, newspaper offices, railroad and telegraph offices, public houses, steamboats and ferry boats, and in all other suitable places, labeled "For Our Sick And Wounded," and that all loyal women meet at such convenient times and places as may be agreed upon in each neighborhood or social circle, to work upon the materials which shall be so procured.[5]

"Our Heroines" from *Harper's Weekly*, April 9, 1864. This illustration by Thomas Nast shows women's spheres of service—on the battlefield, in the hospital, at the fair, and in the parlor, respectively nursing, raising money, and producing soft goods for the soldiers.

AID SOCIETIES

Within two weeks of the beginning of the war, more than 20,000 local aid societies had formed around the country, with most of them being in the North. According to Charles Stille in his official report on the activities of the United States Sanitary Commission, written in 1867, more than 7,000 of these northern aid organizations did form as auxiliaries of the Sanitary Commission or changed their focus from general local aid to war aid. Church groups, Sunday school classes, literary societies, groups of friends, and classes of school children raised money to buy materials and gathered to make items to send to the soldiers.[6]

Alert clubs, comprising men, women, and children, organized to collect money, no matter how little, from every citizen in their towns. Children held fund raisers in their front yards; young men and women canvassed their neighborhoods for dimes—not a small sum in the 1860s; and businesses pledged hundreds and thousands of dollars for the purchase of equipment, materials and food supplies.

In *The Tribute Book*, Frank Goodrich gives credit for the first two soldiers' aid societies forming in Bridgeport, Connecticut, on the fifteenth of April 1861. The Bunker Hill Aid Society in Charlestown, Massachusetts, met on the same day, but the vote to make them formally a soldiers' aid society did not take place until the nineteenth. In Lowell, Massachusetts, the mayor called on all residents to initiate "measures for the comfort, encouragement, and relief of citizen soldiers."

In Cleveland, Ohio, the soldiers' aid society was organized on the twentieth of April for the same purposes and also to provide funds for "the temporary support of the families of three months' men." Three months was the term of enlistment for the first round of volunteers at the start of the war. It was generally accepted that the war would be short in duration.[7]

FAIR UPON A DOOR-STEP.

"Fair upon a Doorstep" was one activity in which children could raise money to donate to the cause. *The Tribute Book.*

The US Sanitary Commission stamp from the Vernon, Connecticut, quilt. The quilts with USSC stamps from New York and Connecticut bear this version.

The US Sanitary Commission stamp from the Brandon, Vermont, quilt. The quilts with USSC stamps from northern New England bear this version.

OFFICE OF A SOLDIERS' AID SOCIETY.

Office of a soldiers' aid society. *The Tribute Book.*

Two of the soldiers' quilts included herein were made by individuals, and they were signed only by their makers. Fourteen of the quilts were group efforts, and the wide range of inscriptions and variations in penmanship indicate the work of many hands. Either the inscriptions or the provenance of at least four of these quilts indicates the formal names of the groups who made the quilts. Two were Ladies' Soldiers' Aid Societies; one, a group of Sunday school scholars; and the fourth, a patriotic society.

As to style, the majority of these Civil War quilts have one-pattern repeating blocks of simple construction, such as Nine Patch and Puss in the Corner. Four are variety quilts, a common style for inscribed quilts, with a wide range of block patterns. One is a medallion quilt, its pattern taken from the issue of *Peterson's Magazine* published in August 1861.

Block sizes range from 7½ inches square in a quilt with ninety-three blocks to 18 inches square in a quilt with twenty blocks. Three of the quilts were made with a larger central block containing either a Union shield or a flag, and three more have patriotic blocks with stars, flags, eagles, and the Union shield. The makers of a fourth quilt achieved a central focus by the placement of nine blocks containing red, white, and blue fabrics. All but three of the quilts employ a wide range of scrap fabrics in the piecing or appliqué.

The sewing machine was in common use by the Civil War, as shown by this detail from an illustration in *Harper's Weekly*, September 6, 1862.

Three of the Civil War quilts include one or more blocks that are machine quilted, and at least one also contains machine piecing and machine appliqué. Sewing machines became commercially available during the decade before the war, and women who owned them put them to use in their relief efforts. There are several accounts of women bringing sewing machines to Ladies' Soldiers' Aid Society meetings.[8]

All but three of the fifteen quilts made for Civil War soldiers are inscribed with dates. The earliest was completed in 1861 and the latest in February 1865. Three quilts are inscribed with both start and finish dates, which indicate that one quilt took a few weeks to complete, a second one six months, and the third a full year.

INSCRIBED QUILTS

Inscribed quilts, also called signature or album quilts, were popular in the United States before and during the Civil War. In a study of inscribed quilts, Barbara Brackman found examples ranging from the late 1830s to the present, with the peak in popularity between 1840 and 1865.[9] The majority of surviving quilts known to be made for soldiers' use are inscribed quilts, with persons' names, dates, and place-names written on patches in the blocks. Inscribed quilts carry meaning even when the purpose for their construction is lost. In the late nineteenth and early twentieth centuries, people to whom the inscribed quilts passed would understand the value of the signatures, even if they didn't know the signers or why the quilt was made. They would have understood the importance of the dates inscribed during the Civil War, so these quilts were saved.

The inscriptions on nineteenth-century quilts range from just a first name, or a simple sentiment such as "Remember Me," to elaborately embellished cartouches surrounding Bible verses, entire poems, names with titles, and cities, states, and dates. Inked roses, animals, figures, birds, and buildings ornament some blocks. Riddles, health advice, and dedications are found on others.

When a friendship quilt includes names and places, historians have important information to use and can sometimes determine when and why a quilt was made. Genealogical research can reveal family relationships. When place-names are included, town histories may explain who were considered the important citizens. Better still are the quilts that have dedications inscribed—so much more is known when a quilt states something like "For Mrs. French, from the Young Ladies of the Society, January 8, 1855, Hudson, New Hampshire." Research will tell us about Mrs. French, the young ladies (each of whom signed a block), and the society that was a group organized with a purpose.

Many authors have written about inscribed quilts— Jessica Nicoll states that they were made to "reify" or make real a community important to the makers.[10] The community named in the signatures on the surface of the quilt might be defined as narrowly as a family or circle of friends, or as wide as a church congregation, neighborhood, or town.

Inscribed quilts frequently represent the work of a group for a particular purpose. In some cases, the blocks are signed by the individuals who made them; in others, individuals made blocks that were signed by others.

Some inscribed quilts are *presentation* quilts, created as a gift for a particular recipient. Within the private sphere of friends or family, many presentation quilts were made for an event such as a wedding or for a westward departure. In the public sphere, presentation quilts were made by church congregations to honor ministers, by students and their parents in gratitude to teachers, or by various self-defined communities, whether local or dispersed, as a token of respect for a prominent person.

Some inscribed quilts may be classified as *friendship* quilts. In these cases, a group of friends agree to make a number of blocks to share, so that each participant receives blocks from everyone in the group. Alternatively, an individual may issue a request for quilt blocks of specified size, colors, or pattern. Whether the quilts resulting from these blocks are then

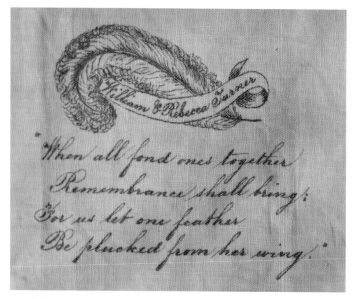

Detail, inscribed quilt with elaborate inscriptions.
Quilt in the collection of K. Triplett; photograph by Pamela Weeks

verses, riddles, proverbs, line drawings, and literary quotations. The Civil War quilts contain health advice and Bible or patriotic verses meant to encourage and inspire soldiers to continue the fight with courage.

POTHOLDER QUILTS

Of the fifteen known Civil War quilts made for soldiers' use, eleven are "potholder" quilts. Potholder quilts are made one block at a time, and each block is finished as it is made—any block from a potholder quilt could stand alone as a finished one-block quilt. To anyone who has participated in the creation of a group quilt, whether for presentation or fundraising, the advantage of potholder construction becomes immediately obvious. Instead of sewing unfinished blocks together to make a top, then layering, quilting, and binding the whole quilt, potholder blocks can simply be sewn together to complete the quilt. We can speculate that many potholder quilts were made for soldiers because they were easier to make as a group

completed individually or with the help of the group, each block becomes a document of the circle of friends or individuals who gathered to organize the project.

When an inscribed quilt is a true signature quilt, also called an autograph quilt, the blocks are signed by their makers and the signatures vary block to block. All but two of the inscribed Civil War quilts presented in this book are signature quilts, with many different people participating in the project of making a quilt to donate to the cause.

Some nineteenth-century inscribed quilts functioned as *fundraisers* for various groups and causes. A small quilt in the collection of Historic New England is the earliest one documented to raise money for a cause; it was auctioned at an 1836 antislavery fair in Boston. Later in the nineteenth century, it was typical for a sponsoring group to collect donations from individuals whose names were then inscribed on the quilt. The resulting quilt was auctioned or raffled to raise additional funds, and then perhaps it was presented to a significant individual, taking on a secondary presentation function.

Although not yet proven, it is possible that three of the Civil War soldiers' quilts were used for fundraising. One is considerably larger than would fit a soldier's cot, and the other two are embroidered and appliquéd with silk, an inappropriate choice of materials for a hospital or camp quilt. Perhaps further research will tell us whether these quilts served in field or hospital, or in meetings of aid societies, or hung at lectures to inspire donors. All were made after October 1863, the date of the only large fundraising fair held in Portland yet to be documented.[11]

The Civil War Union soldiers' quilts had other functions: to entertain, encourage, and comfort. As with the general body of inscribed quilts, they include such data as complete or partial names, place-names, and dates. Some quilts also contain personal messages, Bible

Detail, quilt constructed block by block, 1863.
Collection of Pamela Weeks; photograph by David Bohl

project. The organizer chose a block's size, sometimes dictated a particular pattern, and asked that a certain number of signed blocks be made by the group.

The popularity of potholder quilts during the mid-nineteenth century paralleled that of inscribed quilts and encompassed the years of the American Civil War, 1861 to 1865. Weeks's research on potholder quilts shows that the majority were made between 1845 and 1865, the same peak in the popularity of inscribed quilts. The same research shows that the potholder quilt-making technique was a regional variation, most probably originating in New England. Of the 150 quilts identified in the larger study, 70 percent were made in New England, with quilts made in Massachusetts and Maine predominating. Of the eleven Civil War potholder quilts, nine are from New England towns and one is from a New York town on the Vermont border. The eleventh Civil War potholder quilt was made in Detroit, Michigan, by women who had moved there from Nantucket, Massachusetts, and maintained their New England family connections.

In contrast with the eight potholder quilts that conform to the specifications of the US Sanitary Commission requesting that the quilts be long and narrow to fit a cot, the remaining three Civil War potholder quilts are noticeably wider and feature a limited, more deliberate fabric selection. All the examples feature appliquéd patriotic and military motifs: stars, shields, military insignia, and flags. The size and elaborate designs of these three quilts suggest that they probably functioned as fundraising quilts (or, alternatively, as visual icons of Union patriotism) rather than for soldiers' use. All three quilts were made in Portland, Maine.

The Civil War quilts served two primary functions: to comfort the soldiers and to raise money or support (or both) for relief efforts. Twelve of the fifteen Civil War soldier quilts were made long and narrow as recommended by the Sanitary Commission bulletin, suggesting that they were made for soldiers' use in the field or in a hospital. These quilts were intended to provide not simply physical comfort but mental, emotional, and spiritual solace as well. All fifteen are inscribed with names, place-names, poetry, patriotic slogans, or Bible verses meant to encourage or comfort the reader.

While the sample of quilts made for Civil War soldiers is small, evidence from the fifteen extant examples suggests some findings. Twelve of the quilts appear to have been made for use by soldiers, and three may have been designed to function publicly in raising funds or other support for war relief. The soldier quilts share the characteristics of size, use of a variety of fabrics, and multiple inscriptions. Most share other physical attributes, including central medallions, binding methods, block sizes, and block patterns. All are inscribed with maker's names, towns, and states. Fourteen were made in New England, or a bordering state, and one was made in Michigan and is inscribed with many New England place-names. With the exceptions of the three Portland, Maine, quilts, they may therefore have been made as the result of requests from Civil War aid organizations, and, accordingly, to their specifications.

All were made to improve conditions for the soldiers, either directly in camps or hospitals or to raise money for war relief. Of the tens of thousands of quilts made for these purposes, these few examples survived both the war itself and its aftermath. No doubt, the presence of inscriptions on these quilts contributed to their survival, while countless others, unmarked, were not singled out for safe keeping.

WHERE ARE THE REST OF THE CIVIL WAR SOLDIERS' QUILTS?

There are two parts to the answer. First, conditions in the camps, battlefields, and hospitals were brutal for soldiers and their possessions. During battles, many possessions were lost as men marched and engaged the enemy. When battle lines shifted, camps were abandoned and everything left behind was lost. When a soldier was killed on the battlefield, his body was often raided and possessions were taken by other soldiers, camp followers, or residents of the area. Thousands of men were wounded, and not everything was carried with them if they were taken to a field hospital or eventually transferred to another hospital. Blood-stained uniforms, bandages, and bedding items were burned when they were damaged beyond cleaning.

Second, quilts that survived the Civil War without documentation of the maker, purpose, or recipient lost their meanings after the men who used and carried them died. A utility quilt that survived a soldier's use during the war may have been of simple pattern and probably was stained from hard use. Imagine a nine-patch scrap quilt, long and narrow, badly stained, worn and torn. There was no label sewn on by the quiltmaker—no name, no date, and no presentation sentiment. Further, imagine the soldier who fought in the Civil War and carried that quilt through the last few months before peace was won. When he came home, if he convinced his wife not to pitch it onto the rag heap, she boiled it to remove the insects and the filth, dried it in the sun, and at his insistence put it away in the trunk with his uniform. Three generations later, the trunk is opened, the uniform removed, and its value is recognized, but what about that ragged old brown-stained quilt—why save that? How many thousands of quilts didn't survive the first step of cleaning when soldiers returned? How lucky we are to have some Civil War soldiers' quilts to inspire our work today. ❦

CIVIL WAR

Civil War

QUILTS

Quilts

Inscribed quilts, also commonly called "signature," "album," or "friendship quilts," are distinguished as having two or more names written on the surface of the quilt. Inscribed quilts quickly became very popular in the mid-nineteenth century.[1] Some historians attach this sudden and widespread appearance of inscribed quilts to the invention, first, of the steel-nibbed dip pen, which gave more control to the writer than was afforded by a feather quill pen. Second was the development of ink that was both fade resistant and free of chemicals that corroded. Payson's Indelible Ink is credited with being the oldest manufactured ink suitable for marking fabric, and it was available by 1834. It was advertised as being the best ink for "marking linen, silk and cotton with a common pen without preparation."

Before writing jumped to quilts, it was popular to invite visiting guests, family, and friends to sign an album book and to add poetry, Bible verses, or other thoughts with names, dates, and place-names. Album books were tangible records of visits, events, and circles of family, friends, or a larger community.

Inscribed quilts came to represent these same thoughts, but on fabric that was sewn into a quilt to be used on a bed and cherished for generations. Inscribed quilts were a widespread fad, and their importance was well appreciated by all members of a household, women and men alike. An album quilt was an important piece of history for its owner, whether made by friends, neighbors, or a wider community.

After 1840, cast-metal marking stamps were available for marking household linens and were also used to "sign" quilts. Many have fancy oval cartouches with a blank slot running horizontally across the center. The stamping kit included printer's type with which to spell a person's name, and these were held in place in the horizontal slot with a thumbscrew. Some stamps are simple, with a short, round wooden handle; others are mounted on a cast-metal stand and have a spring-plunger action. The disadvantage in this method is the need to mask the fabric from the possible imprint left by the feet of the stamp.

Inscribed Quilts

Detail, autograph album, Dover, New Hampshire, 1848.
Collection of Pamela Weeks

Nineteenth-century homemakers and quilters had many ways to mark linens and inscribe quilts, including stenciling, stamping, and inking. Note the circular linen stretcher that holds the cloth in place for writing. *Items in the collection of Stephanie Hatch; photograph by Pamela Weeks*

Elaborately inscribed block from a quilt in the collection of K. Triplett. *Photograph by Pamela Weeks*

Album quilt, constructed block by block, possibly organized by Rebecca A. Sibley, Boston, 1865. Cotton (87.5" × 58.5"). *Collection of New England Quilt Museum, Lowell, Massachusetts (2004.17); photograph by David Stansbury*

Stenciling was another way that personal belongings, as well as quilts, were marked. Indelible ink was pounced through a brass or nickel die-cut stencil plate with a short-bristled brush. Ink could also be applied by making a pounce of leather or a ball of stuffed cotton fabric, though these would soak up much ink and be less accurate for applying a controlled amount of ink.

Although both stencils and stamps were available for marking quilts, the majority of inscribed quilts were inked. At the least, there are initials; often a name and date and sometimes place-names are added, including town and state. Others have multiple inscriptions on each block and display elaborate inking, with flags, banners, and soldiers included in the images.

All the surviving Civil War soldiers' quilts are inscribed, and they probably survive because of this. They were cherished by the soldiers who received them—representing comfort and a token of home. They were made by individuals or groups of people wanting to send messages of encouragement, common sense, patriotism, and faith to those serving in the war.

Some of the Civil War soldiers' quilts remained in the families of the soldiers who received them. A quilt in the collection of the New England Quilt Museum was made in Boston, Massachusetts (*see at right*), and before its donation to the museum passed through the hands of several generations of descendants of James George. George volunteered for the 76th Regiment of the New York infantry and served as a private in Company H. He served with his company for nearly three years, fighting at Gettysburg and Fredericksburg, but was captured at the Battle of the Wilderness in May 1864. He was imprisoned at Andersonville for about six months, then released. He may have received the quilt while convalescing in a hospital in Washington, DC, during February 1865, or some other time before he was mustered out in June 1865.[2]

James George's quilt was probably organized by Rebecca Avis Benedict Sibley. It is a potholder quilt, composed of thirty-five pieced cotton blocks individually bound with straight-of-the-grain cotton strips. The blocks

Back of the Sibley Album Quilt, showing the block-by-block construction technique. *Photograph by David Stansbury*

are whip-stitched together from the back. The blocks were made and collected between February 22, 1864, and February 9, 1865, as indicated in an inscription. Although there are thirty-five blocks, there are only seven signers, but the handwriting on several unsigned blocks is the same on blocks bearing signatures. That, and evidence of the same fabrics repeated in the piecing, binding, and backing of several blocks, indicates that some of the makers may have contributed several blocks each. The inscriptions include original poetry, health advice, or Bible verses, and some of the blocks (attributed to R. A. Sibley) display inked pictures of soldiers, a tent, and what appears to be a family or a farm scene, with children gathered around a butter churn.

Rebecca Sibley was born in Rhode Island on October 7, 1812, the third of twelve children. Her father, the reverend doctor David Benedict, was a graduate of Brown University, an ordained Baptist minister, and author of several histories of the Baptist Church in America and of the history of religion that were published in the early nineteenth century.[3]

In 1834 she married Rodney Sibley, who is listed as a clerk in the 1850 census, but as a Boston physician in the 1860 Boston census roll. The censuses of 1850 and 1860 indicate that their household was large, with as many as twenty members—composed of the Sibleys, their children, and several clerks, salesmen, relatives, and domestics. Further research may reveal that the Sibleys were either engaged in business or operated a boardinghouse. The 1860 census includes a student of medicine.[4]

Detail of the Sibley Album Quilt, with inscription and inked drawing. *Photo by David Stansbury*

Rebecca was fifty-three when the quilt was made, and the mother of four children, one a son of an age to serve in the war. She signed several of the blocks and provided the most-patriotic ones, piecing red, white, and blue stars and stripes. One of her striped autographed blocks contains these inscriptions:

> Beat the Rebels, make them run
> Then they'll find it not all fun,
> For the Yankees do agree
> To fight, until the Negro's free.
>
> If you are wounded, sick and sad
> Look to God—he'll make you glad.
> He will hear your humble plea,
> Therefore unto Jesus flee.

> And if to battle you hear the call
> Pray to God; you may not fall.
> But face the foe and stand up right
> Never run, but always fight.
>
> Soldier you have left your home
> in the distant states to roam
> Trust in God and look above,
> He will keep you, God is love.
>
> A true friend to the soldier,
> R. A. Sibley
> Boston, Feb. 22, 1864

There is not enough information inscribed on the quilt to inform us about the relationships of the block makers. The inscriptions do not include an organization name, and none of the signers appear in the Sibley household listed in the 1860 Boston census. Research on these women reveals little beyond their ages, family information, and domiciles, although some of the stories are richer than others. Alice Coburn worked as a mill operative in Lowell, Massachusetts, and was later a teacher in Boston.

We are fortunate that James George treasured the quilt and made clear to his children and grandchildren the importance of preserving it, his letters, and other effects relating to the Civil War. ❖

"Quilt as you go"

is a term that covers several methods used to construct a quilt in sections: piecing or appliquéing blocks, layering them with batting and backing, quilting the layers, then joining the sections to make a larger quilt. Potholder quilts are made in this fashion, but each block is finished individually, usually with binding, and then the finished blocks are sewn together to finish the quilt. What distinguishes potholder quilts from other "quilt as you go" techniques is that each block could stand alone as a small finished quilt.

Potholder quilts are a regional variation on "quilt as you go." In a 2010 study of potholder quilts, Pamela Weeks's data showed that out of eighty-seven potholder quilts cataloged, 74 percent originated in New England.[1] Her work on potholder continues, and the current count is 152 examples. Of those with provenance, 82 percent have New England origins. The data also shows that potholder quilts probably originated in coastal Massachusetts or Maine, since the majority of the New England quilts were made in these states. The earliest dates to 1837, and its blocks are inscribed "Charleston" and "Boston, Massachusetts."

Only a handful of quilts survive that were made for Civil War soldiers, but of these, eleven are potholder quilts, constructed of individually finished blocks. Ten of the eleven Civil War potholder quilts were either made in New England towns or organized by women raised in New England. The eleventh was made in a New York town located on the Vermont border.

POTHOLDER

Potholder Quilts

the Hussey-Fitzgerald
Civil War Quilt
AND
the Beverly Farms,
Massachusetts, Quilt

Detail of pieced quilt made by Sarah A. Leavitt, constructed block by block, 1847. *Collection of Pamela Weeks; photograph by David Bohl*

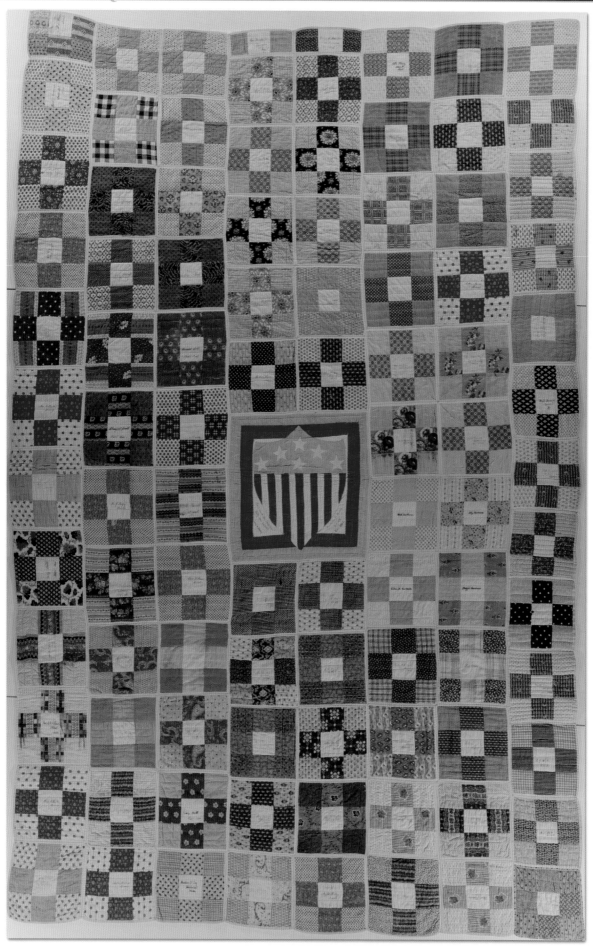

Album quilt, constructed block by block, possibly organized by Charlotte F. Hussey and her daughter, Susan A. Hussey, Detroit, 1864. Cotton (93" × 58"). *Collection of the International Quilt Museum, Lincoln, Nebraska (1997.007.0569)*

All of these surviving quilts are inscribed, some with just the names of the makers and some with town names and dates, and some are covered in verses from poetry, riddles, health advice, or verses from the Bible. Because these quilts were inscribed, they were cherished and saved.

The nature of group work, and especially group relief work (that is, diverse individuals joining to provide tangible items of comfort), probably contributed to the popularity of potholder quilts in the mid-nineteenth century. Imagine how much easier it is to organize a group quilt: a request is made for each member to return to the next meeting of the Ladies' Soldiers' Aid Society with a finished quilt block, 1 foot square, quilted and bound. Once enough blocks were gathered, group members sewed the blocks together, and the quilt was conceivably finished and ready to ship by the end of the meeting.

As evidenced by the variance of styles of the Civil War potholder quilts, a quilt might have all the blocks made with the same pattern, or each block might be different. Fabric could be purchased and distributed to members for framing each block with the same color or for use as a uniform binding. Perhaps a red, white, and blue color scheme was suggested, or the same block pattern was required, but in general only the Portland, Maine, quilt that is attributed to Caroline Davis and Cornelia Dow (chapter 6) shows great continuity among the blocks.

If the collected blocks vary slightly in size, potholder quilts can be forgiving when it comes to sewing all the blocks together. In the Hussey-Fitzgerald Civil War potholder quilt in the collection of the International Quilt Study Center and Museum in Lincoln, Nebraska, the blocks vary enough in size to provide a challenge for the people finishing the quilt. The detail photograph of the upper right-hand corner (*see below*) shows partial blocks and an uneven edge, but the sewers still managed

Detail, Hussey-Fitzgerald Album Quilt, center medallion area

Detail, Hussey-Fitzgerald Album Quilt. Note how the block-by-block construction method allows inaccurately finished blocks to be incorporated into the quilt.

to make the quilt somewhat rectangular.[2]

The quilt contains ninety-five $7\frac{1}{2}$-inch blocks, of which eighty-three are legible and inscribed with names. Some contain town or city names, and one block bears the date of November 1864. There is a larger, centrally placed block with a red, white, and blue shield held within a red square border. With the exception of the double-sized central block, all blocks are the same construction, Nine Patch, with the names inscribed in the white centers of the blocks. Some are partial blocks cut down to fit. The center block contains a line from the chorus of a popular song composed at the start of the Civil War, "The Battle Cry of Freedom." "Rally round the flag, boys! Rally once again!" is a compelling message meant to encourage any soldier.[3]

The center medallion also bears the inscribed names of Charlotte Fitzgerald Hussey and her daughter Susan A. Hussey, who we may assume planned and assembled the quilt, on the basis of that inscription placement. Other inscriptions include Charlotte's daughters Ella Hussey and Mary Elizabeth Borradaile, and two of Charlotte's sisters. While most blocks contain place names in Michigan, four were donated from New Hampshire, eight from Massachusetts, and more from Kentucky, Ohio, Pennsylvania, and California.[4]

The 1850 US Census of Nantucket, Massachusetts, lists Charlotte F. Hussey, her husband, Frederick, and daughters Susan A. and Ella living with Charlotte's father, Timothy Fitzgerald. Only Susan A. Hussey can be

Album quilt, constructed block by block, Beverly Farms, Massachusetts, 1864. Cotton (84" × 56"). Collection of the Rochester Historical Society, Rochester, New York (2004.511). *Photograph by David Bohl*

found in the 1860 census, boarding in the Manchester, New Hampshire, household of Elizabeth Baker and listed as a school teacher. The Massachusetts origin of the family who organized this quilt adds to the evidence that potholder quilts originate in New England.

Augustus Hussey, son of Charlotte and Frederick, enlisted in Company H of the Michigan 24th Infantry on August 13, 1862. Corporal Hussey was wounded on the first day of the battle of Gettysburg, on July 1, 1863, but returned to his unit within a few months. At the Battle of the Wilderness, on May 5, 1864, he was captured and then imprisoned at Andersonville for six months and returned to his unit in December 1864. Augustus was mustered out at Detroit on June 30, 1865, as a second lieutenant.[5]

A small group of people in Beverly Farms, Massachusetts, made a potholder quilt that contains a wide variety of scrap fabrics yet is carefully planned. Its twenty-four 14-inch blocks are bordered with various double-pink, calico prints, and this design element brings the diverse fabric choices together in a more uniform way than is found in other potholder scrap quilts. Two blocks include a fabric, printed during the war era, featuring flags, cannons, and soldiers printed

on a white ground. This and the Hingham Album Quilt are the only Civil War soldiers' quilts that contain pieces of calico printed with military or patriotic motifs—very rare Civil War fabrics.[6]

Only seven unique surnames are found among the inscriptions, since several blocks are unsigned and several people made multiple blocks. Research has not yet revealed the name of the group or if it represented a church or a school, but genealogical information has shed light on some of the signers.

Susan Mary Loring Jackson, who probably organized the quilt, was a forty-one-year-old mother of four children, and the two youngest made or signed blocks for the quilt. She was a member of a wealthy Boston family and married into another. Her father, Charles Greely Loring, was a graduate of Harvard and a prominent lawyer, politician, and author. Susan's mother was Loring's first wife—his third, the widow Cornelia Amory Goddard, was active in the work of the Boston Sanitary Commission during the Civil War.[7]

Her brother, also Charles Greely Loring, joined scientific expeditions from the Great Lakes to Arabia and was an expert on Egyptian art and an archeologist. He served in the Union Army, first on the staff of

Detail, Beverly Farms Album Quilt. Note printed cotton with soldier, cannon, and flag motifs. *Photograph by David Bohl*

General Burnside, then as inspector general in the Ninth Army Corps. Although his position did not require him to engage in active combat, he fought in all the campaigns of the Ninth Corps, receiving three promotions for "gallant and meritorious services," and retired with the rank of major-general. After the war his Egyptian expeditions continued, as did his contributions to the Boston Atheneum, and when it was re-created as the Museum of Fine Arts, he was appointed its first curator.[8]

Susan Jackson's father-in-law, Patrick Tracy Jackson, collaborated with his business partner Francis Cabot Lowell to create the first waterpowered loom used in the United States. Jackson and Lowell organized the Boston Manufacturing Company, which started spinning and weaving cotton in Waltham, Massachusetts, in 1813, founded the Appleton Mills in the manufacturing city of Lowell, and eventually developed or purchased mills in many New England cities, including Amoskeag in Manchester, New Hampshire, and the Cocheco Mills in Dover, New Hampshire. Her husband, Patrick Tracy Jackson Jr., continued in the family textile business.[9]

Patrick Tracy Jackson III, the oldest son of Susan and Patrick Jackson Jr., was a student at Harvard University at the beginning of the Civil War, but in May 1862 enlisted in the Massachusetts 4th Infantry Battalion. He soon mustered out to transfer to the Massachusetts 1st Cavalry Regiment, where he was promoted to second lieutenant in March 1864. In the same month, he transferred to and was commissioned a first lieutenant in Company I, Massachusetts 5th Cavalry Regiment, which was the fifth African American regiment of only seven organized during the Civil War, and the only one from Massachusetts composed only of African Americans, with the exception of the officers, who were all white. The regiment was variously attached to the 22nd Army Corps and the 25th Army Corps near Richmond and Petersburg. In June 1864 the

regiment was ordered to Point Lookout, Maryland, to guard Confederate prisoners there. In June 1865 it was ordered to Clarksville, Texas, and there mustered out in October of that year.[10] After the war Patrick Jackson found employment in the textile industry in Lowell, Massachusetts. Susan Jackson's youngest two children either made or signed blocks.

Anna Pierce Jackson was ten years old when the quilt was made. Later in life, she was the director of the Boston Children's Aid Society and was involved for forty years at the Home for Aged Colored Women.[11]

Inscriptions include verses drawn from the Bible, hymns, and poetry expressing sentiments of comfort, courage, faith, and hope. In one block alone there are excerpts from three sources: Psalm 113, the poem "Bring Flowers" by Felicia Dorothea Hemans, and Robert Burns's poem "Prayer under the Pressure of Violent Anguish." A poem titled "Cheer Up," by an anonymous author, was printed in full in several popular magazines in the 1850s; it urges the reader to take courage and be cheerful:

> All will be right,
> Look to the light,
> Morning was ever the daughter of night;
> All that was black will be all that is bright;
> Cheerily, then! Cheer up!

Some of the inscriptions include dates that range between August 10, 1864, and February 16, 1865. This belies the theory that the potholder method of making quilts always results in a quickly made product. Perhaps the quilt organizer had trouble collecting the blocks from the makers, or perhaps some sewers just kept making blocks until they had enough to make the long, narrow quilt. ❧

Detail, Beverly Farms Album Quilt. *Photograph by David Bohl*

LADIES' AID

Ladies' Aid Societies

Although none of the quilts made by the Bethel, Maine, Ladies' Union Soldiers' Aid Society exist today, the carefully penciled minutes of their meetings—preserved at the library of the Maine Historical Society—are representative of thousands of other groups that formed or refocused their efforts to produce goods for soldiers' aid during the Civil War. The Bethel Soldiers' Aid Society assembled formally in December 1861, elected officers, and appointed a works committee. The copybook that survives dutifully records the activities of the ladies during the war years. In the front and back of the booklet are pasted directions, clipped from newspapers, for making lint for dressing wounds and the dimensions for bandages. The clippings include lists of needed items, such as wool footings (socks), flannel shirts, cotton flannel drawers, and mittens. Supplies, such as dried apples and blueberries, canned vegetables, and jellies for the hospitals, are also requested. The group started with thirty people, and anyone who could pay the ten-cent annual dues was welcome, including men. The meetings were held in private homes for the first year and then moved to a public hall, provided rent free by its owner.

From *Harper's Weekly*, September 6, 1862, this detail of a print titled "The Influence of Women" shows many hands at work in a sewing circle. Notice the woman seated at the sewing machine in the left corner.

Soldiers' Shirts

The biweekly entries are very detailed. On March 17, 1862, a box was sent to the Sanitary Commission rooms in Portland, with the contents to be directed to the 12th or 13th Maine Regiments, in which were enlisted many Bethel men. The contents were typical of future shipments and included

9 pairs slippers	1 feather pillow
1 pair socks	2 hop pillows
5 pairs footings	1 pr. cotton flannel drawers
4 flannel shirts	1 bag dried blueberries
2 cotton flannel shirts	1 bag dried apples
1 bag rags	1 bag lint
4 bundles rags	1 box cranberries
19 towels	box mutton tallow
30 handkerchiefs	1 comforter
4 pr. pillowcases	

Paid freight on the box was 38 cents.

The entry of June 6, 1862, is of interest because it is an early record of the use of sewing machines:

> In compliance with a public notice, Soldier's Aid Society met this day at Patter's Hall, kindly tendered to our use rent free by Mr. Patter. More than thirty ladies interested in this enterprise came provided with their needles and thimbles and willing hands. Two ladies came in with their sewing machines, aiding greatly in forwarding the work making shirts and drawers, sent us from Portland. Many of the ladies took work home to be completed.[1]

Interest and commitment on the home front waxed and waned during the Civil War. There was a great flood of supplies after the North lost the first battle of Bull Run, in July 1861, as a result of the reports in local papers telling of great suffering among the wounded after the battle. Women continued to work to supply soldiers' needs, but as goods became more expensive and as the war wore on, donors' fatigue set in. People were tired of working so hard to provide war materials. Women and the youngest and eldest family members who were left at home took on the manual labor needed to continue working at their farms. They found it difficult to supply the needs of their families, let alone to donate to the war effort.[2]

Album quilt, constructed block by block, Norridgewalk, Maine, 1863. Cotton (84" × 63"). Collection unknown. *Photograph by Laura Syler*

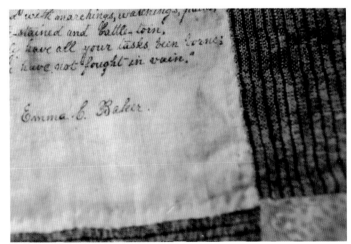

Detail, Norridgewock Album Quilt

Detail, Norridgewock Album Quilt displaying the back. *Photograph by Laura Syler*

In June 1863, the third year of the war, the minutes of the Bethel, Maine, Ladies' Soldiers' Aid Society reported on the 23rd that "Few members present. There is a good supply of work, but little interest manifested. There has never been so much suffering or so great a want as at this time. June 30—met, worked on a quilt."

The US Sanitary Commission recognized the need to reengage the workers in the towns and villages of the North and sent out representatives to encourage more donations. The Bethel Ladies' Soldiers' Aid Society minutes record such a visit on August 4, 1863: "A representative from Portland came and gave an interesting account of their doings." The minutes reflect a renewed interest and effort on the part of the local women, who began to attend again.

The minutes of the Bethel group record continued activity through the end of the war. It is interesting that this group concentrated on quilts in the last months of the war, and the notes of the meetings record which members donated their blocks for the group quilt that was in progress. The last entry is an inventory of their work throughout the war that includes in the long and varied list a total of sixteen quilts and twenty-eight comforters.[3]

A quilt made in 1863, which records the names of sixty volunteers from this small New Hampshire town, is known as the Dublin Quilt. In 2011, after the first edition of this book was published, Loretta B. Chase and Jan Coor-Pender Dodge wrote a research paper about the Dublin Quilt that was published in Volume 32 of *Uncoverings*, the annual publication of the American Quilt Study Group. Their work revealed that this simple quilt held the stories of "the women who made it, the men who served, and the organizations that supported war relief."

Detail of the Dublin, NH quilt, marked in a block on the front of thequilt with the stamp of the United States Sanitary Commission.

In Texas in 2004, a Civil War soldier's quilt was presented for appraisal at a quilt show. The woman and the quilt have since disappeared, but enough information was shared by others who saw the quilt to piece together some of its story.[4] It was made in Norridgewock, Maine, a small town—not unlike Bethel. The quilt is composed of forty 12-inch blocks set in eight rows of five blocks each. The backing of each block is as varied as the front—indigo, shirting, block print, woven checks, and madder prints. Each block is bound and whip-stitched together. It bears multiple signatures as well as the stamp of the US Sanitary Commission. There are several verses, but only this one was transcribed at the time of its appraisal:

> God Bless you, soldier, scarred and worn
> Harried with marchings, walking, pairs
> All battle stained and battle torn
> Bravely have all your tasks been bourne
> You have not fought in vain.
> **—Emma C. Baker**[4]

The census for 1860 informs us that Emma C. Baker was living with her parents and three sisters, one of whom was a school teacher. Joseph Y. Baker was a farmer with a moderate holding. His household included two boarders listed as shoemakers. Emma was twenty when she contributed a block to the Norridgewock quilt.[5]

Unlike the Bethel Ladies' Soldiers' Aid Society, the Ladies' Fort Hill Sewing Circle of Hingham, Massachusetts, was already actively involved in civic affairs years before the start of the Civil War. According to the *History of the Town of Hingham*, a group of women (their names were not included in this history, written in 1893) had raised money to make improvements to the Fort Hill Cemetery, one of the oldest burying grounds in the town. Its care had passed to the town in the late 1700s, and few recent burials had taken place, and so it fell into disrepair.

> [T]he old neglected ground was waiting the advent of the spirit of some "Old Mortality" to redeem it from waste and desecration. This came at last, as so many excellent things do come, from the devotion and labor of woman.[6]

This devoted group called a meeting in November 1851, which resulted in the formation of the Fort Hill Cemetery Corporation. More land was purchased, the acreage was divided into lots, it was fenced, and trees were planted. The Hingham history reports further that the ladies "continued their well-directed efforts, holding a fair each year for the sale of the products of their labor." Their labors were extensive, because the initial expenditure was large. Their proceeds also purchased a monument that was placed in the "old ground" to commemorate the early settlers, and a $2,000 donation followed to set up a fund whose income would be used to maintain the cemetery.

The monument survives, as does the quilt that commemorates their work when they turned to soldiers' aid during the Civil War. The purpose of the quilt and its makers are clearly indicated by an inscription:

> This quilt was made by the Ladies of the Fort Hill Sewing Circle and presented to the soldiers. Hingham, Mass. 1864.

The quilt is a potholder quilt and its fifty-four 9-inch blocks are individually finished in double-pink, straight-of-the-grain binding. Its makers chose a variety of patterns, including Album Block and Nine Patch. They sprinkled in a few unusual blocks, including one appliquéd with white stars, inked flags, and a depiction of George Washington, and a Greek Cross variation.

It is also an inscribed quilt, and many of the blocks bear patriotic messages, Bible verses, and homely sayings meant to send the recipient comforting thoughts from home. One block simply states, "The soldiers' friend, Aunt Betsy."[7] The dates range from June to July

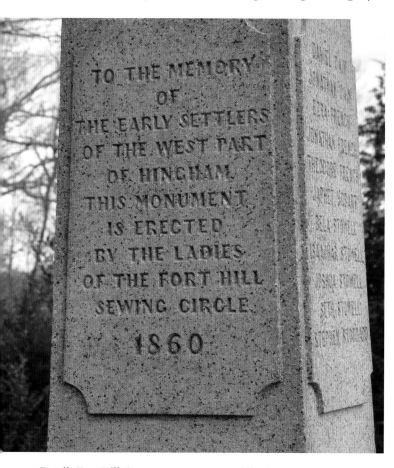

Detail, Fort Hill Cemetery monument, Hingham, Massachusetts. The inscription reads: "To the Memory of the early settlers of the west part of Hingham, this monument is erected by the Ladies of the Fort Hill Sewing Circle." *Photograph by Pamela Weeks*

Monument dedicated to the Early Settlers of Hingham, Massachusetts, erected by the Ladies of the Fort Hill Sewing Circle in 1860. Fort Hill Cemetery, Fort Hill Street, Hingham, Massachusetts. *Photograph by Pamela Weeks*

Album quilt, constructed block by block, made by the Ladies of the Fort Hill Sewing Circle, Hingham, Massachusetts, 1864. Cotton (83" 53.5"). *Photograph courtesy of the International Quilt Museum in the collection of 2017.003.0001*

1864, and the signatures include those of the officers of the sewing circle: The vice president, Rebecca A. Gardner, was the wife of Andrew J. Gardner. He is listed in the 1860 census as a shoemaker. They had four children living at home at the time of the census, and the eldest, at seventeen, is Lucy, also engaged in the shoe trade as a tassel maker.[8]

The history of Hingham lists the directors of the Fort Hill Cemetery Corporation, and Mr. Andrew J. Gardner served two terms in the 1860s and 1870s, and as superintendent from 1879 to 1881. Also listed as directors are Lincolns, Cains, and Stodders, more surnames found on the quilt.[9]

Two of the signers had family members serving in the war at the time the quilt was made. Daniel and Priscilla Lincoln's son, Daniel Stodder Lincoln, enlisted at the beginning of the war as a ninety-day volunteer in the Lincoln Light Infantry, a unit raised from Hingham and surrounding South Shore towns. He mustered out in July but returned to service in the United States Navy, and in 1864 he was serving aboard the supply steamer *Connecticut*, sailing between Boston; Pensacola, Florida; and Mobile, Alabama. He survived the war and returned to Hingham to work as a shoemaker. He died in 1869 of scarlet fever.[10]

Nancy Corcoran, a member of the committee of the sewing circle, signed her name as Mrs. J. J. Corcoran. Her husband, Jeremiah, also enlisted in the Lincoln Light Infantry as a ninety-day volunteer, but at the end of this service he enlisted as a private in Company A of the Fortieth Regiment, Massachusetts Volunteers, for three years. His tours included service in the Department of the South. The book *Hingham in the Civil War* lists the various battles in which he fought and an account of his action at Cold Harbor, a particularly bloody battle in Virginia fought over several days from the end of May to June 10, 1864. In one half-hour period on June 3, the day Jeremiah J. Corcoran was wounded, more than 7,000 Union soldiers died in an assault on Confederate lines. Corcoran died in hospital a week later, on June 10, 1864.[11]

Other Hingham groups made quilts for the war, and from this wonderful excerpt, we confirm that the signature/album quilts *were* intended for hospital use: "The scholars of the Universalist Sabbath School have lately sent a quilt to the Sanitary Rooms, and the pupils of one of our Grammar Schools have made an album quilt and will forward it, as a New Year's gift, for the sick and wounded soldiers."[12] ❧

Caro (short for Caroline) Frances Bowen Fairbanks
hurriedly made a quilt in Brandon, Vermont,
to send to Civil War soldiers through the local
Soldiers' Aid Society. Calico was expensive, nearly
three dollars a yard, another reason to choose a simple
block, with just enough color and piecing to make it
interesting. She chose to recycle a garment to piece the
Snowball blocks, which require only a small triangle of
printed fabric in each corner; careful examination of the
quilt shows fold marks from a released hem in some of
the brown calico patches. She alternated these quickly
pieced blocks with off-white, unprinted squares. Of the
forty blocks in the quilt, only half are pieced.[1]

The quilting was accomplished quickly too—the
pieced blocks are quilted simply, with a large five-
pointed star centered in their white spaces. The
inscribed blocks have six rows of vertical quilting that
slice across the writing. The stitches are large and not
particularly even. The borders are sparsely quilted.

A Vermont Quilt

A view of Brandon, Vermont, in about 1900, showing the Baptist
church where Dr. Chauncey Lee Case, uncle of quiltmaker
Caroline Bowers Fairbanks, was organist for many years.
Photograph courtesy Vermont Historical Society

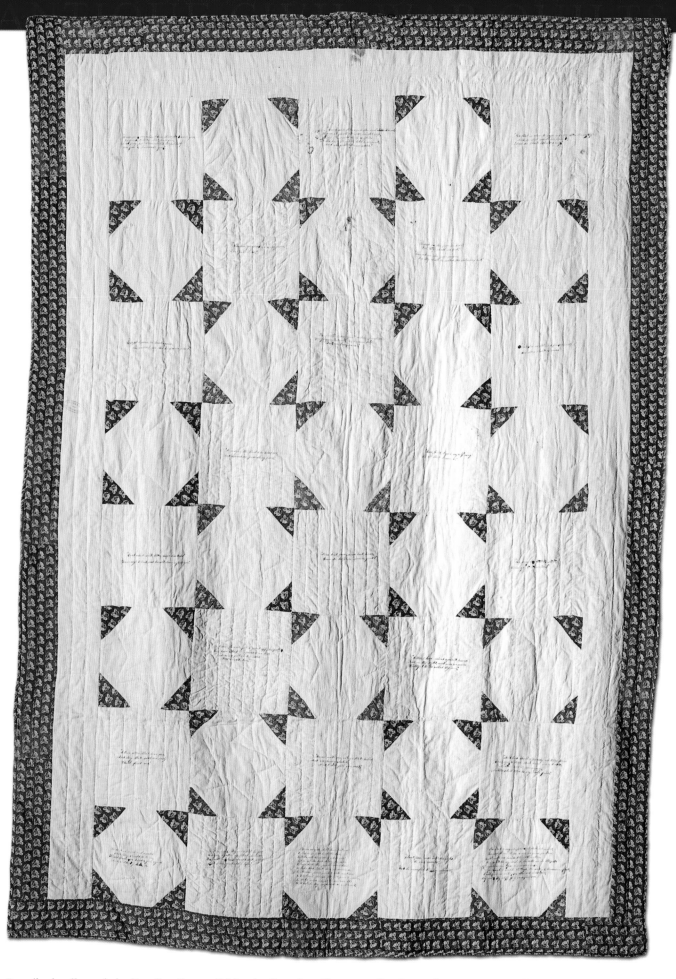

Inscribed quilt made by Caroline Bowen Fairbanks, Brandon, Vermont, after December 25, 1862, and before April 1865. Cotton (82.5" × 57.5"). Collection of the Vermont Historical Society (1987.38.1) Donated in memory of Sophia Wilfong. *Photograph by Paul Rogers*

Caroline Bowen, ca. 1860. *Image courtesy of Grant Fairbanks, great-grandson of Luke and Caroline Fairbanks*

Detail of Fairbanks quilt, showing US Sanitary Commission stamp. *Photograph by Paul Rogers*

Caro inscribed twenty-three different verses on the unpieced blocks for the edification or comfort of the quilt's receiver. Her handwriting scrawls across the large squares, and she left ink blots and scratched-out mistakes on the quilt; other quiltmakers might have replaced the messy blocks with more careful work. There are Bible quotes, lines from hymns, and psalms. A version of the Ten Commandments is the only verse very carefully penned, and it is simplified and rhymed:

> Thou no gods shalt have but me.
> Before no idol bend the knee.
> Take not the name of god in vain.
> Dare not the Sabbath day profane.
> Give both thy parents honor due.
> Take heed that thou no murders do.
> Abstain from words & deeds unclean.
> Steal not, though thou be pour & mean.
> Make not a willful lie nor love it.
> What is thy neighbor's do not covet.

The physical evidence shows that either Caroline lacked skill or that she was in a hurry to contribute a quilt for soldiers' aid. She turned the quilt over, scrawled her name and the name of the town where she lived on the back of the lower border, and called it done. After receiving a stencil mark identifying the Brandon Soldiers' Aid Society as the source for the quilt, it was probably sent to the rooms of the USSC in Boston, where it was marked again, this time with the USSC stamp. The ladies added it to the count in their ledgers and then sent it where it was needed.

Luke and Caroline Fairbanks were half first cousins, descending respectively from the first and second wives of their grandfather, Jonathan Bowen, an early settler of Royalton, Vermont, the small river valley farming town where they both grew up. As a teenager, Luke headed west with his older brother Alonzo. Between 1855 and 1860 they made investments in farms and mills in Iowa and Minnesota, but in the fall of 1860, Luke sold out his shares and returned to Vermont, perhaps in anticipation of the war.[2]

Detail of Fairbanks quilt, showing hastily inscribed Bible verses. *Photograph by Paul Rogers*

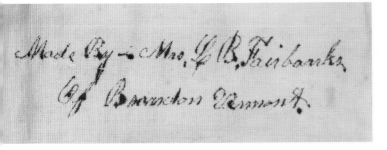

Detail of Fairbanks quilt, signature of Caroline Bowen Fairbanks. *Photograph by Paul Rogers*

Luke Bowen Fairbanks, ca 1861. *Image courtesy of Grant Fairbanks*

Mark Bowen, Caroline's father, died in August 1859, leaving his forty-five-year-old wife, Sarah Harris Bowen, to raise six children between the ages of seventeen and two. Caroline was sixteen when her father died. Within a year, her sister Fannie, who was eighteen, married Charles Waldo, also of Royalton. The 1860 US Census for Royalton lists Charles as head of a household that included his mother-in-law (Sarah), Caroline, Louisa, Ella, Eugene, and Anna Bowen, as well as his two younger brothers, Dillingham and Willis Waldo.[3] A genealogical history of Sarah's Harris family tells us that this was the Mark Bowen family property called Maple Grove Farm.[4]

Little wonder that Caro probably chose to move from that crowded household to the home of her mother's sister in Brandon, Vermont. Her uncle, Chauncy Case, was a prominent doctor and druggist, and in the 1860 census his wealthy household consisted only of him and his wife, Caro's grandmother Hannah Harris, and a domestic servant. Caro was married to Luke from this home.[5] The inscription on the back of the Soldiers' Aid quilt is "Brandon, VT," not her birthplace, Royalton, so she continued to live there after her marriage and while Luke served in the Civil War.

Luke's brother, Charles Bowen, wrote a memoir of his war years and included a story about the enlistment of two of his brothers in the Civil War:

> I well remember the patriotic utterances of my brothers, Luke and John. John was milking one of the cows on the eve of April 12, 1861, when he heard the news of the fall of Fort Sumter. He did not finish milking, but started for the nearest recruiting station, where he, together with my brother Luke, enlisted in Company F, 3rd Regiment, Vermont Volunteers.

This is a lovely story, but the actual military record shows that Luke did not enlist until June 1, 1861.

On April 16, 1862, at Lee's Mills, Luke was severely wounded in the left arm. One account states that he recovered in a hospital, then received a furlough and came home, but another version includes a short spell as a prisoner of war before his hospitalization. The accounts again vary with regard to his time back in Vermont. One version relates that Luke stayed home just long enough to marry Caroline on December 25, 1862, and another account claims he did not return to his unit until the end of January 1863, with time somewhere between June 1862 and April 1863 for him to serve as a recruiter for the Army. He was mustered out in 1865 with the rank of captain.

Captain Luke B. Fairbanks returned to Caroline in Vermont and bought a farm in Royalton, where the first of their seven children was born. Between 1869 and 1895, the family moved several times, homesteading new farms in Kansas, Minnesota, and California. In 1895 Luke and Caro settled in Austin, Minnesota, where he died in 1907 at the age of sixty-nine. Caro moved to Yakima, Washington, to live with her daughter and died there on January 6, 1944, just a few days short of her 101st birthday. She was buried beside Luke in Austin.

Caro's and Luke's graves are located north of the main entrance of the Oakwood Cemetery in Austin, Minnesota, and are marked with two small footstones near a larger monument carved with their last name, and the five-pointed star of the Grand Army of the Republic. A hemlock tree has grown tall to the west of the monument and casts a perpetual shadow on the site. The simple gravestones are of light-gray granite, and the letters of Luke and Caro's names and birth and death dates are raised and polished.

Detail of Fairbanks quilt, showing the Brandon, Vermont, Soldiers' Aid Society stencil. *Photograph by Paul Rogers*

Luke and Caroline Bowen Fairbanks's graves, in Oakwood Cemetery, Austin, Minnesota. *Photograph by Pamela Weeks*

Where the quilt went after being stamped in the Boston offices of the US Sanitary Commission remains a mystery. It was used gently during its service in the war, since the inscriptions are legible and the fabric is still moderately bright. It is most likely that Caro made it late in the war—it does not have a date inscribed, and other surviving Civil War quilts made for soldiers' use are dated 1864 or 1865.

In 1959, the quilt was donated to the Historical Society of York County, Pennsylvania, by Mrs. R. K. Hildebrand in memory of Mrs. Sophia Wilfong. While assessing its collection in 1986, the museum determined that the quilt had no traceable connection to the area, and it was de-accessioned and transferred to the Vermont Historical Society, where it was gratefully accepted as the return of the quilt to its home state in 1987.[6]

PATRIOTIC *Patriotic Quilts*

At the start of the Civil War, in both the South and the North, patriotic fervor encompassed the wearing or display of anything red, white, and blue. Accounts of the musters in small towns and large cities include vivid descriptions of bunting and flags flying from public buildings and private residences. In the book *Wisconsin Women in the War between the States*, Ethel Alice Hurn describes the scene this way:

> Such a display of the national colors had never been seen before. Flag raising was the order of the day. The trinity of red, white, and blue colors were to be seen in all directions. Shop-keepers decked their windows and counters with it. Men wore it in neckties or in a rosette, pinned on the breast or tied in the button-hole. Women wore it conspicuously also. . . . The flag floated not only from halls, stores, dwellings, schoolrooms, churches, doors, windows, and dining-rooms, but even adorned the parlors of cultivated women.[1]

Flag making was popular and considered a patriotic contribution at the time. In every town and city, women were busy making personal versions of Old Glory as well as flags for their local military companies. In the nineteenth century it was common practice for people to make and display their own flags. The proportions of the flag, arrangement of the stars in the blue field, and choice of whether to use four, five, or six points on the stars were decided by the maker.[2]

"The Seventh Regiment, N.G.S.N.Y., Leaves New York April 19, 1861 for the Defense of Washington. Flags fly from every window, flagstaff, spectators' hands." *Frank Leslie's Illustrations: The Soldier in Our Civil War*

Album quilt, constructed block by block, Florence, Massachusetts, 1863. Cotton (85" × 53").
Collection unknown; image courtesy of the American Hurrah Archive, New York City

Newspaper reports included the patriotic activities that people undertook for the cause, and in a retrospective on the Civil War, written up in a Sheboygan, Wisconsin, *Telegram* article in December 1909, the author describes a flag that was

> made in a little country village and raised July 4, 1861. The women of the family made the stripes of muslin and turkey-red calico, and a piece of the daughter's blue apron (for cotton cloth was dear) formed the back-ground for the stars, which were six-pointed and patterned after a drawing by the younger son.

The flag was raised on a pole made by an enlisted son home on leave.[3]

It is not surprising that patriotic elements such as the flag and Union shield translated to quilts made for the war effort. American quilts with patriotic themes date to the founding of the United States. Seven of the fifteen Civil War quilts included in this book exhibit flags or shields in blocks or a red, white, and blue central design element. Another potholder quilt has many red, white, and blue blocks, and nine of these blocks are arranged to form a strong central patriotic medallion. The quilt made for George Teter by his mother, Mary Rockhold Teter, and featured in chapter 8 was made from a pattern found in a ladies' magazine; it is all red, white, and blue, stars and stripes.

A potholder quilt made in Florence, Massachusetts, and dated February 22, 1863, is composed of a white rectangular center, upon which is appliquéd the US national flag with seven red and six white stripes. The blue field has thirty-six stars arranged in the shape of a larger star. This large center medallion is framed with solid blue and bound. It is surrounded by twenty-two individually bound blocks, pieced in the Square in a Square pattern. Some are hand quilted and some are machine quilted, and each of the blocks is signed by a different person, since the handwriting appears to vary from block to block.

Verses are inscribed above and below the flag in the central medallion, and in the largest script above the inked staff that holds the flag is written the final stanza from the first verse of "The Star Spangled Banner"— "The star spangled banner / Long may it wave / O'er the land of the free / and the home of the brave."

Detail, Florence Album Quilt.

Below the flag, the fifth stanza of Joseph Rodman Drake's poem "The American Flag" is elegantly inscribed.

Flag of the free heart's hope and home,
By angel hands to valor given,
Thy stars have lit the welkin dome,
And all thy hues were born in heaven.

Forever float that standard sheet!
Where breathes the foe that falls before us,
With Freedom's soil beneath our fee,
And Freedom's banner streaming o'er us!

—Florence, Mass. Feb. 22nd, 1863[4]

Written before 1820,[5] Drake's poem was resurrected in 1861, when it was published for popular appeal, lavishly illustrated with drawings by F. Darley, and set to music adapted from Bellini by George Danskins. The cover displays a drawing of an eagle, wings spread wide, carrying the stars and stripes in its claws. This patriotic parlor piece certainly influenced the makers of this quilt, as did another popular song of the time. "Rally round the flag, boys!" is a phrase taken from "The Battle Cry of Freedom," composed by George Root in 1862, one of the most popular songs written during the Civil War. More than 700,000 copies of this sheet music were printed, and a version was even adapted by the South. Two other quilts with patriotic center blocks are inscribed with lines from the chorus of this song.[6]

Battle Cry of Freedom

Yes we'll rally round the flag, boys,
    we'll rally once again,
Shouting the battle cry of freedom,
We will rally from the hillside,
    we'll gather from the plain,
Shouting the battle cry of freedom!

Chorus:
The Union forever! Hurrah, boys, hurrah!
Down with the traitor, up with the star;
While we rally round the flag, boys,
    rally once again,
Shouting the battle cry of freedom![7]

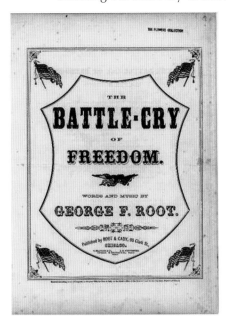

Cover from the sheet music for "The Battle Cry of Freedom," which was one of the most popular songs written and published during the Civil War

The location of this quilt is not known, and it is difficult to puzzle out the names from the available photographs, but it is possible to read four: Irene B. Martin, Mrs. L. Strong, E. P. Hammond, and Abby P. Brown. All added "Florence, Mass." to their blocks, and Mrs. Strong added the date, 1863. These names are also published as members of the Free Congregational Society of Florence, Massachusetts, in a twenty-fifth-anniversary publication celebrating the society's founding in 1863. The basis of this group seems similar to today's Unitarians. Belief in God and professions of faith were not necessary, but equality, free thought, and good works were. "The Free Congregational Society of Florence never declined to adopt any thing practiced by the churches that seemed rational and enjoyable: hence the Society had its 'Sewing Circle' under the name of the 'The Ladies' Industrial Union.'"[8]

Florence, Massachusetts, at the time of the Civil War, was emerging as a manufacturing town. It is not surprising that several of the blocks in this quilt are machine quilted, since the Florence Sewing Machine Company was founded in 1860 and grew during the war, building the first of its three original factory buildings in 1864. By 1866, the company had offices in the largest US cities as well as London and Manchester, England.[9]

"HURRAH FOR THE BOYS OF THE PINE TREE STATE"

{ by **Megan Pinette,**
President of the Belfast Historical Society, Belfast, Maine

On June 17, 1864, the Ladies' Volunteer Aid Society, from the First Church of Belfast, Maine, began work on a flag bed quilt to recognize and honor those who fought to preserve the Union. In mid-July, the finished quilt was sent by express to the Armory Square Hospital in Washington, DC. In March 2011, nearly 150 years since it was made, the quilt was donated to the Belfast Historical Society and Museum. At some point in its long history it was rescued from destruction in a burn barrel and was stored in a closet for thirty years. This time it came by priority mail.

According to the society's minutes, the Ladies' Volunteer Aid Society was formed in 1861, with seventy-eight members, for the purpose of "assisting the noble men of our city and vicinity who volunteer to defend our country in this hour of her greatest peril." They met regularly during the Civil War, each member paying the required sum of 50 cents to belong.

During summer months the society sewed flannel shirts, blue denim pants, handkerchiefs, and havelocks. The society also assembled packets that included sewing kits, combs, scissors, tea, soap, cloves, cornstarch, jellies, a great quantity of lint, and many hundreds of yards of bandages. As winter set in, knitting needles and quilting

Armory Square Hospital

Flag quilt, constructed by the Ladies' Volunteer Aid Society from the First Church of Belfast, Maine, 1864. Cotton and wool (91.5" × 61.5"). *Collection of the Belfast Historical Society, Belfast, Maine; Photograph by Light in the Forest Photography*

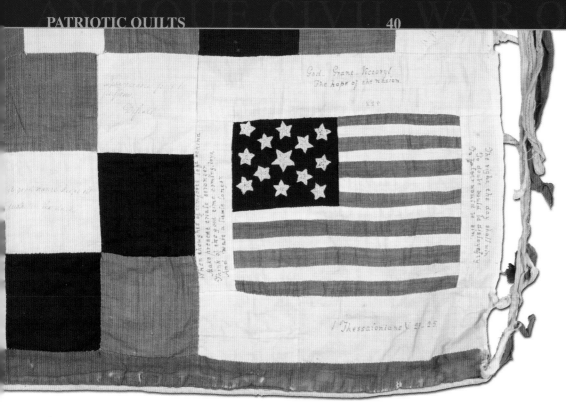

Detail of the Flag Quilt, Belfast, Maine. Each corner of the quilt contains a flag, surrounded by inked inscriptions. *Photograph by Light in the Forest Photography*

frames were brought out and mittens and quilts were made. Most popular and appreciated by the soldiers were dried apples. Farmers in Belfast and surrounding towns produced great quantities of apples, potatoes, and hay, which were loaded on ships sailing out of Belfast's harbor.

The society continued their sewing sessions through the winter of 1863. In June 1864, it was proposed to make a flag bed quilt to send to a hospital; they also renamed the society, using the "Cabalistic Letters" U.S.G. (it is assumed that these letters stand for Ulysses S. Grant). They commenced work on June 17, 1864, and by July 7 the quilt was ready for finishing. The U.S.G. Society did the work at the home of the Hon. Nehemiah Abbott, former US congressman from Belfast (1857–59). After supper, the sewing party and their invited guests danced until the small hours of the morning. The finished quilt was shipped from Belfast the following week.

The top three white stripes contain the following inscriptions:

> Our Nation's Defenders, The Union Volunteers, "U.S.G. Society," Organized 1862, Belle Johnson President, Abby H. Faunce Treasurer, Belfast, Maine, June 17 1864.

Augusta Quimby Frederick, age thirty-one at the time, was one of the ladies who belonged to the society and took part in the design and sewing of the quilt. Many years later, in 1917 at the age of eighty-eight, she wrote and read her "Recollection of the Civil War" to a meeting of the Women's Alliance of Belfast:

> As a diversion from real work it was proposed to make a Flag Bed Quilt for a hospital. Preparations were made at once, a committee was chosen to purchase the materials, and at a meeting at the Unitarian Parsonage the quilt was designed, cut and prepared for willing hands to finish. It was of good size, made like a flag with a red and white border. The names of all the members were written in the white stripes, appropriate mottoes were in every star and where some pun or play upon the Union Officers names could be made, it was quickly incorporated. The idea was like this: a hard resting place for the rebels—"General Pillow." A bus to the rebel progress, "General Gates." The writing was all done by Mrs. John H. Quimby, whose fine penmanship is still remembered. When the quilt was

Detail of the Flag Quilt, Belfast, Maine. The borders' white blocks contain inscriptions; this one is a pun on the name of one of Maine's generals. *Photograph by Light in the Forest Photography*

Arabella (Belle) Johnson, one of the twenty-three women who assisted in making the Flag Quilt. *Photograph by Light in the Forest Photography*

The First Church of Belfast, Maine. *Photograph by Light in the Forest Photography*

finished and ready for the quilting we were invited to the house of Hon. N. Abbott and a picnic supper was served, to which the young men were invited. The quilt was finished during the afternoon and was displayed in the dining room and was much admired. The following week it was sent to Washington by express, accompanied by a letter from our President Miss Arbella Johnson."

On August 12, the day the quilt arrived in Washington, a letter was sent in return from Miss McLellan, Armory Square Hospital, Ward 26, expressing thanks on behalf of the soldiers in the ward. The quilt was carried and exhibited to each one and "many have been the expressions of surprise and admiration."

Over 800 men from Belfast volunteered and joined the ranks of the 4th Maine and the 26th Maine Regiments. The 4th Maine took part in many of the major battles, including First and Second Bull Run, Fredericksburg, and Gettysburg. The 26th Maine, a nine-month regiment, was based in Louisiana, taking part in engagements at Irish Bend and Port Hudson.

Inscriptions on the quilt include poems and puns based on names of Civil War generals:

Here's success to the boys, whoever they are
That have shouldered their muskets and gone to war
Victorious they'll be, defeated they can't
While they are led into battle by U. S. Grant.
    —by Augusta Quimby

The boys of our army, The flag of our country,
The soldiers of Freedom, And the Red White and Blue
On land and on sea, be they ever victorious
And each to the other forever prove true
Good Maine ham well cured and smoked in many battles
    —Gen Burnham

The dread of the coward
    —Hooker and Howard

A good Union Sportsman
    —Gen Hunter

Our native berry
    —Gen H. G. Berry

A popular Union drink
    —Meade

If the rebs won't pay, We will charge 'em

Freedom to arms! Your country's cause
In this dark hour your aid
God's blessing on the hand that draws
In her defence a patriot's blade.

Hurrah! Hurrah!
For the northern sights. Hurrah!
Hurrah for the dear old Flag
With every stripe and star"

Flag of the brave, thy folds shall fly
The sign of hope and triumph high.

Here's success to the boys, whoever they are
That have shouldered their muskets and gone to war
Victorious they'll be, defeated they can't
While they are led into battle by U. S. Grant.
    —by Augusta Quimby

Flag quilts were important to those who made and received them, and letters concerning flag quilts appeared in the Sanitary Commission *Bulletin*:

To the Editor of the *Bulletin*:

Perhaps your readers will be interested in the following items respecting two flag quilts. Some time in April, we received from a country town a quilt made in the form of a flag—red and white stripes and a blue field with the white stars sewed on, all nicely quilted. It was sent to the commission, with a note attached requesting the soldier who had the comfort of sleeping under this UNION quilt to acknowledge it, that we might have some proof that the soldiers received the donations designed for them.

In less than three weeks, the following letter was received at our rooms. Knowing that the exact words of a soldier's letter are always more interesting and effective than any abstract account, I send a copy of it:

Headquarters, 202nd Reg't PA. Vols., Fairfax Station, VA., May 10, 1865.

Fair Sex: I am a soldier in the above named regiment, and also am in receipt of a few lines pinned on one of your quilts; and feel heartily glad to know that we are not forgotten by the fair ones at home. You ask the question for me to inform you whether us soldiers receive such articles. I will answer by saying to the Society that we do. Also, my bed has on a very nice, clean white sheet and pillow, with the white slip on. I need not tell you of the pleasant dreams I had, but the first night the flag quilt was spread over me, I did dream of the loved ones far away.[10]

And that might have been the end of the story for the Belfast quilt, but for a fortuitous twist of fate. When the Armory Square Hospital, where the quilt was sent, closed in January 1865, the quilt disappeared for 147 years, before it turned up in a closet in Lewistown, Montana, from which it was offered to the Belfast Historical Society in 2011. It arrived safely packaged, and funds were raised for the restoration and conservation of the quilt. Shortly afterward, through a series of letters and emails, the history of the quilt after 1865 was revealed.

D. Willard Bliss, physician, of Washington, DC, was born August 18, 1825, at Brutus, New York. He graduated from Cleveland Medical College in 1846 and attained great celebrity as a physician and surgeon. Dr. Bliss entered the Union Army during the Civil War and had the following service record: surgeon in the 3rd Michigan Infantry (May 31, 1861); major and surgeon with the US Volunteers (September 21, 1861); surgeon in charge of Armory Square Hospital at Washington (July 1862–August 1865); brevet lieutenant colonel with the US Volunteers (March 13, 1865); mustered out December 8, 1865, and honorably discharged.

Armory Square Hospital was established in 1862, on the National Mall; the site is now the Smithsonian's National Air and Space Museum. Dr. Bliss was placed in charge in July 1862 and in his three-year tenure oversaw the laying out of the grounds of the hospital and the erection of more buildings. He is credited for his untiring devotion to the care and welfare of his patients. The 1,000-bed hospital complex consisted of twelve pavilions and overflow tents, spread across the Mall, and included quarters for officers, service facilities, and a chapel. The wounded from battlefields of Virginia were brought here.

When the hospital closed in the summer of 1865, all inventory was turned over to the medical staff.

Doctor D. Willard Bliss, photograph by Matthew Brady, sourced from the United States Library of Congress

According to Diana Milburn Brady, the doctor's great-great-granddaughter, it is possible the quilt was presented to him by his devoted staff. Dr. Bliss opened his own practice in Washington, DC, after the Civil War and continued to be a highly respected surgeon in that city. He was one of a group of doctors that tried to save President Lincoln when he was shot. He was an ardent advocate of recognizing real merit wherever found, and therefore of admitting well-qualified physicians into the Medical Association of the District of Columbia regardless of the color of their skin. This, in a politically charged medical association that included ex-Confederate surgeons, did not always sit well, and he was ripe for criticism when he tried working with an indigenous doctor from South America to try to find a cure for cancer.

When President Garfield was shot on March 4, 1881, Dr. Bliss headed the group of doctors who were to care for him. His condition improved and worsened during the two and a half months before he died and there were those who criticized when the patient became worse. A clipping from a Washington paper at the time says this: "There is something magnificent in Dr. Bliss's endurance, fidelity, courage and hope. The attempt to injure him in the estimation of the anxious people is followed by a reaction which makes him one of the most admired men of the day.

The restored Flag Quilt, constructed by the Ladies' Volunteer Aid Society from the First Church of Belfast, Maine, 1864. Cotton and wool (91.5" × 61.5"). *Collection of the Belfast Historical Society, Belfast, Maine; photograph courtesy of Megan Pinette*

The quilt was later given to Bliss's youngest child, Eugenie Prentiss Bliss. She married a young Yale-educated lawyer, George R. Milburn, in 1875, in Washington, DC. Milburn was appointed special Indian agent to the Dakota and Montana Territories in 1882. He moved his family to Miles City, Montana, in 1885, when he was elected that area's first county attorney. In 1889, he was elected judge of the Seventh District Court of Montana, the first year of Montana's statehood. He and Eugenie had four children; the last was George R. Milburn II, born in 1894. Then in 1901 the family moved to Helena, the new state capital. Eugenie died that year, followed by the death of her husband, Judge Milburn, in 1910. It is thought by the family that the quilt was then kept by one of the older sons, the youngest being only seven at the time of his mother's death.

George Milburn II had an interesting life; he went on to become a World War I pilot, then a respected rancher, establishing and managing a large ranch in central Montana, the N-Bar Ranch. After the older brothers' deaths, George became the keeper of the quilt until his death in 1980, while living in Billings, Montana. At that time, his house was cleaned out,

family treasures distributed among remaining family members, and some treasures discarded. For whatever reason, the bed quilt, sewn in Belfast, Maine, in 1864, went into a burn barrel. It was then that Matt Rickl, a family friend and neighbor, rescued it and brought it to his sister Mary's house, where it remained in storage for thirty-one years. It was Mary C. Rickl, daughter of Mary, living in Lewistown, Montana, who first contacted the Belfast Museum about the quilt and then returned it to Belfast.

A few last words from the Bliss/Milburn family, written in a letter to the Belfast Historical Society and Museum in August 2011. "Our family has been the keeper of many treasures . . . historic, sentimental, as well as valuable, so it is ironic that this quilt was nearly lost while in our care. It is a lesson to all of us to write the story and attach it to our treasures so that the next generations can know and appreciate why it has been saved. This special quilt has ended up where it belongs . . . right where it started. What a story it could tell!"

Album quilt, constructed block by block, Ladies' Aid Society of the Munjoy Hill section of Portland, Maine, 1864. Cotton, silk, silk embroidery, paint (86.5" × 68.5"). *Collection of the Brick Store Museum, Kennebunk, Maine (2543); photograph by C. A. Smith*

Two elaborate potholder quilts, one in the collection of the Brick Store Museum in Kennebunk, Maine, and the second in the collection of Mystic Seaport in Mystic, Connecticut, are presumed to have functioned as fundraisers to support the war effort, or they may have been used to decorate hospital wards. The skillful, heavy, and elegant silk embroidery and the use of silk fabrics belie an intention to donate them for use on hospital beds or for soldiers in the field.

Both quilts are attributed to the Ladies' Aid Society of Portland, Maine, and are inscribed with names of women (and two men), many of whom lived in the Munjoy Hill neighborhood, a few blocks north and east of the port and city center. Both quilts are potholder quilts, with blocks constructed from tan cambric for backgrounds. Cambric is a finely woven cotton that was often used for lining clothing. Each block is bound with red cotton, and the blocks contain hand and machine quilting and display military, patriotic, and local landmark motifs. Many of the appliqué motifs are cut from silk fabrics, and silk floss was used for the elaborate chain-stitch embroidery in many of the blocks, notably in the eagle, drum, and saber motifs on both quilts. Thirteen of the Brick Store Museum blocks are heavily machine quilted, and two of the blocks contain machine appliquéd motifs. The Mystic Seaport Museum's quilt contains nine blocks that are machine quilted.[1]

Local Stories from Portland, Maine

Detail, Munjoy Hill Album Quilt, silk embroidery depicting the Great Shield of the United States of America. *Collection of the Brick Store Museum, Kennebunk, Maine; photograph by C. A. Smith*

Detail, Munjoy Hill Album Quilt. Machine appliquéd block of a soldier's canteen and haversack. *Collection of the Brick Store Museum, Kennebunk, Maine; photograph by C. A. Smith*

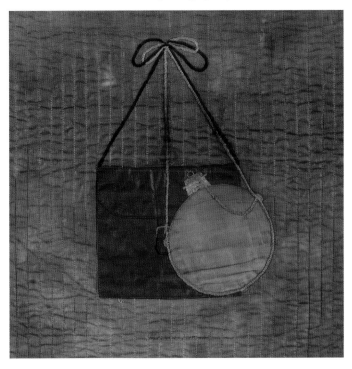

The blocks on the quilts are inscribed with names, some street addresses, and the date 1864. The Brick Store Museum quilt has a poem inscribed on a block depicting a fouled anchor:

> Ye have fought our battles for us
> Showing how the brave can die
> We are waiting to receive you,
> When ye lay your armor by.
>
> We'll stitch with the needle
> And fight with the tongue
> 'til every old rebel
> Is conquered or hung.
>
> Hope is the Anchor of the soul.
> 'Tis Jesus makes the wounded whole;
> Believe in Christ, the victory's won,
> Look up, by faith receive thy crown.

The 1860 census for Portland includes many of the signers of both of the Munjoy Hill Civil War quilts. Some of their husbands, specifically George W. Beal, James V. Poor, his son Samuel V. Poor, and Edward H. Capen, are listed as machinists, and it is possible that they were employees of the Portland Company. The Portland Company was founded in 1846 and operated until 1978. Some of the buildings still stand on Fore Street, at the foot of Munjoy Hill. In its many decades of operation, the Portland Company produced 600 steam locomotives, 160 merchant and naval vessels, railcars, and Knox automobiles, to name just some of its output.

Both quilts contain a depiction of a double-ended, side-wheel steamship, but there are no distinguishing details that would let us conclude the makers had a particular ship in mind. The Civil War side-wheel gunboats Agawam and Potoosuc had steam engines built at the Portland Company. Both were commissioned in 1863, in the summer before the quilt was made. They were gunboats of the Sacassus class and were shallow draft, with rudders at the bow and stern, allowing them to operate in either direction without having to turn around in the narrow waterways for which they were intended.[2]

Four women made or signed blocks in both quilts. Susan Hood signed a block appliquéd and embroidered with cannon balls in the Brick Store Museum quilt, but her block in the Mystic Seaport Museum quilt depicts a protractor and parallel, and both of her blocks are machine quilted.

Album quilt, constructed block by block, Ladies' Aid Society of the Munjoy Hill section of Portland, Maine, 1864. Cotton, silk, silk embroidery, paint (80.5" × 58.5"). *Collection of the Mystic Seaport Museum, Mystic, Connecticut (1968.24); photograph by Pamela Weeks*

Album quilt, detail. Block depicting the Portland Observatory on Munjoy Hill. *Collection of the Mystic Seaport Museum, Mystic, Connecticut (1968.24); photograph by Pamela Weeks*

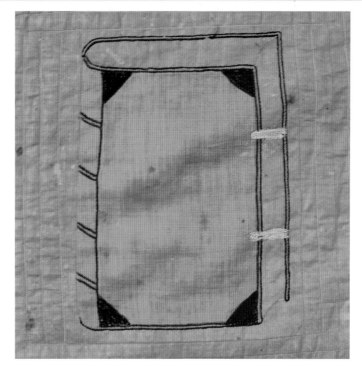

Album quilt, detail. Block depicting a bible or album. *Collection of the Mystic Seaport Museum, Mystic, Connecticut (1968.24); photograph by Pamela Weeks*

Mrs. Clara E. Gray made a block for each quilt, and both are painted. The Brick Store Museum quilt's block, signed by Mrs. Gray, contains a painted circle with "Portland" and "1864," and her block in the Mystic quilt is simply painted "1864." The 1866 *Portland City Directory* lists John Gray as owning a paint manufactory at 2 Munjoy Street.

Elmira K. (Hood) Sargent signed the block depicting the Portland Observatory in the Brick Store Museum quilt, but for the Mystic Seaport Museum quilt she signed the block containing a stack of twenty-one cannon balls.

Only Mrs. George W. Beal's two blocks are the same—beautifully appliquéd and embroidered red books, with gold clasps, but no markings; are they meant to be Bibles or albums?

Abbie J. (Sargent) Randall made or signed twelve of the blocks in the Mystic Seaport Museum quilt, and she signed one block with her husband's name, Joseph P. Randall. Was Abbie's mother, Elmira Hood Sargent, the organizer of both quilts, or was her aunt, Susan C. Hood, the organizer? Continuing research will reveal further family and neighborhood connections between the signers.

The inscriptions on the twenty blocks of the Brick Store Museum quilt include the names of women, addresses in the Munjoy Hill neighborhood, and the dates of August 1 and 4, 1864. The signatures vary from block to block, as does the quality of the workmanship, from rather crude piecing in two blocks to exquisite embroidery in ten others. Blue ink is used in two of the blocks, and two different blocks have painted or inked motifs.[3]

The Mystic Seaport Museum quilt contains thirty-five blocks, but only twenty-one distinct signers. Besides, Abbie J Randall, Mrs. Martha A. Berry, Mrs. Lydia A. Wood, and Mrs. C. E. Gray each made two blocks. The inscriptions are faded on many of the blocks, and the author relied on a transcription made at the time of the donation of the quilt to interpret some of the information.

A recognizable rendition of the Portland Observatory, a Munjoy Hill landmark, also appears on both quilts. Munjoy Hill is a physically prominent Portland neighborhood at the northern part of the city, named for one of its first seventeenth-century settlers. The

Detail, Munjoy Hill Album Quilt. Silk appliqué and embroidery depicting an unidentified paddle-wheel steamship. *Collection of the Brick Store Museum, Kennebunk, Maine (2543); photograph by C. A. Smith*

Detail, Munjoy Hill Album Quilt, silk and cotton appliqué depiction of the Portland Observatory. *Collection of the Brick Store Museum, Kennebunk, Maine (2543); photograph by C. A. Smith*

The Portland Observatory, December 2010. *Photograph by Pamela Weeks*

Cornelia Maria Dow, ca. 1890, Portland, Maine. *Photograph by Pamela Weeks, taken with permission of the Maine Women's Christian Temperance Union, Neal Dow Memorial, Portland, Maine*

observatory, built in 1807, towers over the neighborhood and has an important place in the history of the city. It was built to observe shipping, and signals were devised to alert the merchants in the harbor as to which ships were approaching. This gave them time to organize wharf space and arrange for the sale of the cargo. Since ships under sail could be seen up to 30 miles off shore, and if the wind was light or changed, it could take a day or more from the first sighting for the ship to make port.[4]

The observatory played a role in the only attack on Portland during the Civil War. Late in the day of June 26, 1863, a Confederate crew in command of the captured United States Ship (USS) *Archer* sailed into the harbor and anchored near the US revenue cutter *Caleb Cushing*. During the night, the Confederate crew overpowered the *Caleb Cushing*'s crew and towed both ships out of the harbor, but the wind died and they were becalmed 15 miles off the coast. In one version of the story, credit is given to Captain Enoch Moody, who, in the habit of early-morning observations from the tower, saw the ships and raised the alarm. The passenger steamers *Forest City*, *Casco*, and the *Chesapeake*, manned by armed citizens as well as soldiers and sailors, overtook the Confederate-held ships and, after a short battle, captured them.[5]

Another Portland, Maine, quilt survives to tell a story. It was attributed to Cornelia M. Dow, the daughter of Generla Neal Dow, a national temperance leader and celebrated Union officer.[6] This attribution was assumed because of the prominent placement and the number of her inscriptions that could be seen from photographs. The whereabouts of this quilt was unknown for three decades, but it had been well photographed in the mid-

Album quilt, constructed block by block, probably organized by Carrie Davis and Cornelia Maria Dow, Portland, Maine, 1864. Cotton (81" × 71"). *Collection of the Maine State Museum, 2015.11.1; photograph by Hearts & Hands Media Arts*

Detail, Davis/Dow Album Quilt. *Photograph by Hearts & Hands Media Arts*

Detail, Davis/Dow Album Quilt. *Photograph by Hearts & Hands Media Arts*

The Neal Dow House as it was in early 1900. It was donated to the Maine Women's Christian Temperance Union and is kept as a museum in Neal Dow's memory. *Photograph by Pamela Weeks with permission of the Maine Women's Christian Temperance Union, Neal Dow Memorial, Portland, Maine*

1980s, and information about it published in several places. In 2015, the quilt was acquired by the Maine State Museum in Augusta, and examination revealed many other signers. Also found in the prominent central medallion area of the quilt is the signature of Carrie E. Davis, the daughter of an associate Supreme Court judge for the Portland District, Woodbury Davis. Research will continue on Carrie Davis, but more is currently known about Cornelia Maria Dow. This quilt is 71 × 81 inches, much wider than the 48 inches recommended by the US Sanitary Commission, and it contains sixty-six appliquéd, red or blue, 8-inch star blocks bound in off-white twill tape and surrounding a large center block depicting a Union shield. Each block contains four or five inscriptions, and the center block includes both inscriptions and line drawings.

The inscriptions are especially patriotic in nature, all antislavery and pro-Union, and there are inked depictions of flags, eagles, rifles, anchors, and banners. Cornelia Dow made several blocks, and these are placed in prominent positions near the center of the quilt. One block includes this inscription:

We'll let them alone when the contest is ended,
And the fall of Fort Sumter is fully avenged
When the Stars and Stripes every stronghold shall cover,
And the fires of treason forever are quenched.

We march to conquer treason;
Our purpose is our might;
And we do not fear the issue,
For we know that we are right

There are also many temperance slogans inscribed on the quilt. Neal Dow is known as the "Father of Temperance," and he devoted his time, wealth, and influence to this cause. While serving as the mayor of Portland in 1850, he enacted the first temperance ordinances to pass in any American city. His daughter, Cornelia, never married and lived in her father's stately home on Congress Street in Portland, managing the household after her mother's death. Cornelia served on the executive committees of both the Maine Women's Christian Temperance Union (WCTU), and the national organization.

The family home was donated to the Maine WCTU by Neal's son, Frederick, and stands today at 714 Congress Street, Portland. Although its nineteenth-century exterior elegance has faded, the interior is carefully maintained and the house is open to the public for tours. Neal Dow's extensive collection of books on temperance is intact in his library, and his Civil War field trunk, hat, gloves, and other uniform elements are on display. In a corner of the front parlor is a late-nineteenth-century "biscuit" quilt made by Cornelia, and to the author's knowledge it is the only quilt discovered to date that was made by a woman who also had a hand in the construction of a quilt made for use in the Civil War. ❦

Biscuit Quilt attributed to Cornelia Maria Dow, c. 1890. Silk, cotton lining (75" × 75"). *Photograph by Pamela Weeks with permission of the Maine Womens' Christian Temperance Union, Neal Dow Memorial, Portland, Maine*

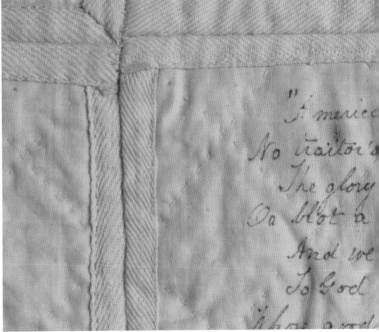

Detail, Davis/Dow Album Quilt, showing the applied tape binding

Letter writing was an important volunteer activity during the Civil War. Correspondence between soldiers and civilians provided comfort and encouragement on both sides, sustaining ties between family and community members. "Letter writing . . . functioned in both private and public ways: as a gendered form of war work, as romantic and economic labor . . . and as a coping method for feelings of impotency as the war continued."[1]

Letters to soldiers connected them to home, motivated them, and provided encouragement and a diversion from their daily conditions, which ranged from humdrum to horrible. The letters were morale boosters, and many accounts record a mail delivery as a major camp event. Letters also served an important romantic function during the war. Conventional contact between men and women was disrupted since the men were away at war. Courting was possible only in letters, and many correspondences were started in hopes of later marriage.

Soldiers placed advertisements in newspapers, soliciting correspondence. These were answered by both men and women wanting to provide boosting letters to the men at war. Notes and letters were often stuffed into the mittens or socks knit by their makers and donated to the war effort. Women and children pinned notes to shirts, handkerchiefs, or quilt blocks, and soldiers returned the kindness by writing to thank the makers.

THE VERNON, CONNECTICUT, U.S. SANITARY COMMISSION QUILT

In the summer of 1864, Sunday School students in Vernon, Connecticut, sewed blocks for an album quilt to be forwarded to the soldiers. The participants inscribed the blocks with their names, and some added the name of their town; one has the date and a verse. There are twenty-two signatures on the quilt, and the names indicate family relationships, friends, and neighbors.[2]

The blocks were sewn together, layered with a backing and thin cotton batting, and lightly quilted. The quilt was packed up and sent to the offices of the US Sanitary Commission in New York City, where it was stamped with the official seal. The quilt traveled to an Army camp near New Berne, North Carolina, and was given to Captain Robert Emmett Fisk, in command of Company G, of the 132nd New York Infantry.[3]

Thanks to a lovely, romanticized version of the story, titled "The Autograph Quilt," written by Fisk's daughter, Florence Fisk White, we know that Company G went to forage for fuel, and while they were gone the camp was raided for bedding by the enemy. Replacement blankets were sent for, and the supplies included quilts. Captain Fisk was delighted to receive a scrap quilt bearing many

Detail, Vernon Album Quilt, showing the US Sanitary Commission stamp. *Photograph by Jonathan Straight*

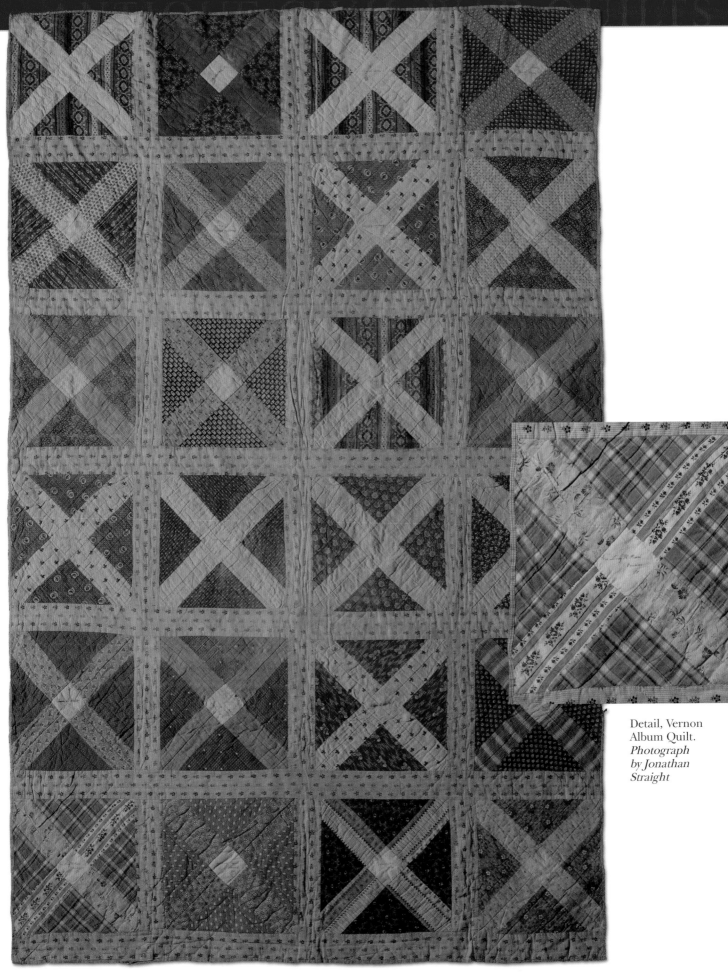

Detail, Vernon
Album Quilt.
*Photograph
by Jonathan
Straight*

Album quilt, Sunday school group in Vernon, Connecticut, 1864. Cotton (84" × 56"). *Collection of the Lincoln
Memorial Shrine (no accession number); photograph by Jonathan Straight*

names, and he wrote to two of the quilters, including Fannie Chester. Her older sister thought her too young for a wartime correspondence to be appropriate, so Lizzie (Elizabeth) Chester answered the soldier's letter and started a correspondence that lasted through the war.[4]

Lizzie Chester's second letter to Captain Fisk expresses the feelings both of a young woman wishing to do well by corresponding with a soldier and of conflict by the pressures of society against the impropriety of contacting a strange man:

South Windsor, Conn.
Nov. 15th 1864

Capt. R. E. Fisk

Since receiving your letter I have been at a loss to know what was best to do with regard to replying. Often we at home are urged to write to our friends in the army to cheer them in their loneliness, and to atone, in some measures for the hardships they undergo for us. Again we are warned against a correspondence of this kind and told that our letters are made subjects of ridicule—but after carefully considering the pros and cons, I have, as you doubtless perceive, ventured to write again.[5]

Captain Robert Emmett Fisk, 132nd New York Infantry, Company G. *Image courtesy of the Montana Historical Society*

Elizabeth Chester, about 1860.
Image courtesy of the Montana Historical Society

Their correspondence continued through the fall of 1864 and the spring of 1865. Fisk mustered out in June 1865 and came to Vernon, Connecticut, via New York City. The couple was engaged to be married, but first Robert accompanied his brother James Liberty Fisk, second in command of an expedition to colonize the Yellowstone Territory. Robert left Lizzie in Connecticut in July 1865 and headed west to meet his brother and prepare for the adventure. They were finally married in March 1867 and traveled to New York on a buying trip, purchasing a household of furniture as well as a printing press and a year's supply of newsprint; Robert and his brother Andrew Jackson Fisk started the *Helena Herald* (Montana) in late 1866.

Lizzie continued to write letters to friends and family back in Connecticut and stated several times that she wanted to write a book about her life and adventures as part of the generation that settled the West, but she never completed that project. Her correspondence survives and is collected at the Montana Historical Society.[6]

Letter from Lizzie to Robert, November 15, 1864. *Image courtesy of the Montana Historical Society.*

The Fisks lived in Helena until the late 1890s, when Robert and his brother sold the newspaper. Robert, Lizzie, and two of their children moved to Berkeley, California, where he died in 1908 and she in 1927. The quilt was donated by their daughter to the Lincoln Shrine, in Redlands, California.

THE SUNDAY SCHOOL SCHOLARS' QUILT

Susannah G. Pullen, a Sunday school teacher in Augusta, Maine, organized her class to make a quilt for the soldiers; it was finished on September 1, 1863. Inscriptions on this quilt were meant not only to comfort and entertain the soldiers who used it, but also to contain information about how and why the quilt was made. Because she also penned a request for correspondence on the surface of it, we know where and how it was used during the Civil War.

We have many dear friends connected with the army & any proper letters from any persons embraced in the defense of our country, received by any whose names are on this quilt shall have a reply. Tell us if nothing more its destination. . . . We meet with many others to sew for you every Wednesday and your letters would prompt us to more exertions for our patriots.[7]

The quilt was used in at least two hospitals: the Armory Square Hospital (see page 39) and the Carver Hospital, both in Washington, DC, as evidenced by letters received by Susannah Pullen and saved with the quilt when it was returned to her after the war; another request she had penned on its surface. In November 1863, Sergeant Nelson Fales wrote to tell her that he "had the pleasure of seeing the beautiful quilt sent by you to cheer and comfort the Maine Soldiers." His letter details his service in the 7th Maine Regiment, Company B, and that he was wounded seven months previous in the battle of Chancellorsville, Virginia.

Album quilt, Sunday School Scholars led by Susannah Pullen, Augusta, Maine, 1863. Cotton (84" × 50") (T7726). *National Museum of American History, Washington, DC*

Reverse, Sunday School Scholars' Quilt

Detail, Sunday School Scholars' Quilt

Letter from William Neal to Susannah Pullen, February 12, 1864. *Accession #138338, National Museum of American History, Washington, DC*

In a letter dated February 24, 1864, Sergeant William M. Neal, of Pennsylvania, wrote to say that he had seen her request for soldiers to write, and decided to accept the invitation. His letter explains that the quilt "has been in several hospitals and in constant use, and yet it looks perfectly new, so clean it is." He expressed the hope that it would be returned in good condition. Sergeant Neal was generous in his praise of the female volunteers who were giving of themselves in the war effort, providing comfort as nurses and providing comfort and inspiration with the quilt.

Mrs. Pullen must have asked the members of her class to provide several verses or sayings each. Virginia Eisemon, in her study of this quilt, charted the participants and their contributions and determined at least ten categories for the quotes. These include nonsense riddles, Bible riddles, practical or health advice, patriotic sayings, and life philosophy. Although the students provided the words for the inscriptions, one inscription indicates that Mrs. Pullen performed the inking. "This quilt contains 3675 words. It was executed by S. G. C. Pullen, the members and ex-members of her S.S. class."[8] On the back of the quilt she wrote these words:

> The commencement of this war took place Apr. 12th 1861. The first gun was fired from Fort Sumter. God speed the time when we can tell when, and where, the last gun was fired; & "we shall learn war no more." If this quilt survives the war we would like to have it returned to Mrs. Gilbert Pullen, Augusta, Me . . . This quilt completed Sept. 1st 1863.

It did survive use during the Civil War and it was returned to Mrs. Pullen, as she requested.[9]

Susannah Pullen's Civil War quilt passed down the generations through her daughters, but at one time it was on loan to the Augusta Historical Society and on display in the public library. In the early part of the twentieth century, a full transcription was made of the inscriptions, for which we are grateful, since they faded and are now barely legible on parts of the quilt. In 1936, Susannah's granddaughter, Gertrude B. Davis, donated the quilt to the Smithsonian Institution in her mother's name, Charlotte Pullen Scruton.[10]

Women in Granville, New York, made an album quilt inscribed with names, cheerful messages, and requests for correspondence. "May God protect you as you have our glorious flag. / Sallie B. Dillingham, Granville, N.Y. / Please address Sallie." Addie Brownell of Cambridge, New York, boldly charged the recipient of the quilt to "Write to me," and Ruth Dillingham, aged twenty-three, included "Write if you please," after her inscription, "In God we trust."

A quick dive into local history yields little on the makers who signed this quilt, beyond identifying the two Dillinghams as sisters, and a third Dillingham as probably a cousin. Ruth Dillingham appeared in the 1860 census still living at home with her parents, George and Amy, and her sister, Amy. The 1870 census lists Ruth boarding in the home of Simeon Brownell, who owns an insurance office, and Ruth is an insurance clerk, probably in his office. Addie Brownell was a signer of the Granville quilt but does not appear in the home of Simeon in 1870, so a relationship cannot be assumed but probably existed. ❦

Album quilt, reverse

Album quilt, made by women in Granville, New York, ca. 1865. Cotton, 79" × 56". *Collection of Wadsworth Atheneum, Hartford, Connecticut; gift of Mrs. Emerson G. Taylor, 1929.212; photograph by Allen Phillips / Wadsworth Atheneum*

This half pattern for a patriotic quilt appeared in *Peterson's Magazine*, volume 40, no. 1, July 1861, as a color-plate frontispiece. *Photograph by Pamela Weeks*

STARS & STRIPES

Stars and Stripes, the Teter Quilt

In July 1861, four months after the start of the Civil War, *Peterson's Magazine* printed a pattern for a Stars and Stripes quilt.[1] The pattern showed thirty-four stars in the central field and thirty-four stars in the border—the number of states in the Union after Kansas was admitted in January 1861. This pattern inspired many quilters; a number of quilts based on this pattern survive in private and museum collections.[2]

Detail of the Stars and Stripes Quilt.

The maker of this example, in the collection of the Smithsonian Institution, was Mary Rockhold Teter, of Noblesville, Indiana. *Peterson's Magazine* showed only a half pattern of the quilt and made no recommendations for the size of any of its sections. Mary made her quilt with a 32-inch blue center square set on point in a field of fifteen red and fourteen white, 2½-inch stripes. The blue border is 6¾ inches wide.[3]

Mary Teter made the quilt for her seventeen-year-old son George and inscribed his name in ink on the back. She quilted names in some of the stars in the border, including "Ab Lyncoln" to honor the president, Abraham Lincoln, and the names "Scott," "Butler," and "Genral Lyon," all prominent Civil War generals. The date, 1861, also appears in the quilting. Perhaps making such a patriotic quilt helped calm Mary's worries about both of her sons, who were enlisted in different units of the Indiana Infantry.

Stars and Stripes Quilt, Mary Rockhold Teter, Noblesville, Indiana, 1863. Cotton (87" × 86").
National Museum of American History, Washington, DC (8420)

Born in Ohio in 1817, Mary Rockhold married Thomas E. Teter in 1838. They moved to Indiana in 1847 and to Noblesville in 1850. Mary gave birth to six children, three boys and three girls, but only the boys survived infancy, and only George and younger brother Newton, born in 1848, married and had children. Thomas and Mary celebrated their golden anniversary in 1888. Mary died in 1897 in Noblesville, Indiana.[4] Her obituary states:

She was of a family of strong, patriotic Revolutionary stock, and inherited a willingness to do and to labor that the country might grow. Her grandfather was Capt. John Rockhold, a native of Pennsylvania, who served in the War for Independence. Her father, Joseph Rockhold, moved from Pennsylvania to Ohio in 1800. He was a captain in the War of 1812. This trait of patriotism was one of the strongest in the character of Mrs. Teter. During the late war she showed her great love for the soldier boys in many ways, aiding in every way she could to encourage and help in the country's peril.[5]

George Teter tried three times to join the army to fight for the preservation of the Union, like his brother Joseph, who was two years older and enlisted in Company B, 101st Indiana Infantry. At the age of sixteen, in 1861, George enlisted as a private in the 75th Indiana Infantry, but the quota of that regiment was full and he served only two weeks. He next tried to enlist in the 39th Indiana Infantry but injured his knee while hunting wild turkeys on foraging duty and was mustered out. He was successful in his third try in the spring of 1864 and became a member of Company B, 136th Indiana, and served for 100 days. His duty was at Memphis, Tennessee, where he was under fire in several skirmishes. He was honorably discharged September 2, 1864, at Indianapolis, at the expiration of his enlistment.

Joseph Teter was wounded at Chickamauga on September 19, 1863, and died in a hospital there a month later.[6]

At the end of the Civil War, George Teter returned to Noblesville to attend business college and then Indiana University. After his marriage to Mary Alice Paswater, in October 1869, he worked in the family's mill with his brother Newton and then expanded into the furniture and undertaking business for several years.

The family moved many times during the years to come, living for a time in Bangor, Iowa, where George owned a mercantile business for nine years and served as the postmaster. Next, the family went to Colorado for a short time, hoping for an improvement to George's health. They then returned to Frankfurt, Indiana, where he bought a mill. In 1885 he moved back to Noblesville, and in 1887 he moved north to Tipton. "He was successful in all his business undertakings and is the owner of considerable valuable real estate and residence property in Noblesville, Kokomo and Tipton."

Despite these many moves, George and Mary were active members of the Methodist Church, and George was a longtime member of the Independent Order of Odd Fellows, a fraternal organization widely known at the time. He was one of the early members of the Grand Army of the Republic (GAR) post at Noblesville, and was also a member at Tipton. He served in leadership roles in the local, state, and national levels of the G.A.R,, which was founded as a fraternal organization for Civil War veterans. The GAR also served to advocate for disabled veterans and those requesting pensions for their service.[7]

Public records concerning George Teter are scarce after 1900. In 1920, the US federal census lists him in the household of his son, Edward, along with Edward's wife and their eldest son, Eugene. George's pension record confirms his service in the Indiana Infantry and states that he died on November 21, 1927, in Aurora, Illinois.[8]

Eugene Austin Teter, George's grandson, married Martha A. Brown of Oklahoma in 1920. The donation records to the Smithsonian Institution state that George Teter gave the quilt to his granddaughter-in-law, Martha, to honor her service in World War I. She was a nurse and worked for many years as supervisor of nurses at Trinity Hospital in Little Rock, Arkansas. She and Eugene donated George Teter's Civil War Stars and Stripes Quilt to the Smithsonian Institution in 1940, thus preserving an important icon of a family's patriotism.[9]

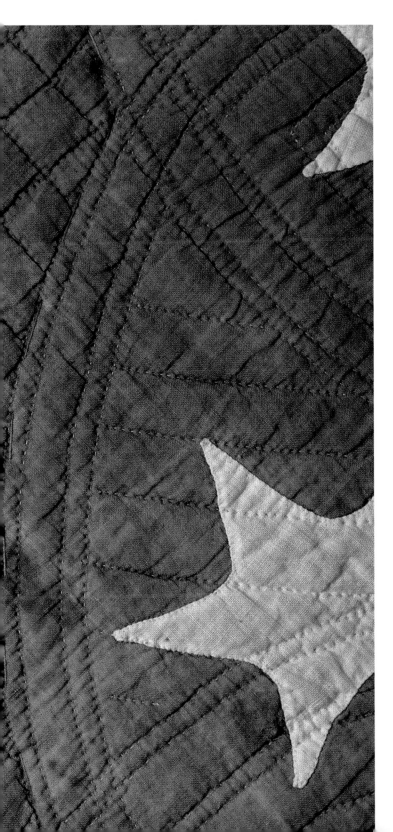

Detail of the Stars and Stripes Quilt

{ contributed by **Sherry Massey,**
Senior Registrar, Oklahoma Museum of History

A Soldier-Made Quilt

Sergeant Stephen A. Lewis, Company C, 10th Ohio Voluntary Infantry.
Collection of the Oklahoma Historical Society, Oklahoma City, OK

Stephen A. Lewis was born April 5, 1838, at Edinburg, Beaver County, Pennsylvania. During the Civil War, he served with two units: Company E of the 19th Ohio Voluntary Infantry and Company C of the 104th Ohio Voluntary Infantry, where he obtained the rank of sergeant. Mr. Lewis was engaged in the Battle of Franklin, Tennessee, on November 30, 1864, when he was wounded. A musket ball passed through one side of his face and out the other. His Union comrades left him behind, thinking he had perished. When Mr. Lewis regained consciousness, he discovered Confederate soldiers scouring the battlefield for Union survivors. Along with others of the wounded, he was forced to start marching to the infamous Andersonville prison.

Along the trail, Lewis found an ax head that he hid in his clothing. That night, after the guard had fallen asleep, Lewis struck him with the ax head and ran for his life, with dogs tracking his scent. He happened upon a slave woman's cabin, where he explained who he was and what was happening. She took him in and hid him under a corn husk mattress, where she lay to disguise his scent. When Confederate soldiers came to her door, he was not found. At dawn, his rescuer walked him to Union lines, from which he was taken to the Union hospital in Louisville, Kentucky. Here he made this quilt from old blankets, Confederate and Union uniforms, and any scraps he could find. Unfortunately, his wound never fully healed and he wore a beard the rest of his life to disguise his scars.

Mr. Lewis returned to Ohio and eventually relocated his family to Alva, Oklahoma Territory. He farmed there until his death on February 20, 1923. In gratitude to the slave woman who saved his life, Lewis offered a safe haven to any African American who needed his help during the turbulent racial conflicts of the early 1920s.

The quilt made by Stephen Lewis was passed down in his family and came into the possession of Denzel D. Garrison, a former Oklahoma state senator and Oklahoma Historical Society board president, who graciously donated the quilt in 1979. It measures 84 by 86 inches and is pieced in squares and rectangles of blue, green, black, gray, and tan wool. It is tied with red wool yarn. The red cotton backing overlaps the edges to form the binding. According to the donor, Mr. Lewis considered this quilt one of his most prized possessions. ❧

Detail of the Sgt. Stephen A. Lewis Quilt

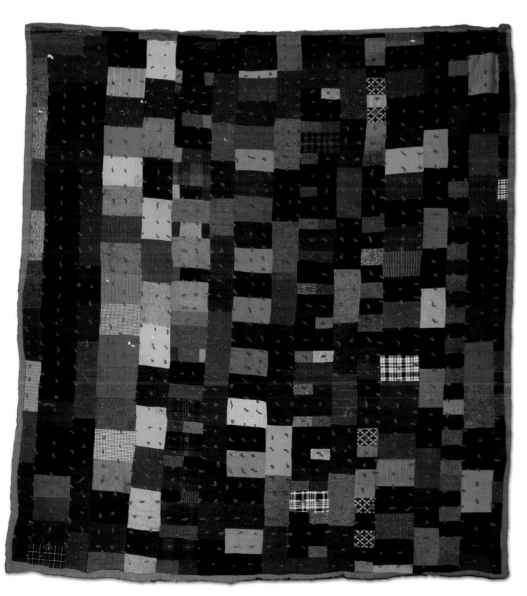

Wool scrap quilt, Sergeant
Stephen A. Lewis, Edinburgh,
Pennsylvania, 1864. Wool (84" ×
86"). Collection of the Oklahoma
Historical Society, Oklahoma City,
Oklahoma. *Photograph by Sherry
Massey*

Chapter 10

The Little Boy Who Went to War

G. H. PLIMPTON,   Foxboro', Mass.

Photograph of Henry Pratt, ca. 1860, in civilian clothes.
Courtesy of Dione Stuart

Wee sister, see my little sword-
And here my wooden gun-
When I have grown a taller boy
I'll have a larger one.
And then I'll be a soldier brave
With buttons new and bright,
And I'll be off to Mexico
And teach them how to fight.

—*Henry Pratt, Mansfield, Mafs. age 6*

Photograph of Pratt Family, ca. 1845. *Pictured from left to right, back row*: Charles W. Pratt, Levi F. Pratt, Sally W. Pratt, Sarah Pratt, Eunice W. Pratt, and Amasa Pratt Jr. *Pictured from left to right, front row*: Henry B. Pratt, Mary A. Pratt, and John Quincy Pratt.
Courtesy of Dione Stuart

Pratt Family Quilt. Dated and signed 1847. *Collection of the International Quilt Study Center & Museum, Lineola, Nebraska, 2011.050.0001; gift of Dione Stuart; photograph Jonathan Strait*

The Pratt Family Quilt was signed in April 1847 at the height of the Mexican-American War, when feelings of patriotism were running rampart in the United States; thus the reference by little Henry Pratt to being "off to Mexico and teach them how to fight." Fourteen years later, the little boy who wanted to go to war got his chance to fight in the Civil War.

The Pratt Family Quilt was made and signed as a going-away present for the seventeen-year-old daughter, Eunice Pratt, and was given to her in mid-1847. Where Eunice was going is not known. Perhaps it was meant as a trousseau gift, in anticipation of a wedding in the near future. However, all of her siblings, her parents, her aunts, and two close friends signed blocks:

Amasa Pratt block close-up. *Courtesy of Dione Stuart; photograph by Jonathan Strait*

Sally Pratt block close-up. *Courtesy of Dione Stuart; photograph by Jonathan Strait*

Henry Pratt block close-up. *Courtesy of Dione Stuart; photograph by Jonathan Strait*

Henry Pratt, ca. 1862, in military uniform. *Courtesy of Dione Stuart; photograph by Jonathan Strait*

Poem by Amasa Pratt, age 46,
Mansfield, Massachusetts (father):

> The sky is clear and bright as then
> And all around as gay;
> But when around I look again
> I find thou art away.
> A love now starts; I'll tell thee why
> 'Tis thee I fain would see;
> But till we meet I bid goodbye;
> Without a word to thee.

Charles W. Pratt, age 15, Mansfield (brother):

> Oh, sometimes in thy hour of woe
> When pleasures are forgot,
> Just cast one hasty glance on this
> And read "Forget me not."
> Affection like a golden chain
> Binds kindred hearts together.

L. Franklin Pratt, age 14, Mansfield (brother):

> On summers eve when oft you see.
> Beneath the pale moon cheering ray;
> Say will you sometimes think of me
> When I am absent far away,
> Please accept this as a token
> Of friendship from your Brother.

Sally W. Pratt, age 40, Mansfield, Mass (mother):

> A mother's blessing on her daughter
> Remember who gave thee life
> When other days shall come;
> When she who had thy earliest kiss,
> Sleeps in her narrow house.
> And bade thee keep the gift that when
> The parting hour would come
> We might have hope to meet again
> In an eternal home.

And Eunice W. Pratt, age 17, reply:

> When you look on this, oh think of the friend
> To whose lonely hours you
> Pleasure did fend
> Whose best wish attends you,
> Wherever you may be,
> Who cannot forget you,
> Who says think of me.
> In this album quilt of mine,
> Let fair friendships name appear
> Framed by assuming print
> Prompted by a heart sincere.
> There let friends present their offerings
> And with kindly feelings great;
> Then let names long loved and cherished
> In harmonious concert meet.

Little Henry Pratt got his wish. Fifteen years later, on September 26, 1862, Henry Bradford Pratt, age twenty-two, enlisted in Company G, 3rd Massachusetts Infantry. Sometime later, he was wounded in battle and spent the rest of the Civil War in and out of military hospitals. He was released from active service on March 19, 1863.

He wrote at least one letter home to his father and mother on US Sanitary Commission stationary, dated August 23, 1864, from the Judiciary Square Hospital

Henry Pratt's letter home, page 1, from Judiciary Military Hospital, Washington, DC. *Courtesy of Dione Stuart; photograph by Jonathan Strait*

Henry
Pratt's letter
home, page 2,
from Judiciary Military
Hospital, Washington,
DC. *Courtesy of Dione Stuart;*
photograph by Jonathan Strait
Envelope, Henry Pratt's letter home,
addressed to Mrs. Amasa Pratt, his mother.
Courtesy of Dione Stuart; photograph: Jonathan Strait

in Washington, DC:

> My Dear Father and Mother I once more take my pen in hand to inform you whare I am and how I am getting along. I am not very well at present. I have had head like lice very bad fore sum time but I don't think thare is much danger and at present I hope when these few lines come to hand they may find you all well and doing well. I don't want you to get friten at this when it come to hand I [?] that I would rit you a few lines to let you no whare I was. I am at Judiciary Square Hospital, Washington, D.C. Rit as soon as they come to hand, send your letter to Judiciary Square Hospital, Washington, D.C., Ward 3. This is from your Dear son to his Dear Father and Mother.

His parents may not have been overly reassured when they received the note, since all the family was well educated. This note sent to his parents was penned by someone else with poor grammar and writing skill, and they must have worried about how bad his wounds were. At least he was alive.

Henry Pratt's wounds were serious. He died August 31, 1865, and is buried in his home city of Mansfield, Massachusetts.

The remarkable story of this family could be seen as a history of America in the first half of the nineteenth century. Little Henry Pratt's grandfather, Amasa Pratt Sr., served during the War of 1812. Not only did Henry serve in the Union forces during the Civil War, but so did his brothers Levi Franklin and Charles W. Pratt. They also both signed blocks on Eunice's quilt.

The little boy seated on Amasa Pratt Jr.'s knee, George F. Pratt, and his father, Charles F. Pratt, served with both the Ohio and the Massachusetts Infantry. Thus, this one family contained at least five Union soldiers.

The Pratt family's Union beliefs probably stemmed from their long participation in the abolitionist movement. Sally Pratt, the quiltmaker, had led a successful movement in her church in the 1830s, the Mansfield Orthodox Congregational Church, to splinter the church between those who believed in slavery and those who did not. There were Pratts in Mansfield who owned plantations in the South and supported their rights to own slaves, but Amasa, Sally, and their branch considered slavery to be wrong and immoral. ❦

Henry Pratt's enlistment/muster-out card.
Courtesy of Dione Stuart; photograph by Jonathan Strait

Receipt for Henry Pratt's 1866 grave monument. *Courtesy of Dione Stuart; photograph by Jonathan Strait*

"Trust in the Lord" half block close-up.
Courtesy of Dione Stuart; photograph by Jonathan Strait

Back of Pratt Family Quilt, showing early-nineteenth-century chintz. *Courtesy of Dione Stuart; photograph by Jonathan Stuart*

In 1863 Jane A. Blakely Stickle of Shaftsbury, Vermont, made a quilt. It is an unusual quilt for its time, in that the blocks are smaller than average—there are 169 4-to-5-inch squares in the large central area of the quilt—many are intricately pieced, some are very simple, and some are appliquéd. Jane Stickle knew geometry, since many of the unique block patterns require the hand of an expert draftswoman. There are some common quilt blocks in use, such as Nine Patch and basket squares, but many more are original patterns.

The pieces making up these small blocks range from less than a quarter inch to 2 inches, and some of the blocks have as many as thirty-five to forty pieces. Each block is pieced with just two fabrics, a printed calico or even-weave gingham and a white fabric. She also had a deep scrap bag from which to draw, and perhaps many neighbors to swap scraps with, since not one fabric is repeated in the squares or triangles.

In War Time: The Jane A. Blakely Stickle Quilt

The Jane Stickle Quilt, detail showing corner block inscribed "In War Time, 1863. Pieces. 5602. Jane A. Stickle."

The Jane A. Blakely Stickle Quilt, made in Shaftsbury, Vermont, 1863.
Cotton, hand pieced, appliquéd, and quilted, 80¼" × 80¼". *Collection of the
Bennington Museum, accession number 2064*

The calicos were carefully arranged by color in the layout of the quilt. Jane placed a green block in the center and chose this block carefully—the only other green blocks are in the outermost corners, placed there with the only blue block in the quilt. This center green block is surrounded by others pieced in yellow, and those in turn by alternating concentric rounds of color, including purple, pink, and reddish-brown calicos. Many of the blocks that were once purple have faded to brown, a common occurrence in many early- and mid-nineteenth-century quilts.

This central area is bordered on four sides with 108 sharp isosceles triangles, alternating between solid fabric and more intricately pieced blocks. Set in each corner is a larger pieced or appliquéd triangle, with one bearing the name of the maker, and the inscription "In War Time, 1863." and "Pieces. 5602." It is also very unusual for mid-nineteenth-century quilts to have a scalloped border, and Jane applied long strips of light-colored fabric to the edges of her quilt, cut scallops, and bound the quilt with straight-of-the-grain green cotton.

Less unusual is the fact that each block is of a different pattern. Sampler or variety quilts composed of blocks pieced in multiple patterns were part of the popular fad of inscribed friendship quilts, which had its peak in the 1860s. Generally, however, a unique maker contributed each block and inscribed her name on it, often including messages or place-names.[1]

The quilt was donated to the Bennington Museum in Bennington, Vermont, at some time in the 1930s by Jane's niece, Sarah Blakely Seymour Bump,[2] and in 1991 it was published in *Plain and Fancy*, Donna Bister and Richard Cleveland's book on Vermont quilts.[3] Brenda Ganges Papadakis saw it, and so began a fascination that resulted in her publishing, in 1996, *Dear Jane: The Two Hundred Twenty-Five Patterns from the 1863 Jane A. Stickle Quilt.* The book is still popular, and thousands of people around the world have made what Brenda calls "Baby Janes," versions of the quilt from nearly exact to wild and bold.[4]

Brenda did extensive research with the help of the staff of the Bennington Museum and others and sketched a picture of Jane Stickle and her life from the available resources.

The Jane Stickle Quilt, detail showing unusual triangular border

The Jane Stickle Quilt, detail showing the reverse of the quilt, pieced of linen and containing her mother's initials—"S B" for Sally or Sarah Blakely

This watercolor painting is the only other work of art known to have been made by Jane A. Stickle. *Photo courtesy of Bennington Museum*

In 2013, author Pam Weeks was invited by Jamie Franklin, curator of collections of the Bennington Museum, to examine the Jane Stickle quilt and refresh the research, which resulted in an article in the museum's publication in the summer of 2013.[5] Several things about the quilt and the families were found, thanks to a team effort and the increasing ease of doing research on the internet. Other items donated by Jane's family were examined and gave insights to the family's history, and freshly discovered newspaper articles from the period yield more information about both Jane's family and the quilt.

That Jane A. Blakely was well educated is proved by both the quilt, which required great needlework skill and a thorough knowledge of geometry, and a watercolor painting, also in the collection of the Bennington Museum. The painting is done in the style of theorem works stenciled on velvet, frequently made during this part of the nineteenth century, and the schools where it was taught advertised the teaching of this technique. In the painting, stylized flowers are formally arranged in a vase, likely traced from a pattern or copied from a master design. It does show some refinement in execution and choice of colors.

Jane recycled a linen sheet for the majority of the backing of the quilt. The sheet is made of two panels joined by a center seam that is butted and hand sewn. Letters were found embroidered at the bottom portion of the sheet that makes up the reverse of one of the scallops. "S B" is embroidered in tiny cross-stitches less than one-quarter inch tall. These are her mother's initials and represent Sarah (also called Sally) Blakely.[6]

Jane's father died in 1831, and the very thorough household inventory of her father's estate included two sets of linen sheets as well as quilts.[7] It was customary in the early nineteenth century for a homemaker to mark

MARRIED,

In Shaftsbury, on the 13th ult. by the Rev. R. R. Bennett, Mr. AARON GIBBONS, and Miss FANNY PRATT, both of White Creek, N. Y.

Also. by the same in Shaftsbury, on the 29th ult. Mr. WALTER STICKLES, and Miss JANE BLAKELY, both of Shaftsbury.

Also, by the same in White Creek, on the 23d ult. Mr. EMMONS RUSSELL, and Miss MARTHA CHASE, both of the same place.

Also, in the same place on the 20th ult. by Rev. R. R. Bennett, Mr. EDWARD BURCHARD, and Miss DIANTHA RICE.

Vermont Gazette; Bennington, VT; Tues., 12 Nov 1844

A newspaper announcement of the marriage of Jane A. Blakely and Walter P. Stickle, October 29, 1844

her household linens with her initials and an inventory number, either in ink or with embroidery. The initials identified the owner, and the inventory number ensured proper rotation of the sheets in household use.[8]

A great mystery was solved when Kathy D. Duncan reported in her genealogy blog that she found Jane Blakely and Walter Stickles's wedding announcement as reported in the *Bennington Banner* in 1844. It was assumed that Walter and Jane were married sometime before the 1850 census, when they appear on the same farm in Shaftsbury, Vermont, but Duncan's discovery pins the date to October 29, 1844. Jane is twenty-seven at this time, and, as Duncan points out, this is late for a woman at this time to marry.[9]

The 1850 census lists W. P. Stickles as head of the household, which includes her brother, listed as E. M. Blakely (Erastus, Jane's younger brother) with his occupation "Tailor"; her mother, Sarah Blakely; and two other adults with relationships unknown. It should be noted that no record has been found that Jane and Walter Stickle had children. No one younger than twenty is listed in this census record.[10]

Vt. Regiment,

of the Commis- few days with e all been down ns the last of

Hon. John R. and wood shed he east part of

—We regret to f this place, was rown from his air at Wilming- ever are not of in doors many beast, became onsequently un- uite a number of iderable bodily

in this Village, g head on Sun- Arlington, oth- , Rev. I Jen- the Congrega- tudent of this

quality, so that what was lacking in quantity was made up in quality.

"Floral Hall" was never so attractive as on the present occasion. The fingers of "our fair ones" must have been very busy during the past year, to have got together so much that was so attractive and valuable. The Hall was richly decorated with fine paintings, rich embroderies, and croshaing. Among the specimens of painting that struck us as possessing great artistic skill, were those of Mrs. Joseph Niles, of Shaftsbury, and Miss Jennie Carpenter, of Pownal. There were a number of others, which possessed great merit, but we do not now remember their names. Mrs. J. B. Smith, of Manchester, Mrs. Taft and Mrs. Stickles presented each a very extra bed quilt. Mrs. Stickles is an in-valid lady, having been for a long time confin-ed to her bed, but her ambition to do some-thing to kill time induced he to put together this quilt. It contains many thousand different pieces of cloth, no two of which are exactly a-like. Upon one corner is marked in plain let-ters, "made in the war of 1863."

There were several specimens of Hair Work," on exhibition which were very neatly executed; those of the young invalid "soldier boy" of Arlington, Mr. F. P Aylsworth, attracted much attention, and justly so, too. Miss Ordway, of Bennington, also had some specimens, which were highly praised,

and $12 for e

There is no Gen. Meade's recent accoun imminent.

All doubts late battles be the actual sig to the dispatc

There is a healthy that t corpse to star

The Union ceded, gives th in the next Co elect the office

The vessels at the taking ed, and the su for distributio lant tars who

A Memphis able expeditio urated, and hi will not interfe Mississippi ar force.

The news fr Blunt had def could be foun ed his comman rs arrive at L

The Hera says : By re

An excerpt from the *Bennington* (Vermont) *Banner*, with descriptions of the quilts submitted and the prizes awarded. *Photograph courtesy of Jamie Franklin*

The gravestone of Jane and Walter Stickle, Shaftsbury, Vermont

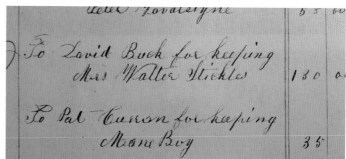

Jane and Walter Stickle were "kept" by the Town of Shaftsbury in one home while Walter was alive, and Jane boarded with David Buck until her death.

The 1860 census reports Jane on one Shaftsbury farm, but her husband, Walter, is enumerated on another, that of Jane's brother Erastus Blakely. His wife and mother, Sarah Blakely, are also included in this household. Because the census is a snapshot of one day in a year, it could be that Walter was counted at the Blakely farm because he was visiting there, not necessarily that he and Jane were legally separated. We learn from a newspaper reference, the *Bennington Banner* of October 1, 1863, that "Blakely and Stickles took a $2 premium" for their horses at the Bennington County Fair. Were they in business together raising horses, and was Walter at the Blakely farm to help with training?

In that same 1863 article on the premiums won at the Bennington County Fair, the writer stated that "Mrs. J. B. Smith of Manchester and Mrs. Taft and Mrs. Stickles presented each a very extra bed quilt. Mrs. Stickles is an invalid lady, having been for a long time confined to her bed, but her ambition to do something to kill time induced her to put together this quilt. It contains many thousand different pieces of cloth, no two of which are exactly alike. Upon one corner is marked in plain letters, 'made in the time of war 1863.'"

Bennington Banner, October 1, 1863

Some writers have opined that Jane worked on the quilt to keep from worrying about her young family members fighting in the Civil War, and perhaps this is true. Work continues on the complicated family relationships of the Blakely and Stickles and other Shaftsbury families. Walter was the fourth to youngest of eleven children, and the author was able to find that he and Jane had seven nephews in Walter's family enlisted in the Union Army by 1863.

Walter and Jane Sickles are listed in the same household in the 1870 census, with the farm valued at $6,000 (about $110,000 in today's money) and personal property at $1,500. Erastus and family are listed on the farm next door. Another newspaper article yields information on Walter's horse-raising success:

"The races at the North Bennington Driving Park association called out a good number of the friends of the turf on Saturday last. The first purse was won by Walter Stickles gray mare; the second purse went to George Barker, Jr., of White Creek; the third purse was won by Wm. Reed's black stallion "Dolan," and the pacing was won by Henry G. Root's bay mare. The meeting was one of the best the association has ever held."

Vermont Gazette, November 6, 1875, p. 3

Jane's brother Erastus Blakely died in 1878, and court records state that a claim on the estate by Walter Stickles in the amount of $2,966 is refused.[11] It is likely that Jane and Walter somehow lost their farm, perhaps due to debts, and perhaps because the executors of Erastus Blakely's estate do not allow Walter's claim against it. In the 1880 census they are boarders in the household of George and Evelyn Eddy. Walter is listed as afflicted with rheumatism. Also in 1880, the Shaftsbury town records record that Walter P. Stickles was given $5 per week, totaling $170, for his own keeping. He and Jane were wards of the town.[12]

The annual report of Shaftsbury includes the report of the Overseer of the Poor and continues listing the Stickles through the 1880s and 1890s. Walter died in 1883 while still boarding with the Eddys. From 1884 until Jane's death in 1896, the records show that David Buck was paid $100 per year for "keeping Mrs. Walter Stickles."

Little changes through these entries—there are usually one or two other people cared for by the town for various periods, all averaging $5 per week. There is a subtle change in the attitude about Jane Stickle—at the beginning of her individual record, she is listed as Mrs. Walter Stickle, but she is slowly downgraded to Mrs. Jane Stickle and, at the last, J. Stickle. Her social status declines over the years she is "kept" by the town. She is buried in Central Cemetery, sharing a headstone with Walter, near the Blakely gravestones.

Jane A. Blakely Stickle's legacy is a masterwork of a quilt made in 1863. She signed it, noting in her inscription an important current event, but also calling attention to the extraordinary feat of needlework she accomplished—5,306 pieces. Each block is unique and uses different fabrics. Jane had access to an amazing wealth of material, and she had time to draft and execute the intricate blocks. She made it during a time in her life when she was enjoying some degree of wealth in both time and resources, which did not last.

How and why did Jane and Walter Stickle lose everything? Why were they boarded out, when, according to census records, two of his brothers continued to live on their farms in Shaftsbury and prosper, and many nieces and nephews lived in the area? Is there a relationship between the Stickles and David Buck, in whose home Jane boarded until she died? And why did the quilt pass to Erastus's daughter, Sarah Louise Bump? Detective work continues, and we may never know, but we are left with an incredible quilt to comfort us while we ponder.

QUILTS to

Quilts to Make Today

make
TODAY

Choosing Fabrics to Reproduce Civil War Quilts

To accurately reproduce antique quilts, a person requires knowledge of textile history and artistic interpretation. The history part involves knowing what block patterns and fabrics were used in which periods, and the artistic part involves selecting fabrics available today and making them work in your quilt. Fabric prints and colors have gone in and out of style at different times as fashions changed with advancing technology of the Industrial Revolution. In fact, fads were created when the technology created new colors or new prints. Quilts can be dated accurately by their fabrics, the block piecing, and sometimes the style of the quilting used to secure the layers.

The art of reproducing antique quilts develops as one comes to recognize that some fabrics available today are similar in print style and color to early fabrics. For example, a quilter seeking the right Turkey Red fabric might find a fabric that has the right color, but the print is wrong for the period or the scale of the print is wrong, or the secondary colors are wrong. Turkey Red is described as a deep red with a blue cast; using a deep red with an orange cast would not be the right choice, and prints rarely had a pattern repeat larger than 8 or 9 inches. Tiny repeating prints are seen most often.

Today, quilters are blessed that there are so many reproduction fabrics available for making authentic-looking nineteenth-century quilts. Many fabric stores carry these fabrics, sometimes in small amounts. However, quilters also have online internet sources that specialize in reproduction fabrics. There are highly reputable online sites, such as www.reproductionfabrics.com and www.schoolhousequilts.com.

Many of the current fabric manufacturers place the appropriate time period in the selvage of the bolt, along with the line's name, designer, and print or design number. (Save these in case you need to purchase more.)

When purchasing reproduction fabrics to make an authentic-looking Civil War quilt, remember these simple guidelines:

1. Fabrics fade with time. Many of the old fabrics may have been much brighter when new, or they may contain fugitive dyes that caused the color to change.

2. Reproduction fabrics from before the Civil War are appropriate to use in Civil War reproduction quilts, since nineteenth-century quilters, just like today, would draw fabrics from their stash or scrap bags.

3. Plaids are always appropriate, as are striped fabrics or grids.

4. Many Civil War fabrics contain small designs. Although you might find paisleys, flags, squiggles, flowers, etc., they tend to be larger than the designs popular in the earlier 1800s.

In this book, we deal with patterns and fabrics that were available before and during the Civil War period, approximately 1850 to 1865. Before the war, when cotton was king, printed cottons were plentiful and cheap and quiltmaking was very popular. As the war progressed, materials became more scarce and cotton more expensive; women must have recycled clothing and household textiles and dug deeper into their scrap bags to make their quilts. Therefore, utilitarian quilts were made with scraps as much as thirty to forty years old.

Records of several Ladies' Soldiers' Aid Societies show that new materials were purchased for war relief work, but of the quilts included in this book, most are scrap quilts. The three exceptions are the Cornelia Dow Album Quilt (see page 49), the Munjoy Hill Album Quilts (see page 44), and the Mary Rockhold Teter Quilt (see page 58).

Scrap quilts exhibit a wide time range of fabrics—some dating as early as the 1830s and some new at the time of the war. The Hingham quilt (see page 30) and the Beverly Farms potholder quilt (see page 24) include two fabrics known to have been printed during the war and contain patriotic Union motifs.

COLORS & PRINT STYLES

Meant to be a guide in selecting accurate contemporaneous fabrics for reproducing Civil War soldier's quilts today, the fabrics shown and described below are reproductions that represent fabrics that would range in date from 1830 to 1865. The names given describe the natural dyestuffs used to produce the fabrics, but the processes are different today.

Although called "homespun," these woven-plaid and woven-stripe fabrics were produced in factories and were used for men's shirts and children's dresses. They are seen in many color combinations, from bright tartan-like fabrics to two-color, even-weave ginhams.

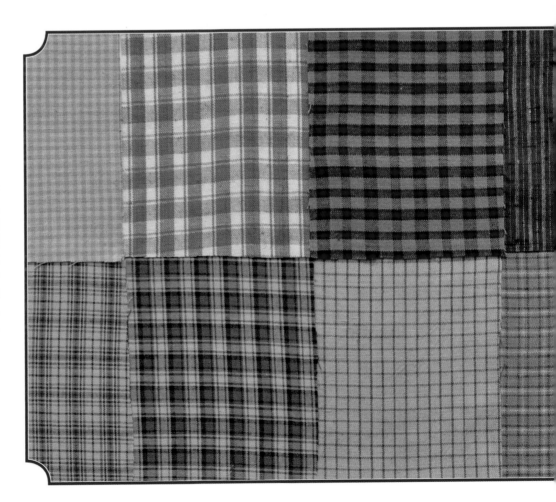

Indigo has been used in dying textiles for centuries. Generally, think "navy blue" and you have indigo, but it can also be a clear medium, or light blue. The dyestuff is derived from a plant grown in many parts of the world. The process involves several steps, including multiple immersions in the dye bath. Prints on a dark-blue field are generally white, or white overprinted with chrome yellow or green. A white or colored ground can be printed with various shades of indigo-blue details. A dark indigo blue might appear blue black.

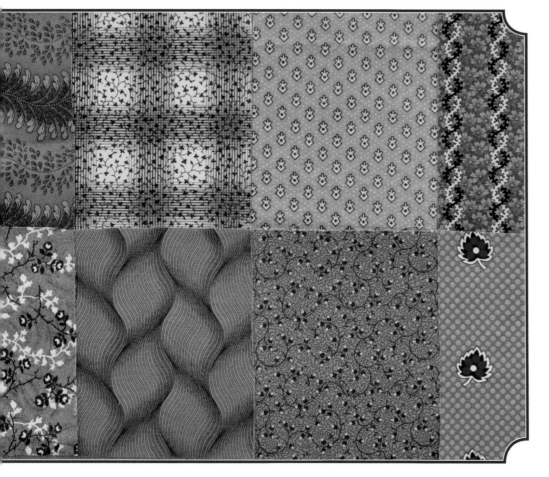

Many tan or grayish fabrics found in early-nineteenth-century quilts were once purple, another madder tint produced with a specific mordant. In 1856, chemist William Perkin accidently produced a purple dye while doing another experiment, and the color mauve was a rage within a few years. It is most often seen in wools and silks in this period but could also produce a medium purple similar to the madder purples on cotton.

Madder styles available before the Civil War were very popular for everyday dress prints and were also used for dressing gowns. These reds have a brownish-rusty cast to them, with many other secondary colors in the prints, commonly brown, blue, green, and black. Stripes were popular, as were paisley prints. Also popular were small floral prints with organic elements in the prints.

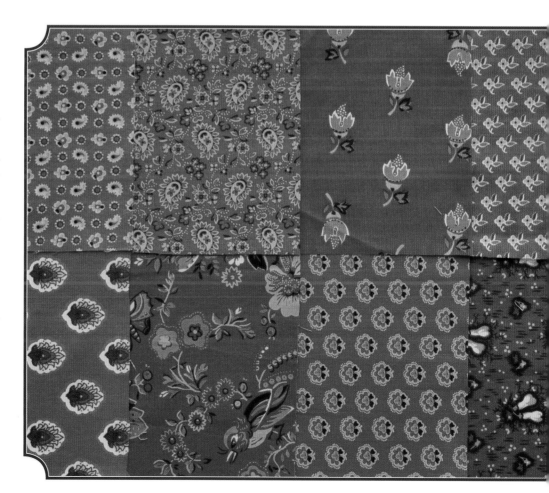

All cotton prints labeled "madder style" and "Turkey reds" are dyed with the same dye stuff—*Rubia tinctorum*, simply known as madder, or madder root. Cotton fibers do not readily accept color and must be treated with chemicals (such as iron or tin) called mordants, to facilitate the dye or printing process. Madder colors depend on the mordants used, which can produce shades of reds, pinks, browns, violets, and black. Turkey red referred to the geographic origin of this distinctive tint that was also extremely colorfast, with a bluish cast to the fabric. Turkey reds were often overprinted in black, yellow, blue, or green (or combinations of these), in very small to large and complex multicolored prints.

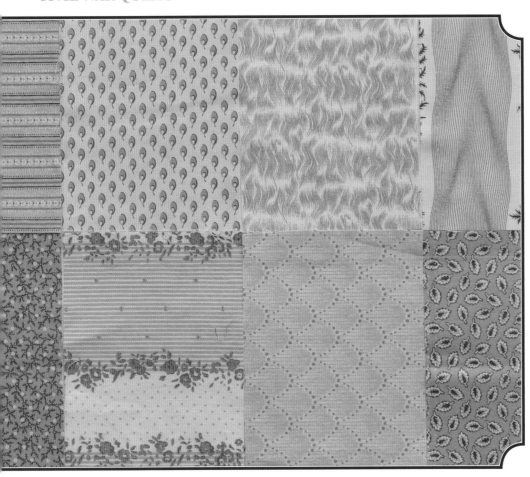

The term "double pink" refers to a fabric that is printed with more than one value of pink (and there are double blues and double yellows too—see above and below) In general, double pinks are seen in quilts from the early 1800s until now, but for some reason, they were very popular for use in inscribed quilts in the middle part of the nineteenth century. Two of the Civil War potholder quilts use double-pink prints to frame or bind the quilts, thus unifying very busy scrap quilts with this common color. Thousands of double-pink prints were produced.

The US Sanitary Commission suggested using dark fabrics for quilts and comforters for the soldiers, and what better color than brown hides dirt? Madder root was also used to produce a medium to dark blackish brown similar to a chocolate color in printed cottons. The same dye source, used with a different mordant to bind it to the cotton fibers, produced a tan or even a very rusty-reddish brown. Logwood was another brown dyestuff for prints seen earlier in the century, and it too could produce a range of colors from black brown, black, and purple, depending on the mordant.

Bright yellows, butterscotch yellow, and orange prints existed before the Civil War, honest! Quercitron is a vegetable dye, extracted from oak bark, and most often producing a brownish yellow that can run to a darker hue. Both antimony and chrome are mineral dyes that produce orangish yellows or yellowish orange, depending on your viewpoint. Sometimes seen is a medium clear yellow on yellow, in prints similar to double blues or double pinks.

Until about the 1850s, any manufacturer desiring a green cotton fabric, or a print that had green elements, was required to perform a two-step process, first dyeing the fabric, or printing the element in yellow, and then redyeing or overprinting in blue, or vice versa. Quilts with green fabrics that have faded unevenly will sometimes have areas of yellowish green or bluish green that seem out of place in the design. There was a medium green that was overprinted with black elements, often seen in quilts midcentury. Another common style midcentury was a green overprinted with yellow and black elements.

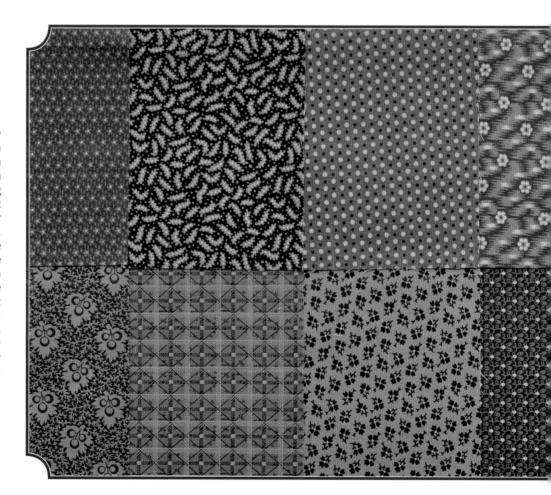

Also seen in this period is a clear medium blue, sometimes with a light and medium value printed in small scale on a white background—called "double blue."
.

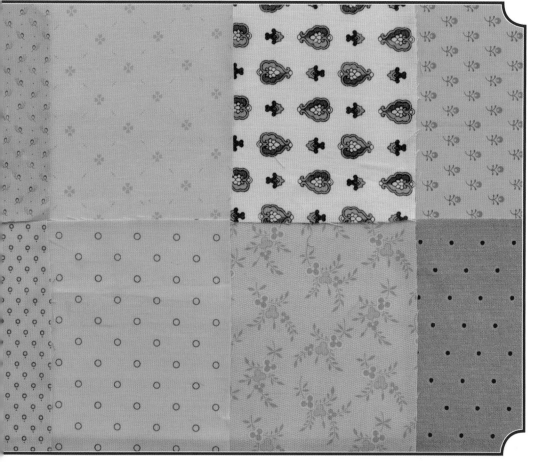

Light-value fabrics found in Civil War–era quilts are often small prints of one or two colors on light solid or printed backgrounds. Floral sprigs, polka dots, and geometric motifs are common. Several patriotic prints were produced for clothing and quiltmaking. See the detail on page 25. ❧

Ft. Hood Memorial Quilt, hand pieced, quilted, embroidered in 30 days from November 6, 2009, to December 5, 2009, by Don Beld. *Photograph by Jonathan Strait*

None of the reproduction quilts found in this book are intended to be exact reproductions of existing quilts. They are made on the basis of personal observation of the quilt, public-domain photographs of the quilt, or private information shared about the quilt and used with the owner's permission. It is the "spirit" of the original quilt that was sought, the use of similar fabrics, color schemes, dimensions, quirks, and oddities found in the original quilt that give the reproduction the sensibility of the real thing.

With three exceptions found in the quilts that may have been used for fundraising purposes, the quilts made for Civil War soldiers' use contain many different fabrics and are very scrappy. The fabric amounts given in some of the instructions assume that you might use the same fabrics for sashings or borders, and you may be more comfortable doing this, which to our twenty-first-century eyes may be more pleasing. But the women making quilts for soldiers' use were generally using up what fabrics they had on hand, as well as purchasing fabrics for the quiltmaking, so feel free to dig into your scrap pile of Civil War–era reproductions.

It is always acceptable to make your own designs and use fabrics you like; machine piece or machine quilt, if you prefer, and let your inner artistic sense be your guide.

GENERAL INSTRUCTIONS FOR USING THE TEMPLATES AND PATTERNS

Don Beld did all of his sewing by hand, while Pam Weeks pieced and quilted by hand and by machine. Handwork is found in the majority of the Civil War soldiers' quilts, but machine piecing, appliqué, and quilting are also seen. It's up to you how to proceed, so we've included instructions for using templates for hand piecing for all of the quilts and rotary cutting for machine piecing for a few of the less complicated quilts and blocks.

If you choose to use the templates for hand piecing and need to trace the sewing line, you'll want to photocopy or trace the patterns provided, and make your own templates of cardboard or template plastic by using the dark inner line, which is the sewing line. Remember when cutting out your pieces to leave at least one-quarter-inch seam allowance on the outside of the sewing line.

If you are rotary cutting, we've given strip width for some of the easier blocks, such as Nine Patch, then piece size for quick cutting. We did not attempt to include strip-piecing methods because the quilts are generally so scrappy, and strip piecing doesn't allow for random scrappiness. There are many good tutorials online, as well as books galore on hand piecing, machine piecing, rotary cutting, and strip piecing.

THE BLOCK PATTERNS GIVEN INCLUDE SEAM ALLOWANCES, AND REMEMBER TO ADJUST THE FINISHED SIZE OF A BLOCK FINISHED "POTHOLDER STYLE" ACCORDINGLY. For instance, our 10-inch pattern for Economy Patch will yield a 10½-inch potholder-style block, because the block is bound as is, not sewn to another block, which would yield a 10-inch block. This is the reason some of the quilt patterns provided, such as the Florence, Massachusetts, quilt, have odd dimensions.

NINETEENTH-CENTURY EDGE FINISHES

A small log cabin doll quilt made with antique 1870s and 1880s fabrics was once presented to a quilt appraiser for dating. She glanced at the quilt and said, "This was finished recently." When asked how she knew, she stated that the fabrics were antique but that the binding was wrong for a nineteenth-century quilt, since it had tightly mitered corners and the binding was wider than those common to nineteenth-century quilts.

Mid-nineteenth-century knife edge finish. *Photograph: Jonathan Strait*

Edge finishes are an important detail when reproducing antique quilts. Many nineteenth-century quilts made before 1850, especially whole-cloth quilts, have a knife edge finish, also called a seamed edge, in which the top and bottom layers are folded under and blind-stitch closed. Some quilts were bound with woven tape, and some had the top brought to the back (or the back brought to the front) and turned under to finish. A very small number had piped edges.

Block showing applied strip binding. *Photograph: Jonathan Strait*

Block showing applied strip binding. *Photograph: Jonathan Strait*

APPLIED STRIP BINDING

The most common edge finish for nineteenth-century quilts was straight-of-the-grain, applied strip binding. In the nineteenth and early twentieth centuries, this was done with a single layer of fabric, not the double layer as is commonly used today. The miter at each corner is more of a gentle bending-around-the-corner style rather than a true miter, but many quilters did employ a miter at each corner of the block. A narrow, straight-of-the-grain strip of fabric was sewn to the front, with an $1/8$- or $1/4$-inch seam allowance, wrong sides together, then brought to the back, turned under, and appliqué-stitched or blind-stitched down. It is unusual to see binding less that $3/8$ inch wide on the front, but rarely as wide as a half inch. The single-layer applied strip-

binding method is flexible compared to the double-folded, machine-sewn bindings used today. Bias binding is rare in nineteenth-century quilts.

Most quilts finished this way have the binding started at one corner and applied all the way around, finishing where it began. Seams were evident, so a single-strip cut the length of the fabric, long enough to bind the entire quilt, was not used. Some quilts have binding applied to opposite sides first, and then they are finished by applying binding to the remaining, opposite sides. After midcentury, when the sewing machine was available to many home sewers, more bindings were applied by machine.

Mid-nineteenth-century applied strip binding, rounded corner.
Photograph by Jonathan Strait

Making Applied Strip, Opposing-Sides Binding: One type of applied strip binding can be called "opposing-sides binding." This technique is done by finishing one side of the quilt binding at a time. It produces a sharp, 90-degree angle on the corners.

Block showing applied strip binding. *Photograph: Jonathan Strait*

Pin binding to edge of quilt after marking sewing line, then sew the binding to the quilt. *Photograph: Jonathan Strait*

Trim binding flush with edge of quilt after it is sewn down. *Photograph: Jonathan Strait*

1. After squaring the quilt, measure the edges of the quilt and add 2" to the measurement of each side. (Your measurements should be the same for the opposite sides.) Cut binding strips 1¼" wide, running along the length of the binding fabric, and if needed, join pieces to achieve the lengths required. For the most authentic look, do not miter the joins. Do not sew the four strips together.

2. On the wrong side of the four binding strips, mark a ¼" sewing line the length of the strip. Use a pencil when the back of the fabric is a light color and a colored pencil (white, red, etc.) when the back of the fabric is a dark color.

3. The binding is applied to one edge of the quilt at a time.

4. Placing the right sides of the fabrics together, pin a binding strip even with the edge on the top surface of the quilt on one side, leaving 1" of binding hanging past the corner of the quilt. The excess will be dealt with later in the process (see page 91).

5. Using a running stitch, sew on the marked line, stitching through the binding, the top layer of the quilt, and the batting. Take a backstitch after every five or six stitches. Do not sew through the back fabric.

6. When the stitching is complete, trim off the excess fabric ends so that the beginning and end of that piece of binding are even with the edge of the quilt.

7. Turn the quilt over to the backside. Fold the binding straight up, so that the back of the binding shows above the quilt when seen from the back. There should be approximately ¾" showing.

8. Fold the binding down toward the edge of the quilt until the raw edge touches the edge of the quilt, and then fold it over once again so that the binding covers ¼" of the back of the quilt. Pin in place.

9. Use an appliqué or blind stitch for sewing down the binding on the back.

10. Repeat steps 5 through 10 for the opposite side of the quilt.

11. For each of the third and fourth (opposite) sides, take one of the remaining pieces of binding and follow step 5, leaving an equal amount of fabric extending past the previously bound edges of the quilt at both ends.

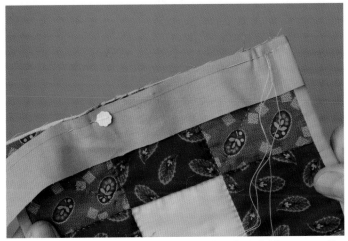

When sewing third and fourth pieces of binding, fold over small piece when starting. *Photograph: Jonathan Strait*

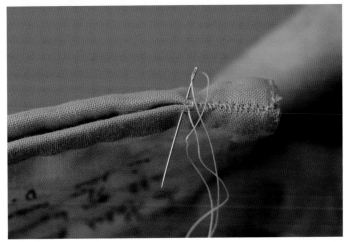

Whip-stitch small space where underlying binding shows through. *Photograph: Jonathan Strait*

12. Before starting to sew the binding to the top of the quilt, fold over a small bit of binding so that the folded edge is flush with the edge of the other binding.

13. Repeat step 6—attaching the binding strip to the edge of the quilt. At the end of the binding, fold over a small bit of it again, so that the folded binding is flush with the binding at the other edge.

14. Repeat steps 7, 8, 9, and 10 to finish the binding.

15. At each of the four corners of the quilt where the binding is folded over, there will be an opening. Sew it closed with whip stitching, or ladder stitching. The same is true for the 90-degree beginning corner in the rounded applied strip-binding technique.

APPLIED TAPE BINDING

Fabric tape was sometimes used in the nineteenth century to finish the edges of quilts. It was commercially available and also woven at home. It usually measured $3/4$ to $1 1/4$ inches in width. It was applied by folding the tape in half over the edge of the quilt and secured by blind stitching or overcast stitching. Tape binding is very sturdy. Refer to the photos on page 51.

When reaching other end, fold over small piece to finish the binding. *Photograph: Jonathan Strait*

Remember to bury your knots whenever starting with new thread or a new position, and bury them before cutting your thread.

This binding technique lies flatter, is more pliable, and uses approximately half as much fabric as today's double-layer binding technique.

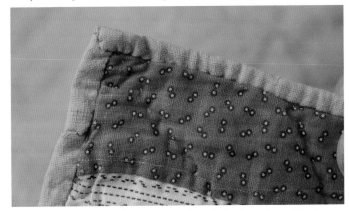

Front of mid-nineteeth-century quilt with back-to-front binding. *Photograph: Jonathan Strait*

Back of mid-nineteenth-century quilt with back-to-front binding. *Photograph: Jonathan Strait*

Detail, knife edge finish. *Photograph: Jonathan Strait*

Block showing final side of back-to-front binding before folding over to front. *Photograph: Jonathan Strait*

KNIFE EDGE FINISH

While not a binding technique, a "knife edge" was used in the early to the mid-nineteenth century to finish some quilts. Once the quilt is quilted and squared up, remove enough batting from the edges of the quilt so that the top and backing extend a quarter inch beyond the edge of the batting. Mark a straight line a quarter inch away from the top edges of the quilt, fold the top edge under on this line, and run a line of basting stitches near the fold to hold it in place. Then fold under the back of the quilt and tuck it under the batting, matching the top folded edge. Baste in place. Use a ladder stitch to invisibly join the front and the back together.

BACK-TO-FRONT
or FRONT-TO-BACK BINDING

The Vernon, Connecticut, Civil War quilt with the Sanitary Commission stamp (see page 52) is finished by folding the backing fabric to the front of the quilt, trimming it, and tucking it under with a blind stitch. It is an easy, fast, and historically accurate method for finishing a reproduction quilt.

Finish the quilting, making sure to leave at least an inch unquilted at the edges. Fold the back fabric away from the edge and pin it in place. Square the quilt, but trim only the top and the batting. (If you make a mistake and cut the backing at this point, you'll have to choose another method for finishing the quilt.) Unpin the backing and smooth it out so that it extends beyond the trimmed edges of the top and batting. Trim the backing fabric so that ½ to ¾ inch remains beyond the front fabric and batting line.

To finish, fold the backing fabric in toward the quilt until the raw edge meets the trimmed edge of the quilt, then fold again onto the top of the quilt. Pin or baste in place. Sew using either a blind stitch or appliqué stitch. At the corners, make a neat fold and whip-stitch in place.

HOW TO MAKE A POTHOLDER QUILT

Quilts made of individually finished blocks (called potholder quilts, or block-by-block quilts) appeared during the mid-nineteenth century. The earliest example is dated 1837, and their popularity peaked in the 1860s. Most of the surviving examples of potholder quilts are inscribed quilts and were made by groups of people for presentation, or for a community service quilt project. Made of individually pieced, quilted, and bound blocks, they were, and still are, a great way to quickly and easily make a quilt. A group of twenty to forty women, making individual blocks, could conceivably complete a quilt in two or three days. Of the fifteen surviving quilts known to be made for Civil War soldiers for use in the field or in the hospital, eleven are potholder quilts.

A potholder quilt is still an easy community service project. One guild in Southern California recently used the potholder quilt method to make a quilt as a thank-you gift for its president and used batik fabrics. Guild members made the individually pieced, quilted, bound blocks, and after they were assembled into the potholder quilt, yo-yos were sewn into the corners where four blocks met.

Use the following guidelines to make a potholder quilt:

1. If the exact final quilt size is very important, decide which block edge finish you will employ before beginning. If you choose to finish each block with a knife edge, you will turn under the outside edge seam allowance, and a pattern for an 8" block will finish at 8 inches. If you choose to bind each block with woven tape or applied strip binding, that same pattern for an 8" block will finish at $8^1/_2$" because the seam allowances at the edges of the block will be covered with the binding, not turned under. Also take into account that quilting and finishing each block individually will shrink it slightly more. It's always a good idea to make a few blocks from start to finish before cutting out an entire project.

2. After piecing the block, layer it with batting and backing fabric. Pin or baste the piece to secure the layers.

3. Note: Harriet Hargrave's preferred batting for historical accuracy is Mountain Mist Blue Ribbon 100% cotton batting. In some potholder quilts, the backing fabrics vary from block to block, but in many more, the backings are the same. The group that made the Hingham Sanitary Commission Quilt used both a consistent back fabric and a consistent sashing fabric. The soldier's quilt made by the Beverly, Massachusetts, group used various backings and bindings (see page 24).

4. Quilt the individual block by either hand or machine. Machine quilting was used during the nineteenth century, as home sewing machines were available, and many machine-quilted examples survive. Several accounts from Ladies' Union Soldiers' Aid Societies mention the use of sewing machines to speed their labors, and four of the Civil War soldiers' potholder quilts have machine-quilted blocks.

5. If hand quilting, be sure that the batting and the back are at least 2" bigger on all four sides of the block so that the piece can be secured into a quilting frame or quilting hoop. This allows for the traditional hand-quilting method to be used and will result in finer stitches. However, because the blocks are small, it is easy to simply quilt the block without a frame. Baste or pin the piece heavily to prevent slippage or bunching and for ease of handling for quilting.

6. Bind the quilt blocks by using one of the techniques found on pages 90–92. Most potholder quilts were made of blocks finished with applied strip binding applied by hand or by machine, running around all sides, starting and finishing on the same corner. The second most common binding method is the opposing-sides binding described on page 90.

Example of finished potholder block. *Photograph: Jonathan Strait*

If you are making a group quilt, you might consider requiring everyone contributing a block to use the same color or even the same fabric for the binding, which gives at least one common design element.

Potholder block layered, basted with enough batting and backing to fit quilting frame. *Photograph: Jonathan Strait*

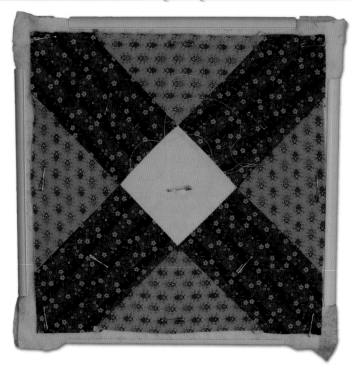

Potholder block in quilting PVC frame, ready for hand quilting.
Photograph: Jonathan Strait

NOTE: If you are applying binding by machine, it is not recommended to use binding cut 2.5" wide and doubled. Doubled binding as we're used to using in this century on full-sized quilts will result in a very stiff potholder-style quilt, and you will not enjoy the result.

7. Complete the quilt by joining two blocks with tops facing each other and whip-stitch from the back, along one side very near the edge of the finished binding. The stitches must be very tight and close together, or the blocks will have gaps between them. Remember to bury the threads when beginning and ending lines of stitching.

   Although the whip stitching shows on the back, on the front the block bindings look like narrow sashing with a quilting line running down the center. Continue to add one block at a time in this method until the desired width of the quilt is reached. Complete more rows and then sew the rows together until the desired length is reached.

8. When the quilt is completely assembled, wash in cold water with a mild soap*. Lay the quilt out in a flat area such as a bed, floor, or table to dry. Be sure to block and straighten the quilt while it is wet, since it sets when drying. The whip stitching on the back will recede somewhat into the quilt with time and repeated washings.

   NOTE: If your quilt contains inscriptions, make sure your work is washable!

WRITING ON QUILTS

Inscribed quilts were a widespread fad in the mid-nineteenth century and reached the height of popularity during the Civil War. It is not surprising that all of the surviving Union soldiers' quilts are inscribed. Writing on quilts was one way to send messages of support, comfort, faith, and advice to the men on the battlefields and in hospitals. These quilts were probably saved because they were inscribed, and carried messages and meanings beyond the time of their use.

As described in greater detail in chapter 1, writing on fabric in the 1800s was made easier with the invention of the steel-nibbed dip pen, giving more control to the writer than was afforded by a feather quill pen. Ink that was both fade resistant and free of chemicals that corroded fabric was commercially available soon afterward. Payson's Indelible Ink is credited with being the oldest manufactured ink suitable for marking fabric, and was available by 1834. It was advertised as being the best ink for "marking linen, silk and cotton with a common pen without preparation."

Writing on quilts was made popular not only because the tools were easier to use, but because this practice followed another fad of the time—autograph albums. They were found in every parlor and carried by many people to be inscribed by friends and family. The fad translated onto fabric, and inscribed squares were sewn into quilt blocks.

In the nineteenth century, there were formulas for preparing the fabric for inking, and the process took several steps and many hours waiting for the coated fabric to dry before the writing could commence. Then the patch had to be washed, and some processes required it to dry in the sun.

Writing on cloth is so much easier with the tools we have available today. Instead of starchy formulas for stiffening the fabrics, we can press cloth to freezer paper, then peel it off when the inscription is finished. Instead of mixing ink, or dipping pens into an inkwell, we remove the caps from our Pigma or other textile pens.

Inscribe the light-colored fabric patches before completing the blocks, but if you feel courageous, by all means, piece your blocks and then write on them. Many nineteenth-century quilts exist with blotches and cross-outs, and several exist where the name was inscribed on a small patch that was appliquéd onto the block. This probably was done to cover a mistake, or to add the name after a very elaborate block has been created.

A potholder block inspired by the Dow Album Quilt, inscribed by Pamela Weeks, November 2010

The easiest way to stiffen the patches you will write on is to iron freezer paper onto them. Freezer paper is used for wrapping meat—obviously for storage in the freezer—and is easily available in grocery stores. Quilters have adapted it for lots of things, including writing and drawing on fabric that will be sewn into patchwork.

Freezer paper has a shiny or waxy side, and a paperlike side. Draw the shape of the finished patch on the paper side with a bold pen and cut it out, outside the line. Then cut a piece of light-colored fabric the size of the finished patch plus seam allowances; center the freezer paper on the patch and, using a dry iron at the cotton setting, press the freezer paper to the patch.

Using the same bold pen, draw lines on the paperlike side of the freezer paper to guide your inscription. Writing on the fabric on a light-colored surface allows the line to show through enough to act as a guide. Use a light box or hold the patch on a window while writing. Make sketches on the freezer paper to trace, but remember, the image will be reversed when it's turned over and traced onto the fabric.

Practice penmanship before beginning to write on fabric. Generally, nineteenth-century quilts display gorgeous, small-scale handwriting. Find a calligraphy book that features a Spencerian alphabet. Spencerian script was taught at the time that inscribed quilts were so popular, and the flowing script is beautiful. Practice the inscriptions planned for the quilt on paper first, then make some practice patches of fabric stiffened with freezer paper.

There are many choices for pens, but be sure to select a brand that has "pigment marker" written somewhere on the pen. This indicates that it is a dye marker and will penetrate the fabric, which makes it lightfast and washfast. DO NOT USE SHARPIES brand—they are not made for use on fabrics. They will run and the inscription will look fuzzy.

Included in the text are many inscriptions taken from the Civil War quilts for copying onto quilts. Each of the Sanitary Commission quilts listed in the "Making Quilts in the Style of US Sanitary Commission Quilts" chapter also list inscriptions for those quilts. Add favorites from the Bible, or poems, or hymns popular in the period.

There are six known surviving quilts with the US Sanitary Commission stamp. Information on and photos of the remaining six do exist. Three were made as potholder quilts and three were made as standard pieced quilts; all come from New England. Don Beld has made a quilt in the style of these quilts, using standard hand-piecing and hand-quilting techniques. Information for making your own version of these priceless, historical quilts is found in this chapter.

BRANDON, VERMONT

Many quilt guilds today make quilts to donate to community service projects, such as the homeless; hospitalized people; newborn babies; fire, hurricane, and flood victims; battered women; and veterans, to name just a few. They often consist of many squares sewn together and then quilted. The Brandon, Vermont, Sanitary Commission quilt is a one-person community service project and is made in this fashion. It uses only two fabrics: an off-white solid and a dark-brown print, and it contains Bible verses, religious sayings, and hymns that reflect the maker's spiritual beliefs.

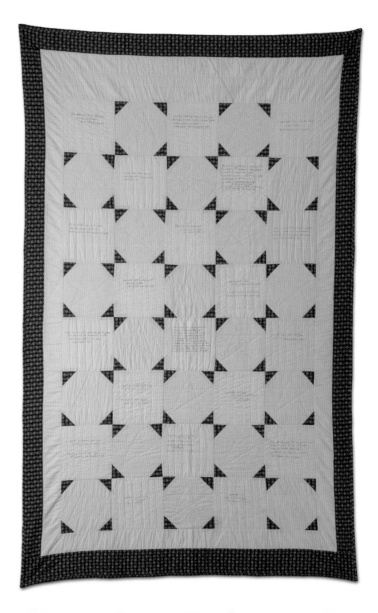

Quilt in the style of the Brandon, Vermont, quilt. Quiltmaker: Don Beld. *Photograph: Jonathan Strait*

The basic information for making a version of this quilt includes:

The block that Caro Fairbanks used to make her quilt is quickly and easily pieced. This block is often called Snowball or Octagon. The following instructions replicate Don Beld's quilt pictured on page 96.

1. Quilt size: 56" × 84"

2. Block size: 8" finished

3. Number of blocks required: 20 pieced, 20 8.5" solid light color

4. First border: 4" light-colored fabric on two long sides and one short side, and 7" light-colored border on the "top." Second border: 4" dark-brown print on all four sides.

5. Inscriptions are found in many of the light-colored areas of the quilt. See page 98 for the transcriptions from the original, and refer to page 95 for how to write on quilts.

6. Quilting: Five-pointed stars in the Octagon blocks, and vertical parallel lines about an inch apart in the solid light-colored blocks

7. Binding: straight-of-the-grain binding applied front to back

8. In addition, the original quilt was stenciled on the back with the mark "Brandon Soldiers' Aid Society" and stamped by the Sanitary Commission.

"Love your enemies" block in Brandon quilt. Quiltmaker: Don Beld. *Photograph: Jonathan Strait*

"Made by Mrs. L. B. Fairbanks Of Brandon, VT" is inscribed on the front, as are the following verses, with their sources in italics. Most of the sources were not included on the quilt. All Bible quotes are from the King James Version, including a lovely nineteenth-century children's poem that children used to memorize the Ten Commandments. All the sayings were inscribed in the one-piece squares.

"And God shall wipe away all tears" block in Brandon quilt. Quiltmaker: Don Beld. *Photograph: Jonathan Strait*

Close-up of children's poem of the Ten Commandments. Quiltmaker: Don Beld. *Photograph: Jonathan Strait*

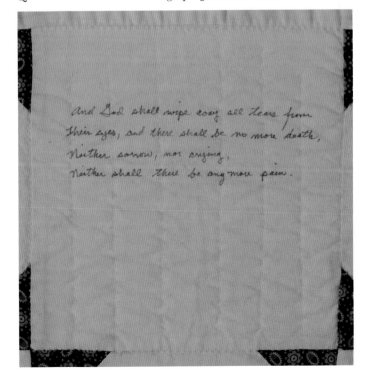

When using the rotary cutting instructions, cut the fabrics, then sew each piece A to the corners of piece B. Trim and press open to form the block.

1. Come unto me, all ye that labor, And are heavy laden, And I will give you rest. *Matt. 11:28*

2. And God shall wipe away all tears from their eyes, And there shall be no more death, Neither sorrow, nor crying. Neither shall there be any more pain. *Rev. 21:4*

3. The Lord is my Sheppard; I shall not want. He maketh me to lie down in green pastures; He leadeth me beside the still waters. He restoreth my soul; He leadeth me in paths of righteousness for his name sake. Yea though I walk through the valley of the shadow of death, I will fear no evil: for thou are with me. Thy rod and thy staff, they comfort me. *Psalms 23:1–4*

4. Thou no gods shall have but me.
Before no idol bend the knee.
Take not the name of God in vain.
Dare not the Sabbath day profane.
Give both thy parents honor due.
Take heed that thou no murders do.
Abstain from words and deeds unclean.
Steal not, though thy be poor and mean.
Make not a willful lie nor love it.
What is thy neighbor's, do not covet.
Children's rhyme of the Ten Commandments

5. I love those that love me. And they that seek me early Shall find me. *Prov. 8:17*

6. To do to all me as I would That they should do to me. *Book of Common Prayer*

7. Would make me kind and just and good and so I'll try to be. *Unknown*

8. God so loved the world that He gave His only begotten son, that whosoever Believeth in Him should not perish But have everlasting life. *John 3:16*

9. When he was yet a great way off, his father Saw him and had compassion on him And ran and fell on his neck And kissed him. *Luke 15:20*

10. Lord what wilt thou have me do? *Acts 9:6*

11. Draw nigh to God, and He will draw nigh to you. *James 4:8*

12. None but Jesus, none but Jesus, Can do helpless sinners good! Come Ye Sinners. *Joseph Hart, 1759*

13. Here, Lord, I give myself away. 'Tis all that I can do. Alas! And Did My Savior Bleed. *Isaiah Watts, 1707*

14. Lo, everyone that thirsteth, Come ye to the waters. *Isaiah 55:1*

15. Love your enemies, bless them that curse you. Do good to those that hate you, And pray for those which despitefully Use you and persecute you. *Matt. 5:44*

16. Except a man be born again He cannot see the kingdom of God. *John 3:3*

17. Whatever ye shall ask in my name, That I will do. *John 10:14*

18. Look not thou upon the wine when it is red, When it giveth the color to the cup, When it moveth itself aright. At the end it biteth like a serpent, And stingeth like an adder. *Prov. 23:31–32*

Fabric amounts to make a quilt similar to the Brandon, Vermont quilt:

1. Borders, binding, and triangles in "Octagon" square: 2.5 yards of a medium-to-dark-brown small flower print.

2. 3 yards of a solid white or off-white for inner borders, 20 one-pieced square blocks, and the 20 *Octagon* blocks.

3. Backing fabric: 3.5 yards of 44" fabric cut in half and sewn together will make a 60" by 88" backing. The backing of the original is off-white muslin.

Note: Cut all border pieces first so that they do not have to be pieced.

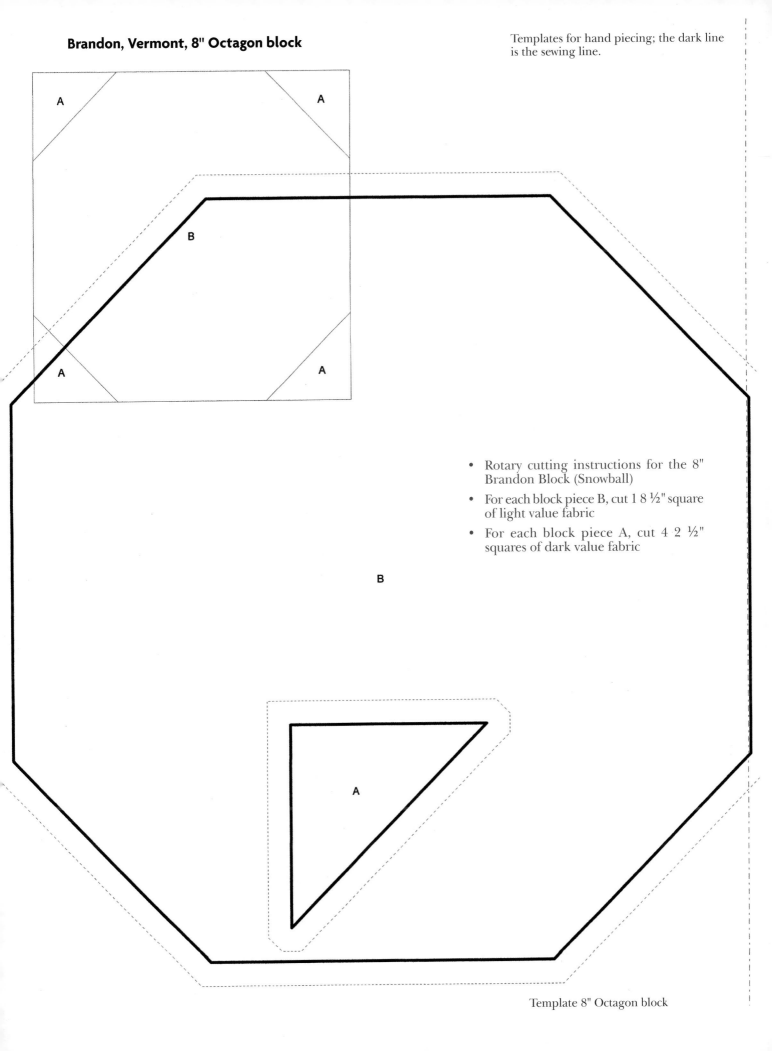

Brandon, Vermont, 8" Octagon block

Templates for hand piecing; the dark line is the sewing line.

A

A

B

A

A

B

- Rotary cutting instructions for the 8" Brandon Block (Snowball)
- For each block piece B, cut 1 8 ½" square of light value fabric
- For each block piece A, cut 4 2 ½" squares of dark value fabric

A

Template 8" Octagon block

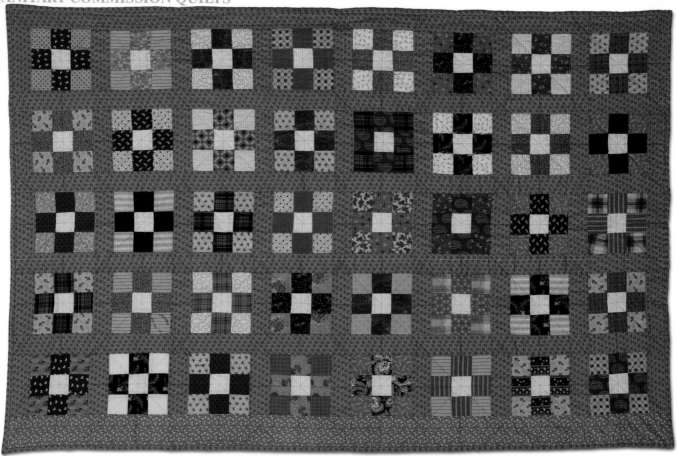

Quilt in the style of the Dublin, New Hampshire, quilt. Quiltmaker: Don Beld. *Photograph: Jonathan Strait*

NEW HAMPSHIRE

A quilt made in 1863 records the names of sixty volunteers from this small New Hampshire town and is known as the Dublin quilt. In 2011, after the first edition of this book was published, Loretta B. Chase and Jan Coor-Pender Dodge wrote a research paper about the Dublin quilt that was published in Volume 32 of *Uncoverings*, the annual publication of the American Quilt Study Group. Their work revealed that this simple quilt held the stories of "the women who made it, the men who served, and the organizations that supported war relief."

There are several interesting features about this quilt. First, it is the only survivor that was stamped by the Sanitary Commission on its front. Second, the simple Nine Patch block has retained its popularity throughout the history of quiltmaking, yet it is rarely used when making an inscribed quilt. And on this quilt, the inscriptions include not just some of the makers of the quilt, but also the names of some of the men serving in the Civil War.

When hand piecing, only one template is required—remember to differentiate between the cutting and sewing lines on the template. When rotary cutting, it's very easy to cut strips (if you are using large pieces rather than scraps), sew the strips together in threes, alternating values, then cut those strips into three-piece slices that can be quickly sewn into Nine Patch blocks.

Detail of Sanitary Commission stamp on front of Don Beld's Dublin, New Hampshire, quilt. *Photograph: Jonathan Strait*

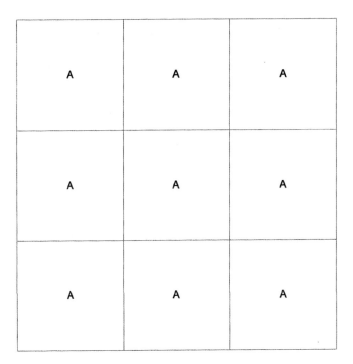

The basic information for making a version of the Dublin Quilt:

1. Size: 54" × 84"

2. Number of blocks: 40

3. Block size: 8"

4. Block name: Nine Patch

5. Sashing: 2" between the blocks

6. Borders: 3". The original quilt has borders on only three sides. Our instructions include a fourth border.

7. Binding: straight of the grain, applied front to back

8. Quilting: The original is quilted diagonally across each block, and in the sashing, ¼" from the seams of the horizontal and vertical strips between the blocks.

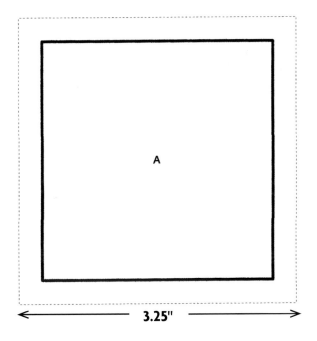

8" template for Nine Patch block

Amounts of fabric needed to make this quilt:

The original quilt has more than 70 different light-, medium-, and dark-value fabrics. The darkest values in each block form a cross, the medium values are placed in the "corners" of the blocks, and every block has a light-colored center square that is inscribed.

1. For the light center squares, one-half yard light-colored cotton

2. For the dark values, the equivalent of 1½ yards of scraps or fat eights, and for the medium values, the equivalent of 1¼ yards in scraps or fat eighths

3. Sashing, borders, and binding: assuming one fabric, 3¼ yards

4. Backing fabric: 3½ yards cut in half and sewn together on the long sides will make a backing 63" × 84", just barely long enough. You may need more fabric to add a 4" strip along one end.

Quilt in the style of the Florence, Massachusetts, quilt.
Quiltmaker: Don Beld. *Photograph: Jonathan Strait*

Basic information for making this quilt:

1. Size: 54" × 85.5"

2. Number of blocks: 22 pieced blocks;
   1 center medallion

3. Block size: 10"

4. Block name: Economy Patch

5. Sashing: This is a potholder quilt and there
   is no sashing; however, if you choose to make
   the quilt as a standard quilt, use 0.5" sashing
   around all the blocks.

6. Borders: 6"

7. Quilting: The reproduction quilt has
   in the ditch quilting in the blocks and
   small diagonal grid quilting in the center
   medallion, with larger diagonal grid quilting
   in the border. In a printed description of the
   quilting, it states that in the antique quilt, the
   quilting ranges from very good to extremely
   poor. This is often the case in potholders,
   since different people with different levels of
   skill made the blocks.

8. Binding: applied strip binding around each
   block and around the outer borders of the quilt

9. Center medallion panel: 20.5" × 31".
   Flag appliqué: 13" × 21"

"Touch not tobacco" block in Florence quilt.
Photograph: Jonathan Strait

FLORENCE, MASSACHUSETTS

The Florence, Massachusetts, quilt is an unusual potholder quilt in that it has a large center medallion, twenty-two pieced Economy Patch blocks, and long rectangular borders. From the available photographs, it does not appear that the borders are finished as large potholder sections, but we think that this may be the easiest way to add the borders. The center part of the quilt, composed of the flag medallion and the Economy Patch blocks, will be assembled first, then quilted and bound sections of the borders will be added.

Listed below are some of the sayings and slogans found on the quilt:

1. Yes, we'll rally 'round the flag, boys,
   we'll rally once again.
   Shouting the Battle Cry of Freedom.
   We will rally from the hillside,
   we'll rally from the plain,
   Shouting the Battle Cry of Freedom.

   This should be placed on the

center medallion below the flag.

2. The Star Spangled Banner
   Long may it wave
   O'er the land of the free
   And the home of the brave.

   *This should be placed on the
   center medallion above the flag.*

3. Quiet conscience gives quiet sleep.
   Touch not tobacco A curse upon it.

4. Be true to humanity and freedom, Ye are martyrs
   to a good cause.

5. Union Forever

6. Forever float that standard sheet! Where breathes
   the foe but falls before us, With freedom's soil
   beneath our feet, And freedom's banner streaming
   o'er us.

7. Flag of the free hearts hope and home By angel
   hands to valor given Thy stars have lit the welkin
   dome And thy hues were born in heaven.

8. Safely home to wife and child.

Detail of two blocks with sayings in Florence quilt.
Photograph: Jonathan Strait

Amounts of fabric to make a quilt similar to this quilt:

1. Sashing: The original quilt is a
   potholder quilt and does not have sashing.

2. Borders and binding: 3 yards. If you wish
   to also use 5" sashing rather than make a
   potholder quilt, use the same fabric for the
   sashing, border, and binding and add 1 yard
   for a total of 4 yards.

3. Blocks: 22 Economy Patch. Several different
   fat quarters from your stash to equal 2 yards,
   with a mixture of darks and lights. 1.5
   yards of an off-white for the background of
   the center medallion and the centers of the
   blocks.

4. Flag: 1 yard solid-red fabric; 1 yard solid-
   white fabric; ½ yard of an indigo-blue fabric

5. Back fabric: 3.5 yards. Note that this is a
   potholder quilt, so the back fabric in the
   original quilt was usually made from odd
   pieces of fabric found in the maker's stash.
   But if you are making it as a standard quilt,
   3.5 yards is needed.

Center flag medallion block in Florence quilt. *Photograph: Jonathan Strait*

How to make the center medallion:

1. From the off-white fabric, cut one piece that measures 21.5" × 32", which gives you a piece that includes a half-inch seam allowance on all sides. If you wish, cut the piece slightly larger (23" × 34"), and you can trim it after the flag is added so that it measures the requisite size of 21.5" × 32".

2. From the blue-indigo fabric, cut one piece 7.5" square and mark sewing lines so that the finished piece will measure 7" × 7".

3. From the red fabric, cut 3 pieces 1.5" × 21.5" and 4 pieces 1.5" × 14.5".

4. From the white fabric, cut 3 pieces 1.5" × 21.5" and 3 pieces 1.5" × 14.5".

Referring to the photo above, piece the short strips together, starting with a red, then a white, etc. Add the seven pieced strips to the indigo-blue fabric. Piece the remaining six long pieces together in the same fashion, starting with a white strip, and add to the indigo square and pieced strips. The finished stripes should measure 1" wide. The short stripes should be 14¼" long and the long stripes should be 21.5" long.

After completing the flag, baste it to the off-white medallion piece and needle-turn appliqué stitch the outer edges down. Remove the basting thread. Note that in the original quilt, the center medallion was made as a potholder block and thus has to be quilted and an applied straight edge binding added before joining the square within a square block to -the medallion.

Florence, Massachusetts, 10" Patch

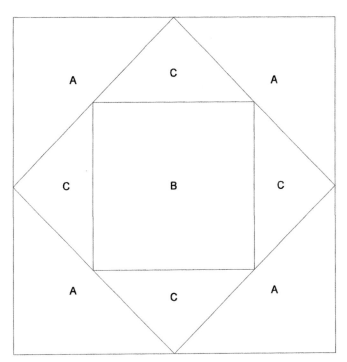

Templates for hand piecing; the dark
line is the sewing line.

See templates A and C on page 106.

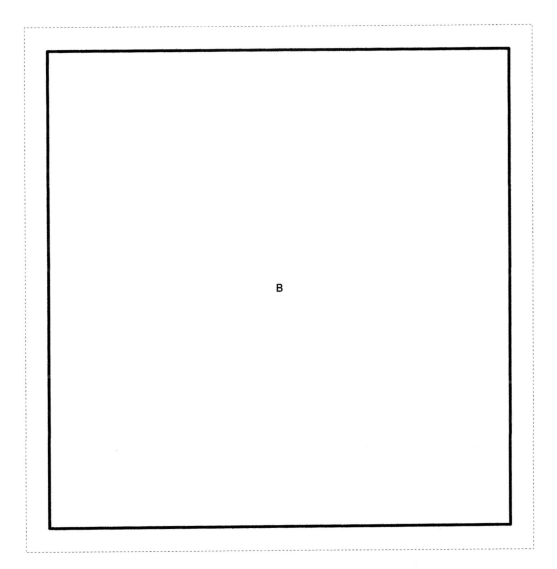

10" templates for Economy Patch

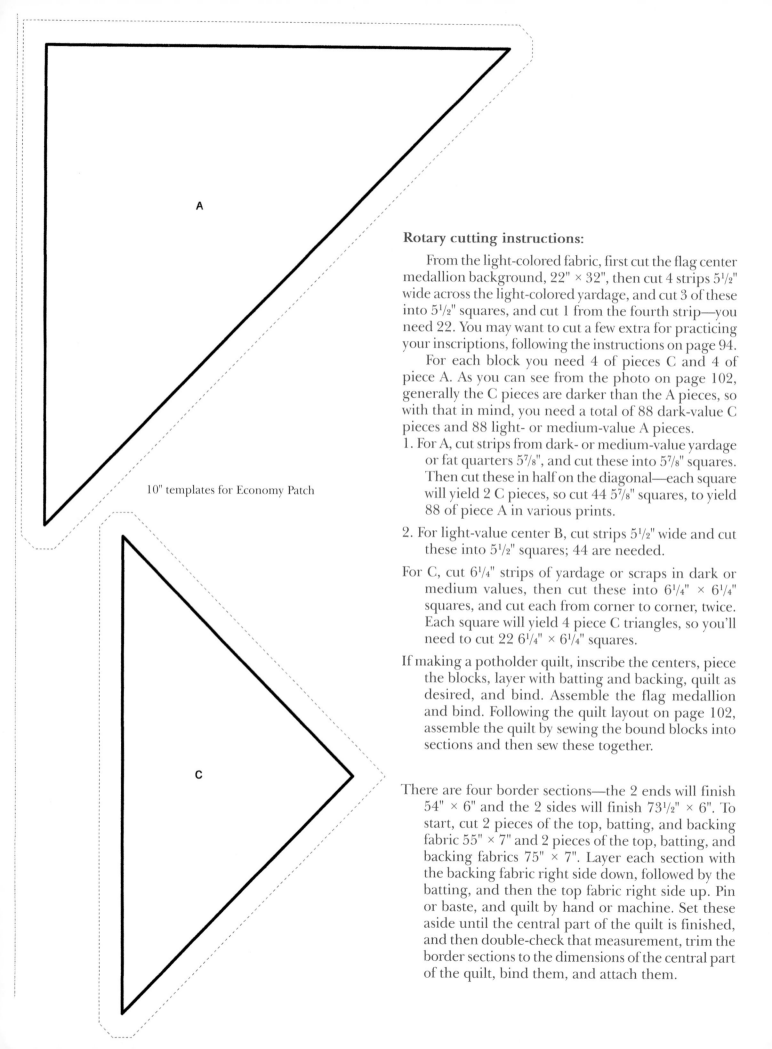

A

10" templates for Economy Patch

C

Rotary cutting instructions:

From the light-colored fabric, first cut the flag center medallion background, 22" × 32", then cut 4 strips 5½" wide across the light-colored yardage, and cut 3 of these into 5½" squares, and cut 1 from the fourth strip—you need 22. You may want to cut a few extra for practicing your inscriptions, following the instructions on page 94.

For each block you need 4 of pieces C and 4 of piece A. As you can see from the photo on page 102, generally the C pieces are darker than the A pieces, so with that in mind, you need a total of 88 dark-value C pieces and 88 light- or medium-value A pieces.

1. For A, cut strips from dark- or medium-value yardage or fat quarters 5⅞", and cut these into 5⅞" squares. Then cut these in half on the diagonal—each square will yield 2 C pieces, so cut 44 5⅞" squares, to yield 88 of piece A in various prints.

2. For light-value center B, cut strips 5½" wide and cut these into 5½" squares; 44 are needed.

For C, cut 6¼" strips of yardage or scraps in dark or medium values, then cut these into 6¼" × 6¼" squares, and cut each from corner to corner, twice. Each square will yield 4 piece C triangles, so you'll need to cut 22 6¼" × 6¼" squares.

If making a potholder quilt, inscribe the centers, piece the blocks, layer with batting and backing, quilt as desired, and bind. Assemble the flag medallion and bind. Following the quilt layout on page 102, assemble the quilt by sewing the bound blocks into sections and then sew these together.

There are four border sections—the 2 ends will finish 54" × 6" and the 2 sides will finish 73½" × 6". To start, cut 2 pieces of the top, batting, and backing fabric 55" × 7" and 2 pieces of the top, batting, and backing fabrics 75" × 7". Layer each section with the backing fabric right side down, followed by the batting, and then the top fabric right side up. Pin or baste, and quilt by hand or machine. Set these aside until the central part of the quilt is finished, and then double-check that measurement, trim the border sections to the dimensions of the central part of the quilt, bind them, and attach them.

Quilt in the style of the Hingham, Massachusetts, quilt. Quiltmaker, Don Beld. *Photograph: Jonathan Strait*

HINGHAM, MASSACHUSETTS

In late 2007, Don Beld received a telephone call from Mrs. Debbie Knapp of Michigan, who had been given his name by a textile expert at Michigan State University. It seemed that she had been given a quilt by her mother-in-law that she thought might be an unusual survivor of the Civil War, and had been told that Don could help her verify its importance.

It was (at that time) the fifth known surviving US Sanitary Commission quilt. Since its discovery in 2007, another, the sixth Sanitary Commission quilt, has been discovered, in July 2010. It is hoped that there are more out there in attics, trunks, and even in museum storage.

Don was graciously sent photographs, including close-ups, of the quilt and authorized to spread the word about this quilt, for purposes of having it both authenticated and appraised for inheritance purposes. Authorization was subsequently given to make a reproduction quilt based on the quilt.

It is now known as the Hingham, Massachusetts, Sanitary Commission quilt. Of the Sanitary Commission quilts found in this book, it is unusual because it contains thirteen different patterns. It is also a potholder quilt with two distinctions: there was a uniform fabric used for all the bindings, which gives the appearance of sashing, and a plain white fabric had been uniformly used for the backing.

Basic information for making this reproduction quilt:

1. Size: 57.5" × 86"

2. Number of blocks: 54

3. Block size: 9"

4. Block(s) name(s): multiple names with 13 different patterns found in the quilt

5. Sashing: none. This is a potholder quilt and there is no sashing; however, if you choose to make the quilt as a standard quilt, substitute 0.5" sashing strips between the blocks and as an outer border.

6. Borders: none

7. Quilting: varied

8. Binding: applied strip binding to each individual block

9. Stamped on the back in an oval "Sanitary Commission".

"The soldier's friend, Aunt Betsy" block.
Photograph: Jonathan Strait

Detail of Album (Fat X) block.
Photograph: Jonathan Strait

Detail of Nine Patch block.
Photograph: Jonathan Strait

"Our starry banner" block.
Photograph: Jonathan Strait

Broken Dishes "Let us not be weary" block.
Photograph: Jonathan Strait

Names of officers of the Ft. Hill Sewing Circle.
Photograph: Jonathan Strait

"Come man to fellow man" Mosaic block.
Photograph: Jonathan Strait

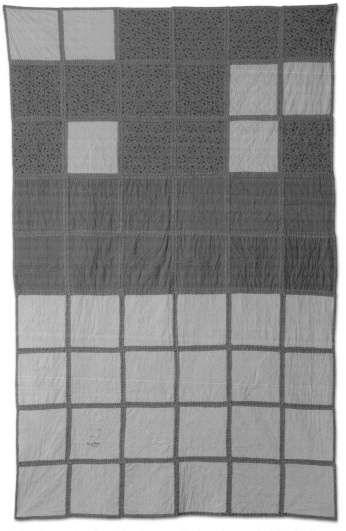

Back of reproduction Hingham quilt, showing potholder backs.
Photograph: Jonathan Strait

Listed below are some of the sayings, slogans, and signatures found on the quilt:

1. Let your watchword ever be, country, God, and Liberty. Hingham July 10, 1864

2. Our starry banner, O long may it wave, Over the land of the free and the home of the brave. N. Remington July 12, 1864

3. Let us not be weary in well doing. For in the due season we shall reap if we faint not. July 4, 1864 Priscilla Lincoln

4. Be of good courage and he shall strengthen your heart, all ye that hope in the Lord. July 11, 1864

5. Come man to brother man. Come in the hand of peace. Let strife and war with all their trials of darkening horrors cease. Hingham June 1864

6. The soldier's friend, Aunt Betsy

7. This quilt was made by the ladies of the Ft. Hill Sewing Circle and presented to the soldiers, Hingham, Massachusetts, July 1864, Mrs. Josepephat [indecipherable] President; Mrs. Matthew Stoddard and Mrs. J. J. Corcoran, Committee; Mrs. Andrew J. Garner, Vice President; Mrs. Daniel Cain, Treasurer; Mrs. William Lincoln, Secretary.

Amounts of fabric to make a quilt similar to this quilt:

1. 4 yards Civil War–era double pink for binding

2. 4 yards white or off-white for backing, or scraps 10" square

3. Fat quarters or fabrics from stash in Turkey reds, nineteenth-century pinks, poison greens, indigo, browns, off-whites, plaids, and blues. You will need approximately 30 to 40 different fabrics.

Hingham, Mosaic

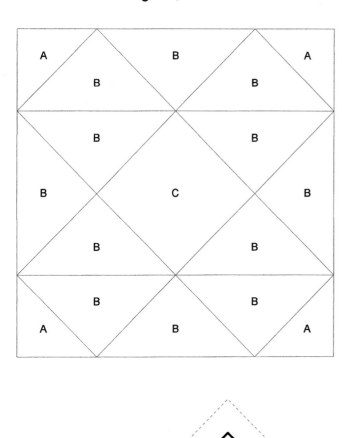

9" template for Hingham Mosaic

Rotary cutting instructions for 9" Mosaic block

- For piece A, cut 2 squares $3^{1}/_{16}$", and cut on the diagonal, yielding 4 color 1.
- For piece B, cut 2 squares $5^{11}/_{16}$" and cut on the diagonal twice, yielding 8 color 1 (6 needed), and cut 2 squares $5^{11}/_{16}$" and cut on the diagonal twice, yielding 8 color 2 (6 needed).
- For piece C, cut 1 square $3^{11}/_{16}$" light-value fabric and inscribe as desired.

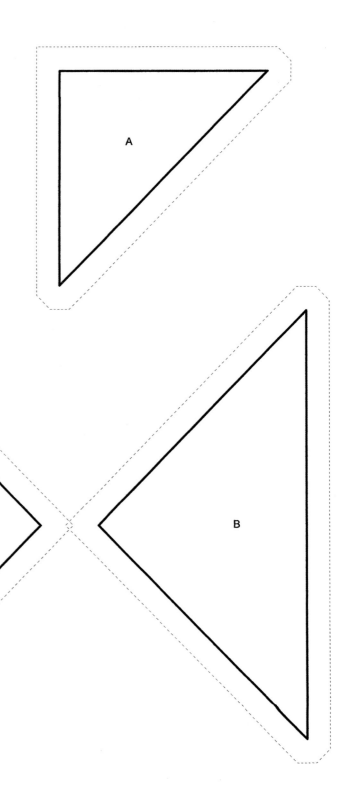

Hingham, Eight-Pointed Star

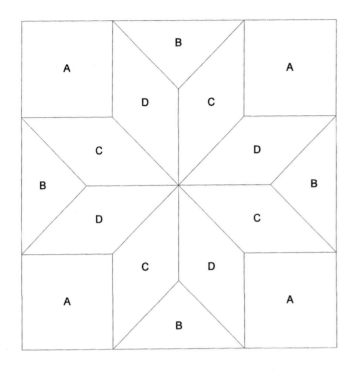

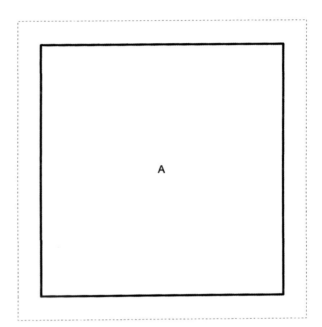

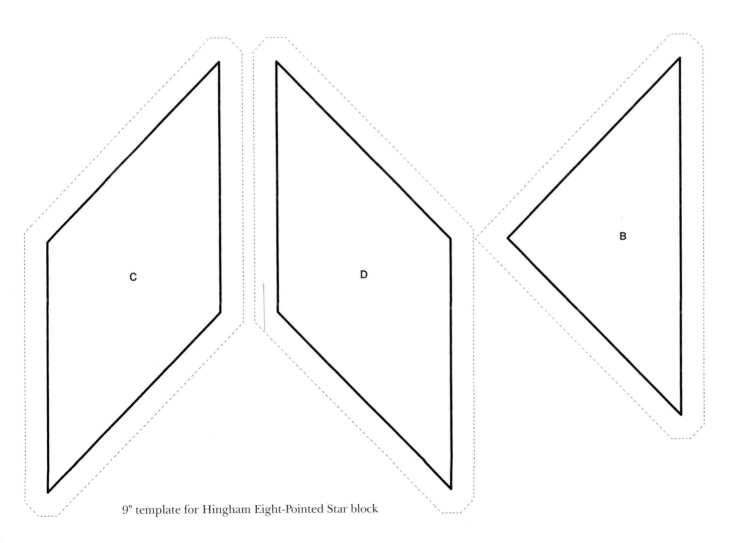

9" template for Hingham Eight-Pointed Star block

Rotary cutting instructions for 9" Broken Dishes block

- For piece A, cut 2 squares of color 1, and 2 squares of color 2, each 5³/₁₆", and cut on the diagonal once, yielding 4 triangles of each color.

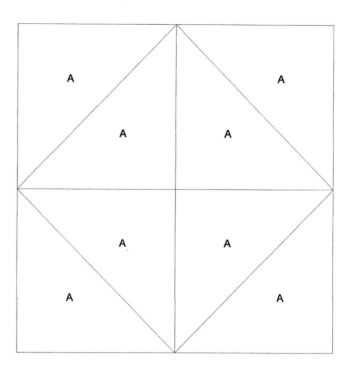

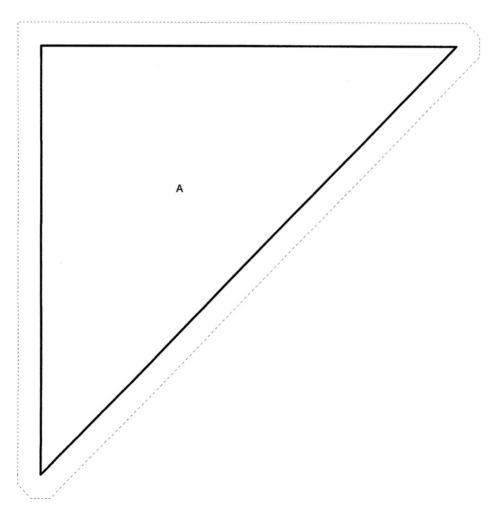

9" template for Hingham Broken Dishes block

Hingham, Flying Geese

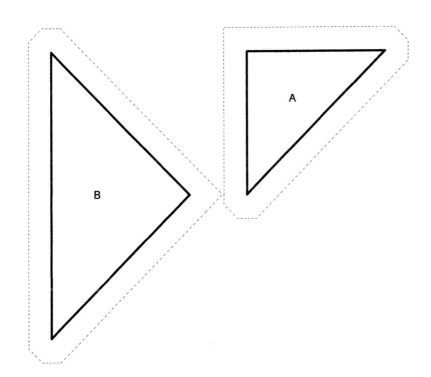

Rotary cutting instructions for 9" Flying Geese block

- For piece A, cut 18 $2\frac{3}{16}$" squares of color 1 and cut diagonally once, yielding 36.

- For piece B, cut 5 $4\frac{3}{16}$" squares of color 2 and cut on the diagonal twice, yielding 20 (18 needed).

9" template for Hingham Flying Geese block

Hingham, Greek Cross

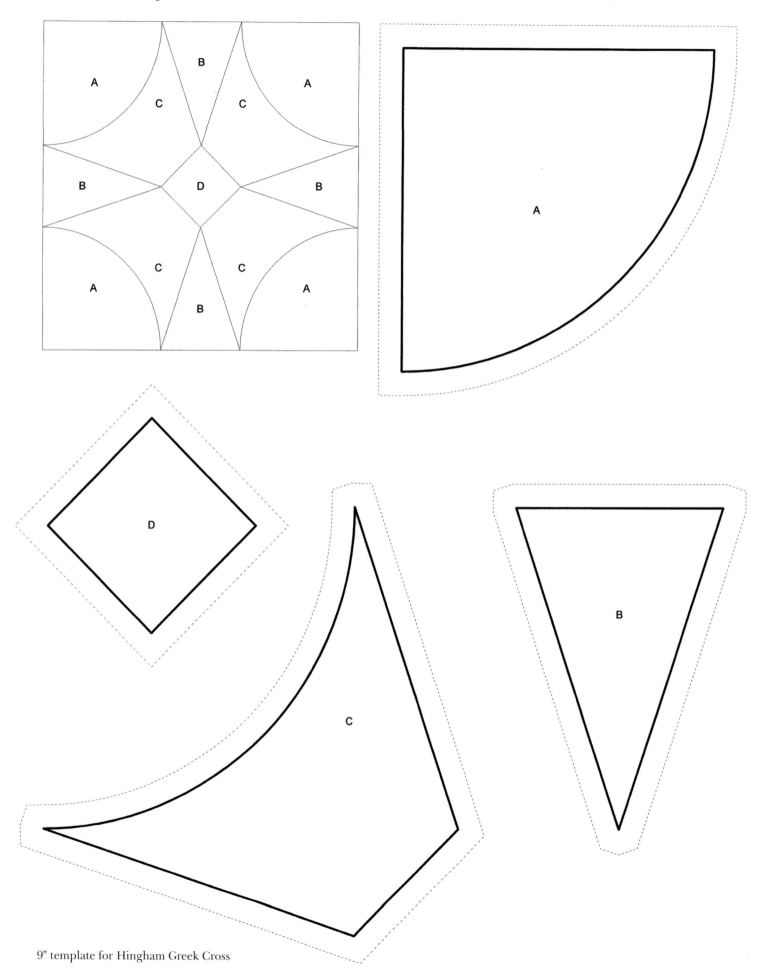

A

B

C

D

9" template for Hingham Greek Cross

Hingham, Nine Patch / Four Patch with sashing

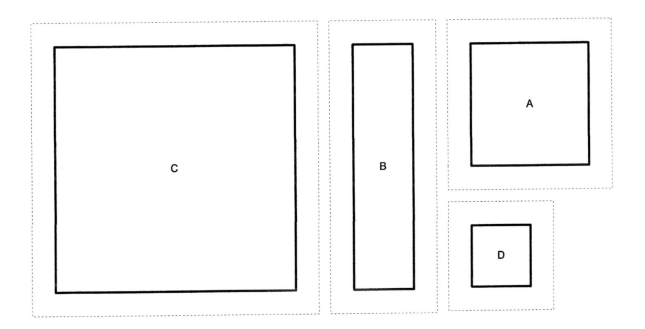

Rotary cutting instructions for 9" Nine Patch / Four Patch with Sashing block

- For piece A, cut 8 color 1 and 8 color 2, 1¾" × 1¾".
- For piece B, cut 8 color 4, 1⅛" × 3".
- For piece C, cut 4 color 3, and 1 color 5, 3 ¹⁄₁₆" × 3 ¹⁄₁₆".
- For piece D, cut 4 color 4, 1⅛" × 1⅛".

9" template for Hingham Nine Patch with Four Patch block

Hingham, Album (Fat X) block

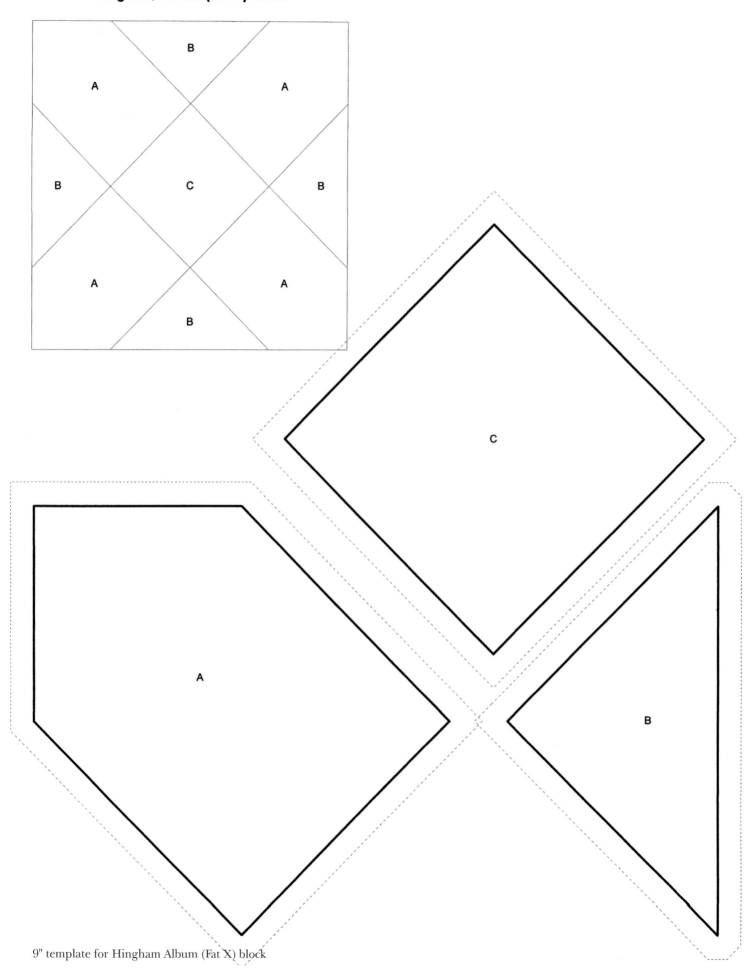

9" template for Hingham Album (Fat X) block

Rotary cutting instructions for 9" Album block (Fat X)

- For piece A, cut 4 of dark-value color 1, 3¾" × 5½" (this rectangle will be trimmed after the block is pieced).
- For piece B, cut one medium- or light-value square color 2, 5¾", and cut on the diagonal twice.
- For piece C, cut one light-value color 3 (for inscribing), 3¾" × 3¾".
- Piece the block—then measure block and trim to 9½" square (the "arms" of the album will be trimmed to square the block).

Piece the "Fat X" block after rotary cutting the "arms" as rectangles, press, and trim all "arms" as shown in the lower right corner of the photo.

Hingham, Flock of Geese

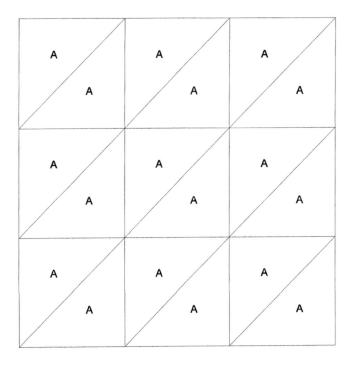

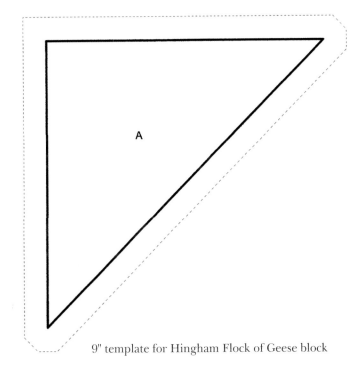

9" template for Hingham Flock of Geese block

Rotary cutting instructions for 9" Flock of Geese block

- From color 1 and color 2, cut 5 ³⁷⁄₁₆" squares, and cut on the diagonal once, yielding 10 of each color (9 needed).

Hingham, Broken Dishes with border

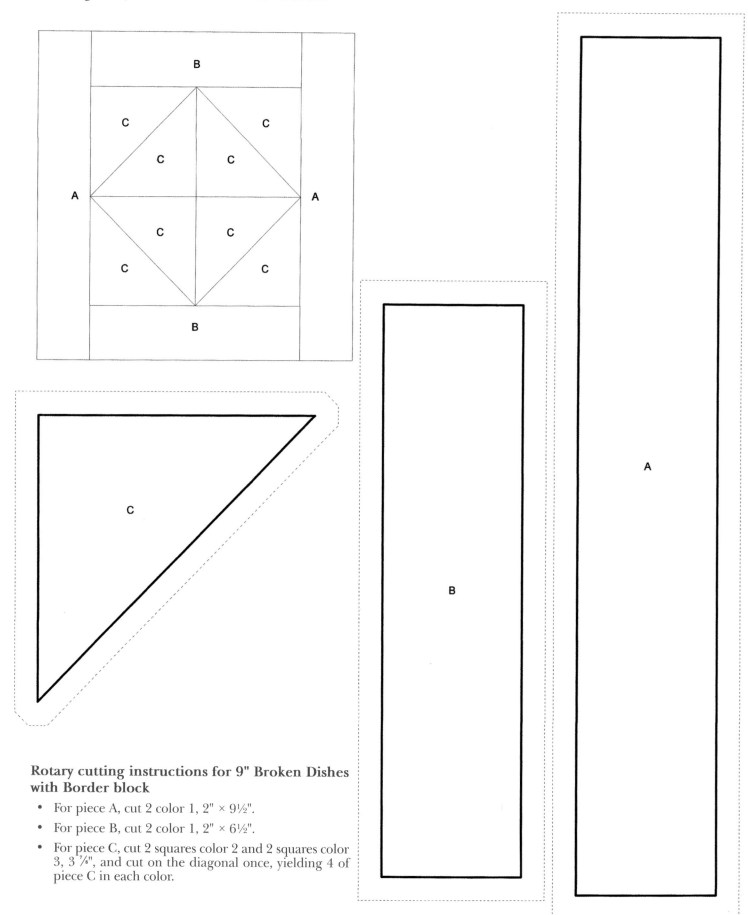

Rotary cutting instructions for 9" Broken Dishes with Border block

- For piece A, cut 2 color 1, 2" × 9½".
- For piece B, cut 2 color 1, 2" × 6½".
- For piece C, cut 2 squares color 2 and 2 squares color 3, 3⅞", and cut on the diagonal once, yielding 4 of piece C in each color.

9" template for Hingham Broken Dishes with Border block

9 Patch with Border

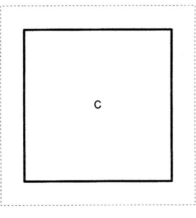

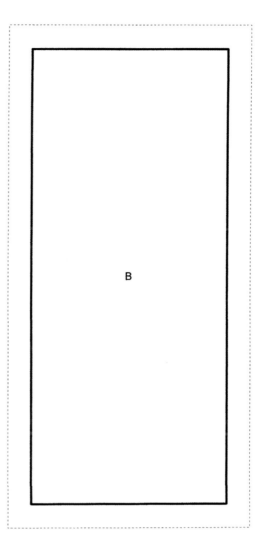

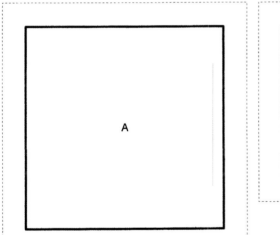

Rotary cutting instructions for 9 Patch with Border

- For piece A, cut 4 color 1, 2 ⅜" × 2 ⅜".
- For piece B, cut 4 color 1 or 2, 2 ⅝" × 5 ¼".
- For piece C, cut 4 color 3 and 5 squares color 4, 2 ⅛" × 2 ¹⁄₁₆".

9" template for Hingham 9 Patch with border block

Hingham, Nine Patch

A	A	A
A	A	A
A	A	A

Rotary cutting instructions for 9" Nine Patch block

- Cut strips of fabric in multiple colors, 3½", and cut again into 3½" squares.

- Each block needs 4 dark and 4 medium colors, and one light value for center inscribed block.

9" template for Hingham Nine Patch block

Hingham, Whirligig

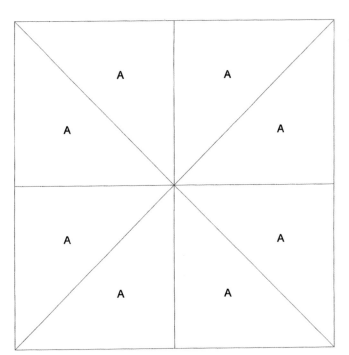

**Rotary cutting instructions for 9"
Whirligig block**

- From color 1 and color 2, cut 2
  5 ³⁄₁₆" × 5 ³⁄₁₆" squares, and cut on the diagonal
  once, yielding 4 of each color (4 needed).

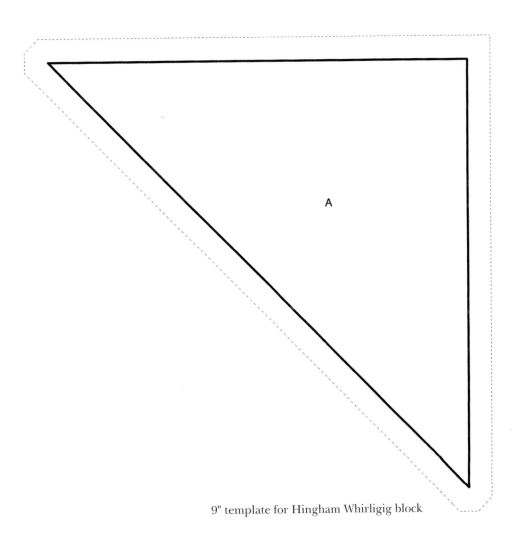

9" template for Hingham Whirligig block

Hingham, Union Star

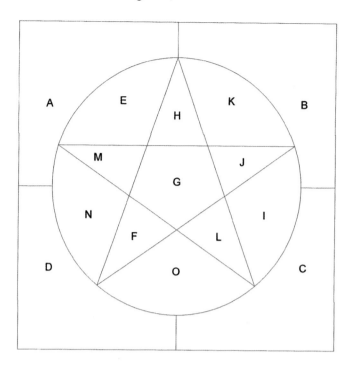

See templates E, F, G, H, J, K, L, M on the next page

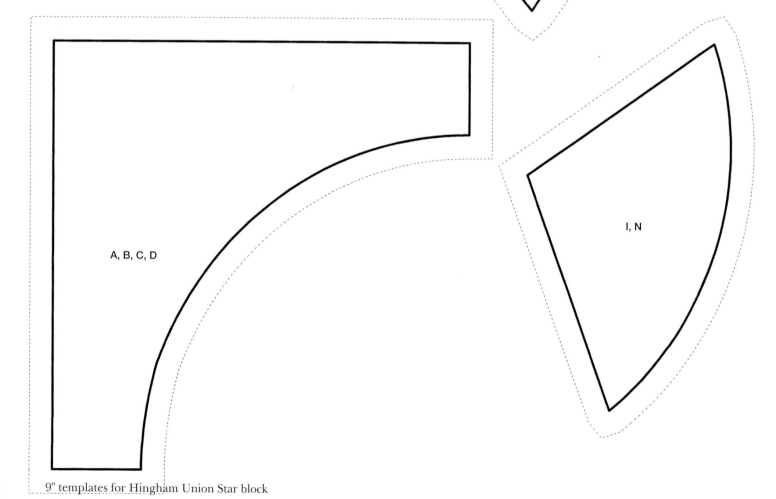

O

A, B, C, D

I, N

9" templates for Hingham Union Star block

E, K

F

H

L

G

M

J

9" templates for Hingham Union Star block

Quilt in the style of the Norridgewock, Maine, quilt, showing half as seen in the first rediscovered photograph of the quilt.
Quiltmaker: Don Beld. *Photograph: Jonathan Strait*

NORRIDGEWOCK,
MAINE

The Norridgewock, Maine, Sanitary Commission quilt was for many years known as the mystery Sanitary Commission quilt. Seen only once in public at the 1998 Dallas, Texas, Quilt Celebration, it was viewed, authenticated, and appraised by three well-known, respected quilt historians. With time, it slipped into the collective unconsciousness of the quilting world and obtained mystical status because no one recollection of it was like another. Communication back and forth between interested persons during the period 2002 to 2010 resulted in several versions of what the quilt looked like. Fortunately, in June 2010, one of the quilt historians found in her files a photograph of the quilt,

and the mystery quilt is now known to be an Album (Fat X) block. It is a similar design to the Vernon, Connecticut, Sanitary Commission quilt, which is an Album (Skinny X) block. Another major difference is that the Norridgewock quilt is a potholder quilt and the Vernon quilt is a standard quilt pieced with sashing and borders. The Norridgewock quilt is unusual in that it is a very long Sanitary Commission quilt. It measures 60 by 96 inches, which is a foot longer than most of the quilts. The reason for this might be that the Soldiers' Aid Society of Northern Ohio, in one of its publications, suggested making "comfortable at least 8 feet long and 4 feet wide."

A "long" quilt in the style of the Norridgewock quilt, showing
entire quilt. Quiltmaker: Don Beld. *Photograph: Jonathan Strait*

The quilt is constructed of forty Album blocks, and it can be seen from the photo on page 27 that although most blocks are the same, there are several with thinner "arms." One of the block's "arms" is pieced with Four Patch blocks, with a triangle in the corner to finish the piece. There is no consistency in the bindings, thus making this scrappy quilt even scrappier.

Basic information for making this reproduction quilt:

1. Size: 60" × 96"

2. Number of blocks: 40

3. Block name: Album (Fat X) block

4. Block size: 12"

5. Sashing. This is a potholder quilt, and there is no sashing; however, if you choose to make this quilt as a standard quilt with sashing, use 0.5" sashing between all the blocks and bind as usual.

6. Borders: none

7. Quilting: unknown, although it can be seen that at least one block has some circular quilting in the triangles.

8. Stamped on the back "Sanitary Commission"

Rotary cutting instructions for 12" Album block (Fat X) for each block:

For piece A, cut 4 rectangles of dark fabric 3⅞" × 7½" (this rectangle will be trimmed after the block is pieced).

For piece B, cut 1 square 6½" and cut on the diagonal twice, yielding 4 triangles.

For piece C, cut 1 square 3⅞" × 3⅞" of light fabric to be inscribed.

Piece the block, then measure and trim to 12½" square (the "arms" of the album will be trimmed to square the block).

"God bless you, soldier" block. *Photograph: Jonathan Strait*

Only one inscription has been documented from this quilt:

God bless you, soldier, scarred and worn
Harried with markings, walking pain
All battle stained and battle torn
Bravely have all your tasks been bourne
You have not fought in vain.
—*Emma C. Baker*

Amounts of fabric needed to make this reproduction quilt:

1. For the inscribed center blocks, ½ yard light-colored cotton. The blocks are very scrappy, but you'll need the equivalent of 20 fat quarters of dark-colored fabrics for the "arms" and 5 fat quarters of medium-value fabrics for the setting triangles. (Each dark-value fat quarter will yield "arms" for two blocks. A medium-value fat quarter will yield the triangles [piece B] for 9 blocks.)

2. Sashing: none

3. Borders and binding: none. Be sure to buy enough fat-quarter material to provide the binding for the individual blocks.

4. Backing: potholder or 3.5 yards

    Remember that the back fabric usually is made up of odd pieces from the maker's stash, but the same fabric can be used if preferred.

Norridgewock Album (Fat X) block

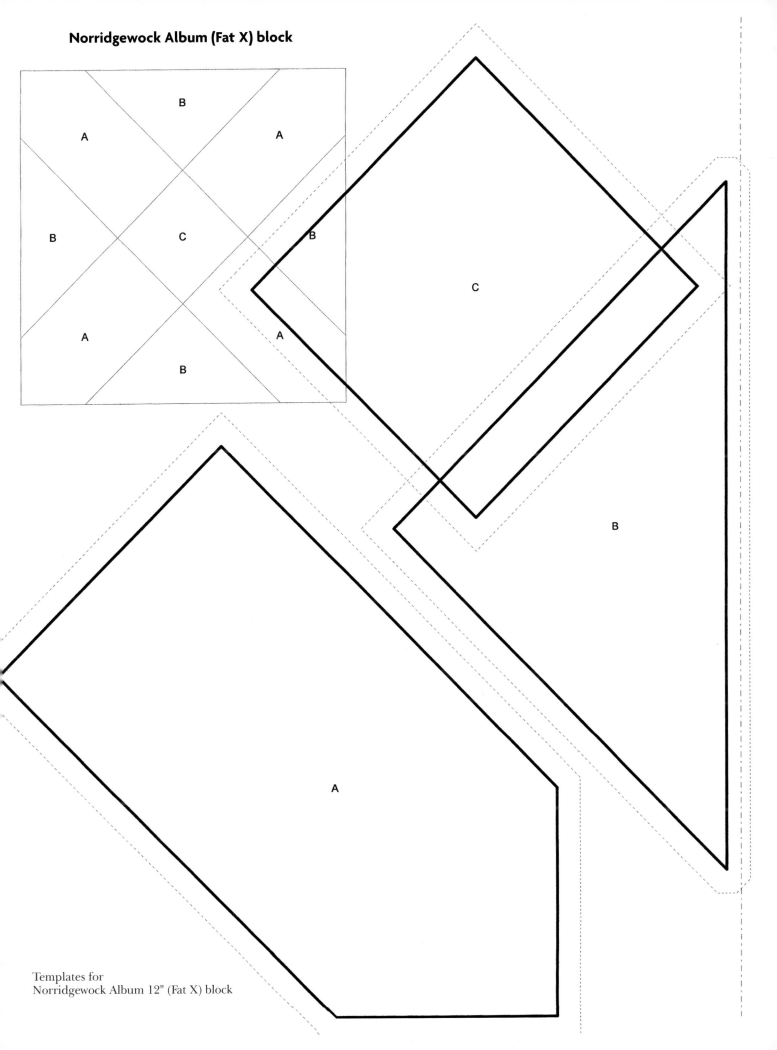

B

A   A

B   C

A

B

B

C

A

B

A

Templates for
Norridgewock Album 12" (Fat X) block

VERNON, CONNECTICUT

The Vernon quilt was used as the model for the Home of the Brave Quilt Project's quilts, which are presented to families of the fallen heroes from Operation Enduring Freedom and Operation Iraqi Freedom. The primary difference is that the HOTBQP uses only 15 12" blocks with 3" sashing, including the top, sides, and bottom, and an additional piece of fabric 3" tall and the width of the quilt at either the top or bottom.

Fannie Chester block (sister of Elizabeth Chester Fisk). *Photograph: Jonathan Strait*

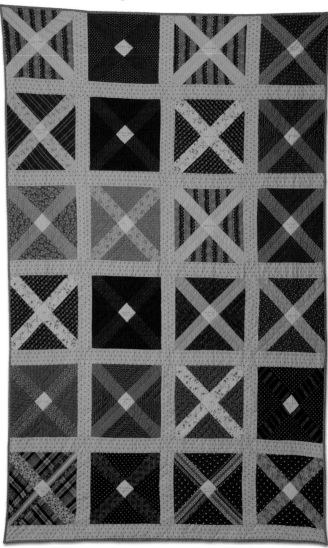

Quilt in the style of the Vernon, Connecticut, quilt, showing fugitive dye fabrics as they might have looked in the 1860s. Quiltmaker: Don Beld. *Photograph: Jonathan Strait*

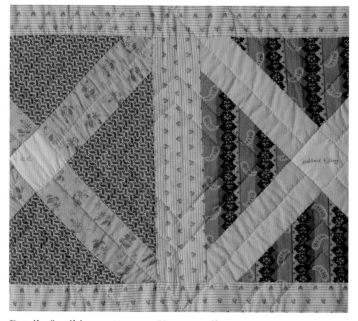

Detail of quilting pattern on Vernon quilt. *Photograph: Jonathan Strait*

The Vernon quilt contains many different fabrics; however, a number of the blocks are actually identical or contain some fabrics that are found in other blocks. Another point of interest is that several of these blocks contain fugitive dyes that, in the quilt as it exists today, appear to be creams or browns but originally were purples or violets. The reproduction quilt made in the style of the Vernon quilt may actually be closer to what the real quilt looked like when it was new.

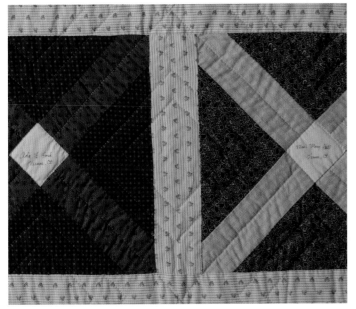

Detail of blocks from Vernon quilt. *Photograph: Jonathan Strait*

Back of Vernon quilt, showing Sanitary Commission stamp. *Photograph: Jonathan Strait*

Basic information for making this reproduction quilt:

1. Size: 56" × 84"

2. Number of blocks: 24

3. Block size: 12"

4. Block name: Album (Skinny X) block

5. Sashing: 2.5". There is no sashing on the top, left side, or right side of the quilt.

6. Borders: none

7. Quilting: Elbow quilting, squares on point within squares on point, with each signature square having in the ditch quilting

8. Binding: Backing brought to front

9. Stamped on back: Sanitary Commission stamp

Names as found on the Vernon quilt

VERNON, CONNECTICUT, SANITARY COMMISSION QUILT SIGNATURES

1 Julia A Sanford	2 Mrs. William David	3 Lucy L. Gilbert	4 Lizzie C. Corbin Vernon, Ct
5 Fannie Chester Vernon, Ct	6 Mrs. Eliza W. Kellogg Vernon, Ct	7 Rowena S. Clark	8 Mrs. H. Roberts
9 blank	10 W. N.	11 Hubbard Kellogg	12 Mary Chapman (?) Vernon, Ct
13 L. Clark	14 Ada F. Ford Vernon. Ct	15 Mrs. Mary Hall	16 Ellen McLean
17 Anna A. Kellogg	18 E. G. Hammond Vernon, Ct 1864	19 S. Clark	20 Mrs. Ruth Baker Vernon, Ct
21 Mrs. Leroy K. Pearl Vernon, Ct	22 Mrs. Emily Chapman Vernon, Ct	23 Elisa A. Ford Vernon, Ct	24 blank

Block similarities when making the quilt:

1. Blocks 1, 3, and 10 contain the same triangle fabric and the same X fabric.

2. Blocks 5 and 13 contain the same triangle fabric and the same X fabric.

3. Blocks 8 and 18 contain the same triangle fabric but different X fabric.

4. Blocks 2 and 20 contain the same triangle fabric but different X fabric. The X fabric in block 2 may be a brocade.

5. Blocks 19 and 20 contain the same triangle fabric but different X fabric.

6. Blocks 7, 13, and 19 contain the same X fabric, and blocks 7 and 13 have the same triangle fabric.

7. Block 21 contains two different fabrics in the X.

The sashing fabric is an off-white or cream print with lines running through it, with bouquets of flowers. In the original quilt, the bouquets were alternating pink and violet. Also note that the sashing is made as strip sashing (i.e., block-length sashing, 2.5" by 12", is found between blocks in each row, with long strips of sashing between the rows. ❧

Rotary cutting instructions for 12" Album (Thin X) block for each block:

For piece A, cut 4 rectangles of dark fabric $2^5/_8" \times 8"$ (this rectangle will be trimmed after the block is pieced).

For piece B, cut 1 square $10^1/_2"$ and cut on the diagonal twice, yielding 4 triangles.

For piece C, cut 1 square $2^5/_8" \times 2^5/_8"$ of light fabric to be inscribed.

Piece the block, then measure and trim to $12^1/_2"$ square (the "arms" of the album will be trimmed to square the block as seen in the photograph on p. 119).

Amounts of fabric to make a quilt similar to this quilt:

1. Sashing: 2.5 yards

2. 24 Album blocks using 17 different fat quarters for triangles, 21 different fat quarters for the Xs, and 0.5 yards of an off-white for the center signature square

3. Back fabric: 3.5 yards. For the back fabric, which is also the binding, cut 3.5 yards of fabric in half and sew together to make a 60" × 88" back panel. If the quilt top is centered properly, this will provide just enough back fabric to make the back-to-front binding. The back fabric should be a medium-brown print.

Vernon, Connecticut (Skinny X) block

Key Block (29/100 actual size)

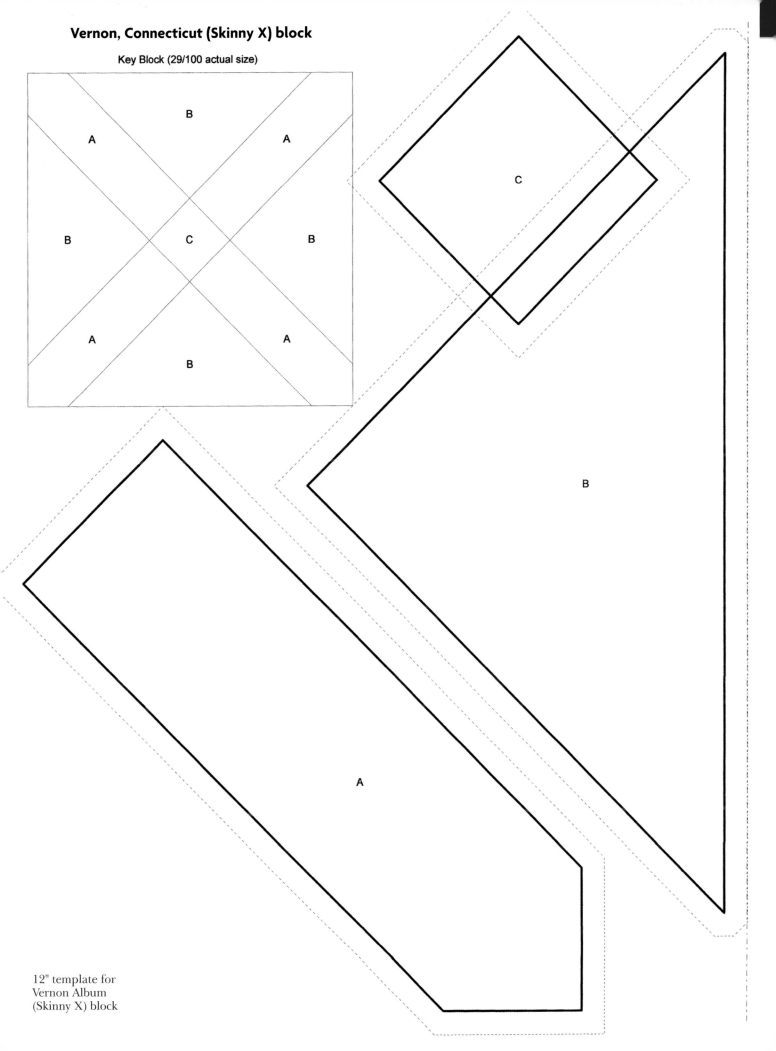

B

A

A

B

C

B

A

A

B

C

B

A

12" template for
Vernon Album
(Skinny X) block

SMALL QUILTS

Small Quilt Projects

The Civil War era was a time of practical quiltmaking for beds, children's cribs, and keeping warm in cold weather. Today, many quilters like to adorn their homes with small quilts and present them as gifts to families or friends.

These small potholder quilt projects are perfect for that. Because they can be inscribed blocks, they make wonderful wedding, birth, anniversary, or family tree gifts. They can be used to celebrate all of life's important events.

Because each block is made separately and then assembled into quilts, the small quilts can start with just four blocks. You can add more to make a six- or nine-block quilt, and expand as the quilter needs or desires. If recording a family tree, new block leaves can be added as new births occur. Even one block makes a perfect birth gift, with the baby's name and date of birth in the center white square.

Three Civil War–era blocks are provided for this project. All are set on point, and all measure approximately 10½ by 10½ inches finished. The finished quilt can be made of multiple blocks of the same pattern, or it can be made by mixing the three patterns together.

If you wish to progress to a full-size Sanitary Commission–style quilt, it takes forty blocks of five rows across and eight rows down. You also can continue to add blocks until you reach a standard-, queen-, or king-size quilt. In short, you can turn the quilt into that long-term hand piecing and hand quilting you have always wanted to work on, but still have a presentable quilt along the way.

GREEK CROSS BLOCK

This block is found in the Hingham, Massachusetts, Sanitary Commission quilt and is a unique block in that quilt. It has no known name from that period; however, Barbara Brackman in her *Encyclopedia of Pieced Quilt Patterns* identifies it with a late-nineteenth-century name of Greek Cross and an early-twentieth-century name of Ice Cream Cone.

Small potholder quilt,
Greek Cross on Point.
Quiltmaker: Don Beld.
*Photograph: Jonathan
Strait*

Basic information for making this quilt:

1. Size: 21" × 21"

2. Number of blocks: 4

3. Block size: 10", plus seam allowance

4. Block name: Greek Cross

5. Sashing: none

6. Borders: none

7. Quilting: as desired

8. Binding: potholder around each block

9. Fabric requirements:

    ½ yard of solid fabric for setting triangles

    ½ yard of fabric for binding

    1 fat quarter of white or off-white for center squares

    4 fat quarters of dark fabric

    4 fat quarters of light fabric

    f. 1 fat quarter of a solid for background in blocks

Small Quilts. Greek Cross

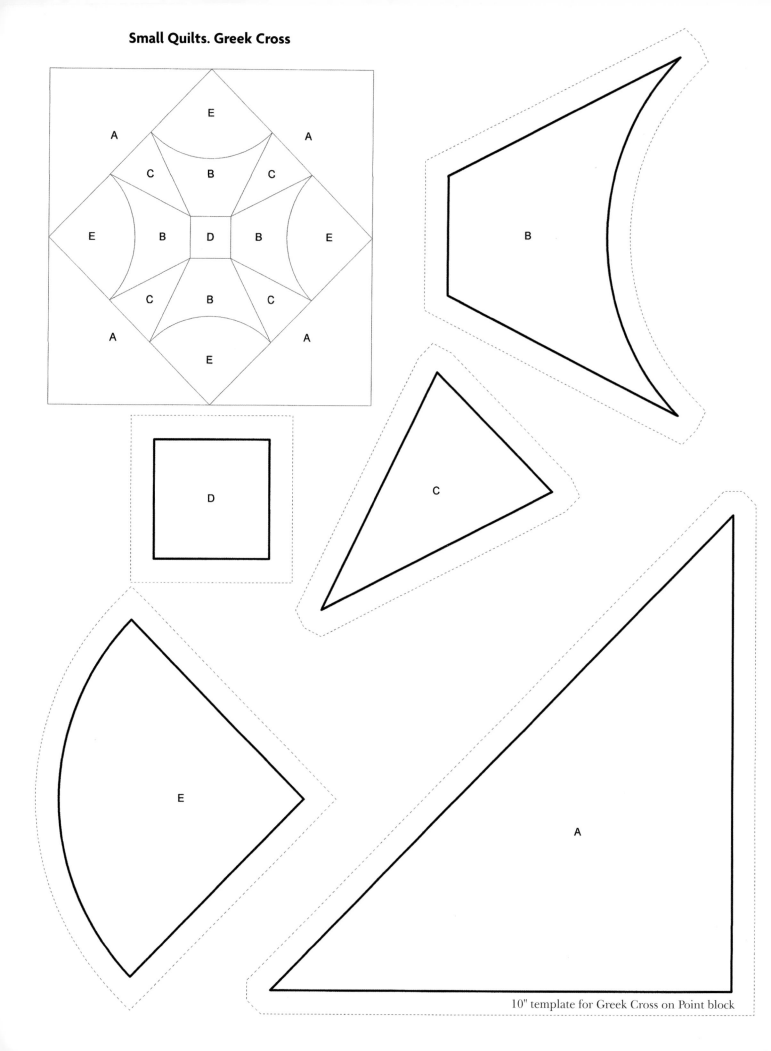

10" template for Greek Cross on Point block

Small potholder quilt-as-you-go quilt,
Crossroads on Point. Quiltmaker: Don Beld.
Photograph: Jonathan Strait

THE CROSSROADS BLOCK

The crossroads block is not found in any of the Civil War soldiers' quilts featured in this book. This wall hanging is included because at one time, it was thought that this was the block used in the Norridgewock, Maine, Sanitary Commission quilt. Because no photograph of this quilt was found until June 2010, the descriptions of the quilt by the three quilt historians who saw the quilt in 1998 were used to try to re-create the quilt. At one time, it was also thought the Norridgewock quilt might be the Album (Chimney Sweep) Block, but that turned out to be wrong as well. At various times, the quilt was described as being a potholder quilt, not a potholder quilt, or a quilt-as-you-go quilt. The recollections are that it was composed almost entirely of medium and dark browns that blended into each other.

Basic information for making this quilt:

1. Size: 31" × 31"

2. Number of blocks: 9

3. Block size: 10" plus seam allowance

4. Block name: Crossroads

5. Sashing: none

6. Borders: none

7. Quilting: as desired

8. Binding: traditional binding of your choice

9. Fabric requirement:

   1.2 yards of white or off-white solid

   9 fat quarters of dark-brown fabric

   1½ yards of medium-brown fabric for setting triangles, which also provides enough fabric for the binding

Fortunately a photograph of the quilt was discovered in June 2010, and it shows the quilt as an Album (Fat X) block, made in the potholder style, and with multitudes of different colors, some of which are very bright. The block in this project, the Crossroads pattern, is very similar to the Album (Fat X) block, except for the small triangle of a different fabric at the end of each X.

This wall hanging was made as a quilt-as-you-go quilt, since that style of quiltmaking is also found in some of the Civil War Union soldiers' quilts. See knife edge finished edges for techniques to make as a "quilt as you go."

Small Quilts, Crossroads on Point

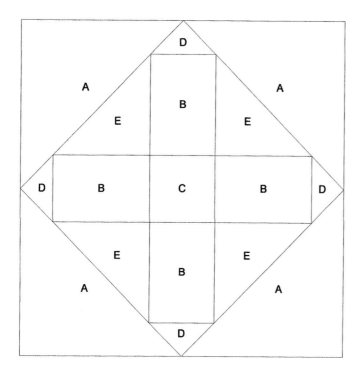

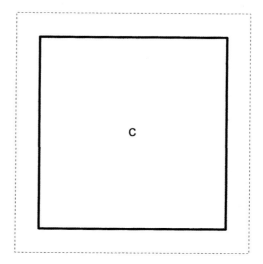

Rotary cutting instructions for each 10" Crossroads block (multiply by 9 if you are making the Nine Block small quilt)

- For piece A, cut 2 squares color 1 (medium value) and cut on the diagonal once.

- For piece B, cut 4 squares color 2 (light value), 2½" × 3½".

- For piece C, cut 1 square color 2 (light value) 2½" × 2½".

- For piece D, cut 2 squares color 3, 2 ⅜" X 2 ⅜", and cut on the diagonal once.

- For piece E, cut 1 square color 3, 4¼" × 4¼", and cut on the diagonal twice.

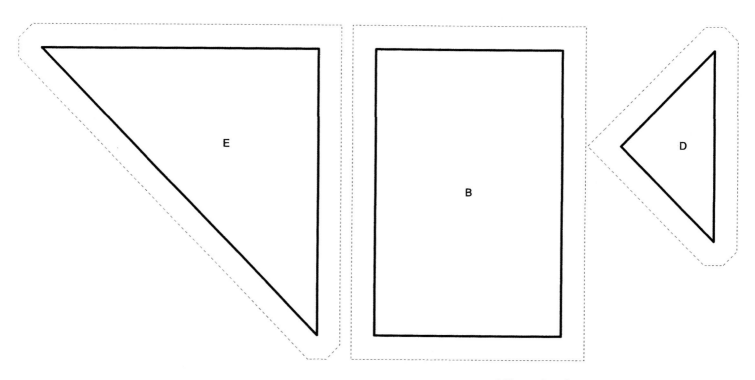

10" template for Crossroads on Point block

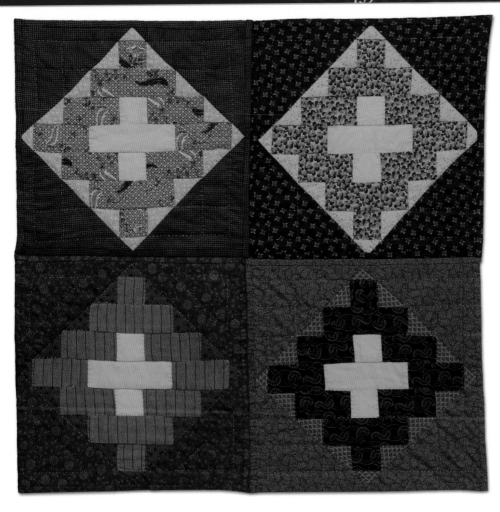

Small potholder quilt, Album
(Chimney Sweep) on Point block.
Quiltmaker: Don Beld.
Photograph: Jonathan Strait

ALBUM
(CHIMNEY SWEEP)
BLOCK

Although the Album (Chimney Sweep) block is not
found in any of the Civil War Union soldiers' quilts
featured in this book, it was a popular (perhaps the
most popular) inscribed quilt pattern before, during,
and after the Civil War. Its popular name of "Chimney
Sweep" was not used during the Civil War, when it was
referred to as the "Album" block. Many other blocks
also used that name.

After the Civil War, members of the GAR Clara Barton
Post in North Oxford, Massachusetts, and their wives made
an inscribed presentation quilt for Clara Barton, and they
used this block. It can be seen today on her bed in the
Clara Barton Museum in Washington, DC. ❦

Basic information
for making this quilt:

1. Size: 21" × 21"

2. Number of blocks: 4

3. Size of blocks: 10" plus seam allowance

4. Block name: Album

5. Sashing: none

6. Borders: none

7. Quilting: as desired

8. Binding: potholder style around each block

9. Fabric requirements:

   4 fat quarters for setting triangles and
   binding

   1 fat quarter white or off-white for center X

   4 fat quarters of dark-brown fabric
   for squares and rectangles in blocks

   4 fat quarters of light or medium
   browns for small triangles in block

Small Quilts, Album (Chimney Sweep) block on point

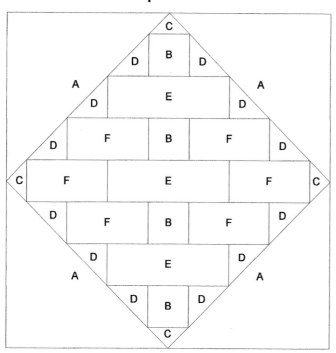

Rotary cutting instructions for each 10" Chimney Sweep block (multiply by 4 if you are making the Four Block small quilt)

- For piece A, cut 1 square color 1 (medium value), 11½" × 11½", and cut on the diagonal once.

- For piece B, cut 2 squares color 2 (light value) and 2 squares 1¾" × 1¾".

- For piece C, cut 2 squares color 3 (light value), 1¾" × 1¾", and cut on the diagonal once for 4.

- For piece D, cut 3 squares color 3, 2 ¾" × 2 ¾", and cut on the diagonal twice for 12.

- For piece E, cut 1 light-color rectangle and 2 color 2 rectangles, 1¼" × 3¾".

- For piece F, cut 4 rectangles of color 2, 1¼" × 2½".

- NOTE: the easiest way to cut pieces B, E, and F is to cut strips 1¾" wide, then cut into desired lengths, as above.

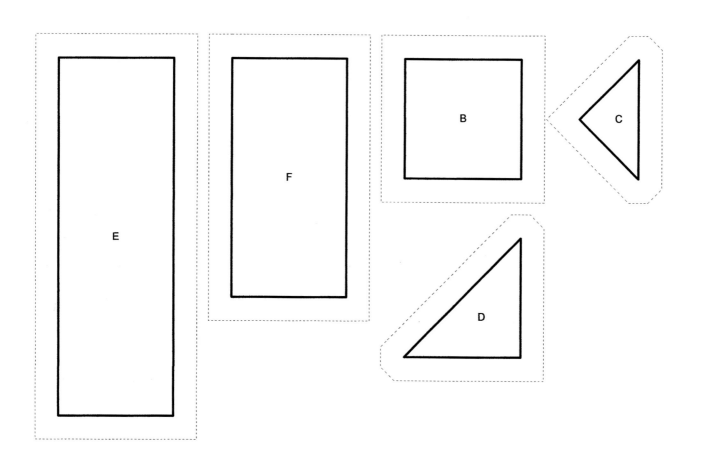

10" template for Album (Chimney Sweep) block on point

Quilts with either pieced or appliquéd stars and shields were very popular during the Civil War era. A number of the Union soldiers' quilts use these motifs: the Dow quilt; the Florence, Massachusetts, Sanitary Commission Quilt; and the Detroit, Michigan, Soldier's Quilt.

The popularity of stars and shields in quilts actually began almost with the founding of the nation and has continued throughout the nation's history. They have been especially popular during times of war and important milestone celebrations such as the 100th-anniversary celebration of the Declaration of Independence, etc. Small wall-size quilts are popular today for home décor during observances of the Fourth of July and Memorial Day.

The Stars & Shield Wall Hanging patterns included here will allow you to make your own patriotic small quilt.

The Stars & Shield Wall Hanging

Basic information for making this quilt:

Size: 32" × 32"

Blocks: 12 Star blocks; one center medallion block

Size of blocks: Star blocks are 8" finished; Shield medallion block is 16" finished.

Block names: Federal Star and Federal Shield

Sashing: none

Borders: none

Quilting: recommend ¾ to 1" grid quilting

Binding: as desired

Embellishments: as desired. The verses from "The Star Spangled Banner" were popular during the Civil War, as were the verses from songs such as "The Battle Cry for Freedom," and "The Battle Hymn of the Republic."

The pattern for the Federal Star block has a one-piece star. You may choose to appliqué this onto an 8½" background.

Tip: if you choose to piece the block, after marking the star piece, cut into the seam allowance at the interior corners to facilitate rotating the star as you piece the outer five white pieces to the star.

The Shield pattern is reversed to make the second part of the shield. Piece the four pieces of the shield together before appliquéing the shield to the background fabric.

Stars & Shield Wall Hanging. Quiltmakers: Bernice Foster (appliqué, embroidery, and quilting) and Don Beld (pieced stars). *Photograph: Jonathan Strait*

Union Star

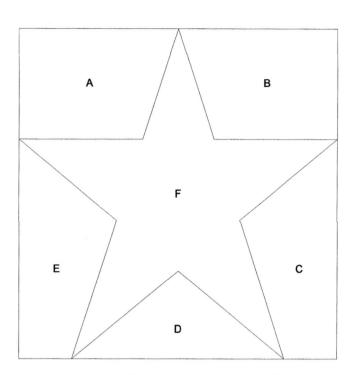

See templates A, B, and F on page 128.

This star can be used as a pattern piece for appliqué. Cut a light-colored background square 8½" and apply the star to it.

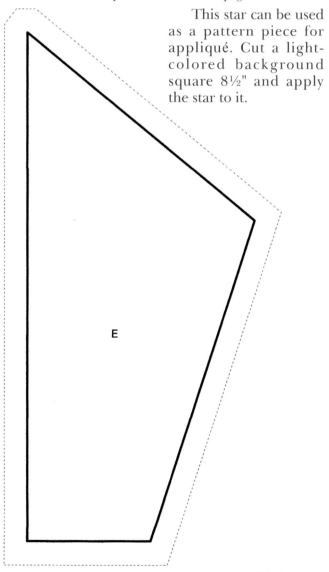

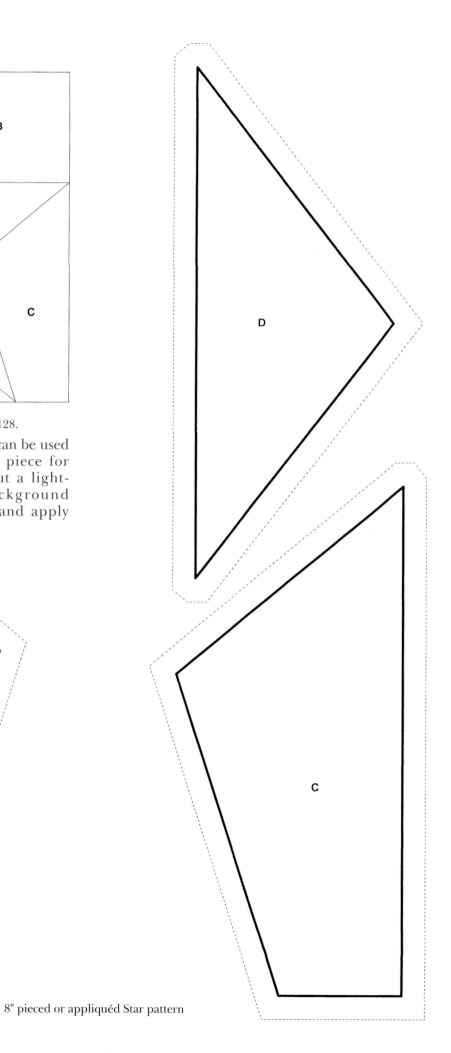

8" pieced or appliquéd Star pattern

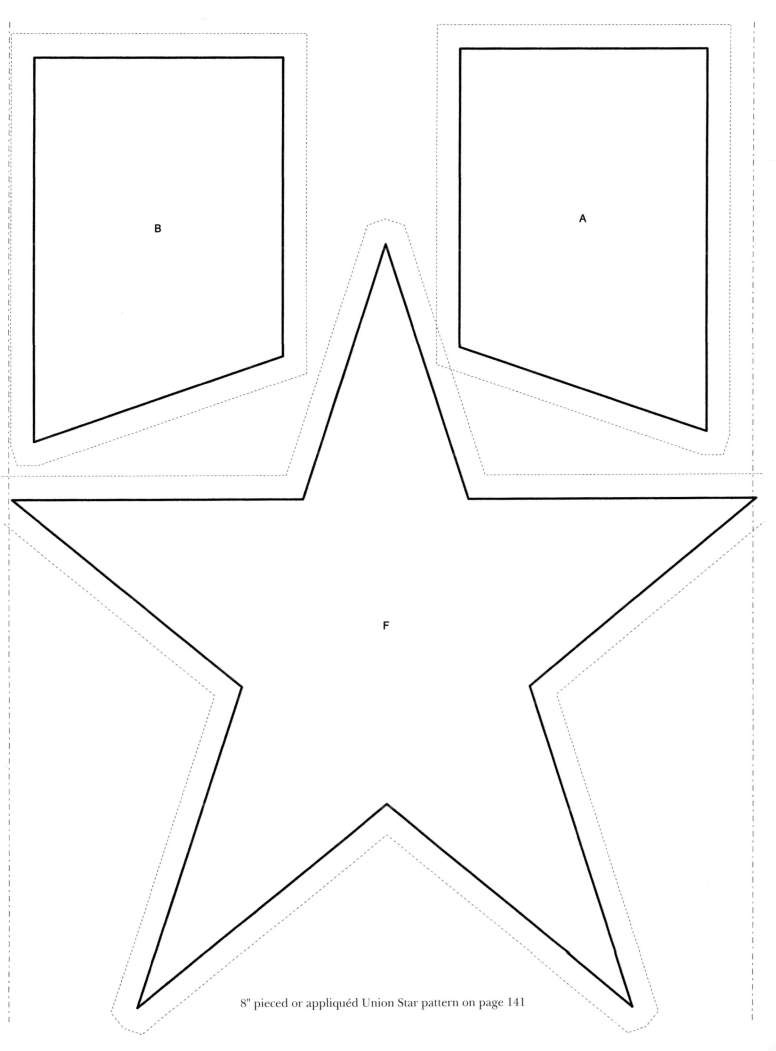

B

A

F

8" pieced or appliquéd Union Star pattern on page 141

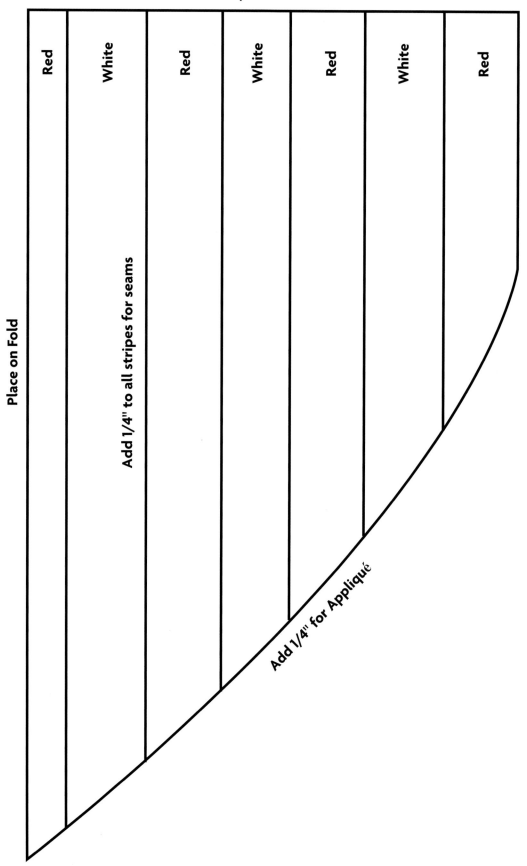

Add 1/4" for seam

Red

White

Red

White

Red

White

Red

Place on Fold

Add 1/4" to all stripes for seams

Add 1/4" for Appliqué

Pattern for half of lower portion of Union Shield. Piece the stripes, add this to the blue field (pattern on page 145) and then applique onto the background fabric.

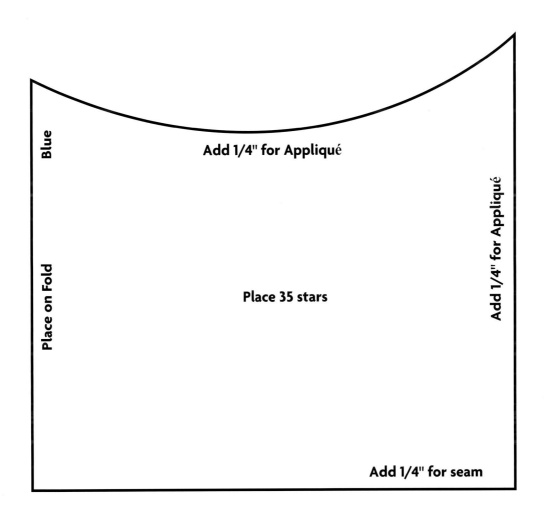

Blue

Add 1/4" for Appliqué

Place on Fold

Place 35 stars

Add 1/4" for Appliqué

Add 1/4" for seam

Pattern for upper portion of Union Sheild. Place on folded blue fabric, trace and cut out 1/4 from drawn line. Embroider stars, add the striped bottom portion, and applique to the background fabric.

*Signature
Block Templates
From 1835 to 1865*

All of the surviving Union soldiers' quilts are inscribed quilts. Inscribed quilts have been popular since the 1830s and continue to be popular today. Guild presidents' quilts and the Home of the Brave quilts are current examples. At the turn of the nineteenth to twentieth centuries, Red Cross quilts were popular—especially during World War I, when they were used to raise funds for the Red Cross relief programs. Crazy quilts are sometimes inscribed quilts, with names, dates, and locations of the quiltmaker embroidered on the squares.

Included on pages 146 to 149 are photos of seventeen 10-inch blocks from existing quilts, dating from the period 1835 to 1865. Most can be found in the antique quilts pictured in this book. Templates for each block are found on page 150 to 167.

You can create your own Civil War Union soldier's quilt by using one, a few, or all of these patterns and putting them together as pieced tops with or without sashing and with or without borders. You can also make potholder blocks and assemble them into a quilt. If you add the three 10-inch blocks from the Small Quilt Projects, and make two of each block, you would have forty blocks, which are enough to make a 50-by-80-inch quilt.

Uneven Nine-Patch Block
See template on page 150.

Friendship Star
See template on page 151.

Unnamed 1.
See template on page 152.

Washington Pavement.
See template on page 153.

Six inscribed potholder blocks. Photograph Jonathan Strait

Square in Square with Sashing.
See template on page 154.

Fractured Star.
See template on page 155.

Eight-Point Star on Point. See template on page 156.

Uneven Nine Patch. See template on page 157.

Robbing Peter to Pay Paul variation.
See template on pages 158 and 159.

Flag. See template on page 160.

Nine Patch on Point. See template on page 161

Basket. See template on page 162.

Unnamed 2. See template on page 163.

Pratt Family Quilt. See template on page 164.

Six inscribed potholder blocks. Photograph Jonathan Strait

Fly Away.
See template on page 166.

Hourglass Variation.
See template on page 167.

Hourglass Variation 2.
See template on page 165.

All photographs by Jonathan Strait

Rotary cutting instructions for each 10" Uneven Nine-Patch Signature block

- For piece A, cut 4 squares color 1 (medium value), 3" × 3".

- For piece B, cut 4 rectangles color 2 (dark value), 3" × 5¼".

- For piece C, cut 1 rectangle/strip color 3 (light value), 1⅞" × 7¾".

- For piece D, cut 1 square color 3, 4⅞" × 4⅞", and cut on the diagonal once.

- HINT for piecing: Cut 1 piece C and 2 pieces D. Fold C in half and finger-press, leaving a ridge at the center. Fold both pieces D to find the centers of the long sides, and again finger-press. Match the center of one piece D with the center of piece C and sew. Repeat with the second piece D. Press seams to the outside, and square and trim this assemblage to make a 5½" square.

Signature Uneven Nine Patch block

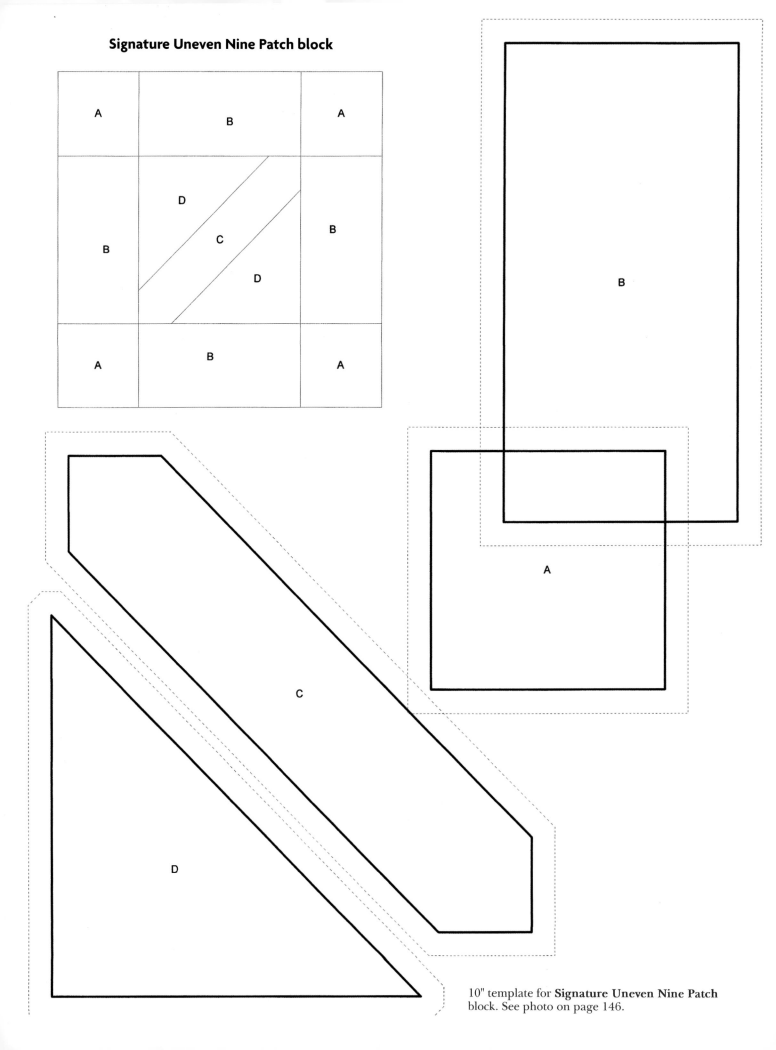

A	B	A
B	D C D	B
A	B	A

B

A

C

D

10" template for **Signature Uneven Nine Patch** block. See photo on page 146.

Friendship Star

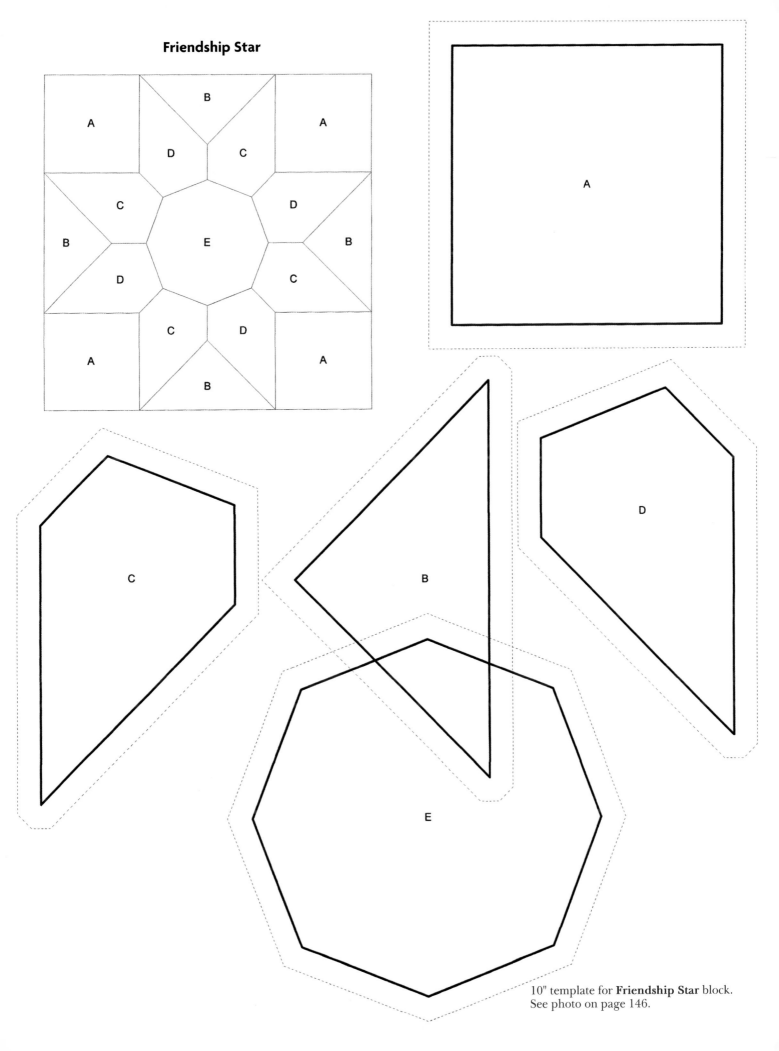

A

B

C

D

E

10" template for **Friendship Star** block.
See photo on page 146.

Unnamed 1

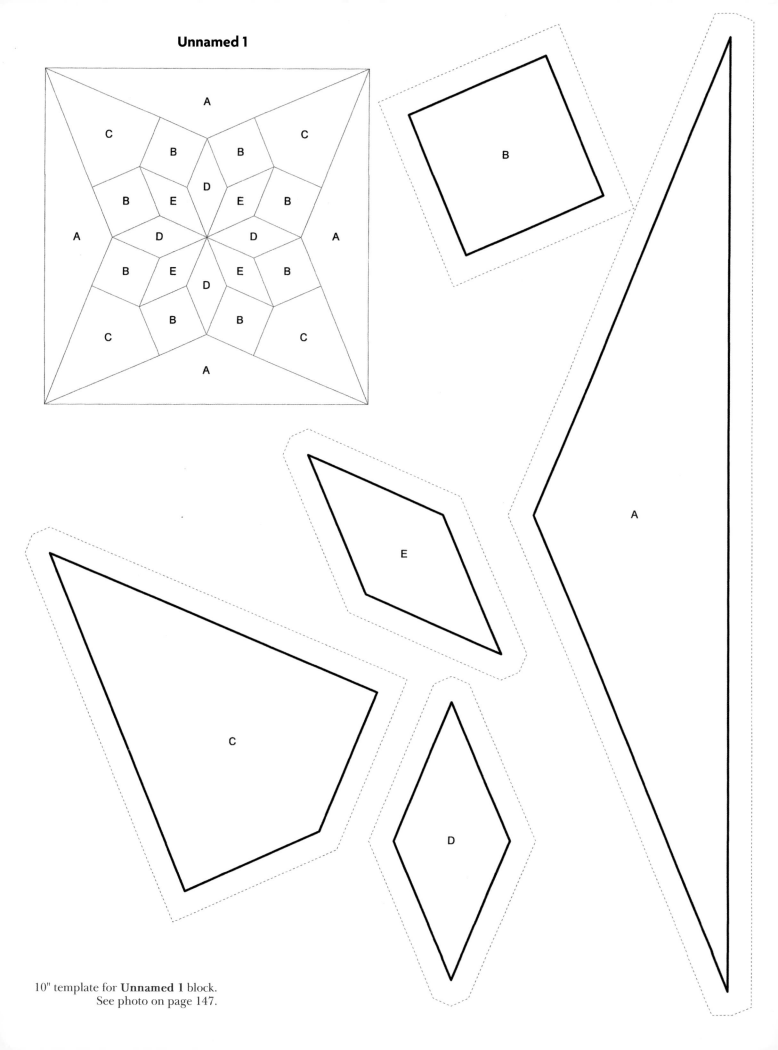

A

C

C

B

B

D

B

E

E

B

A

D

D

A

B

E

E

B

C

B

B

C

A

B

C

E

D

A

10" template for **Unnamed 1** block.
See photo on page 147.

Washington Pavement

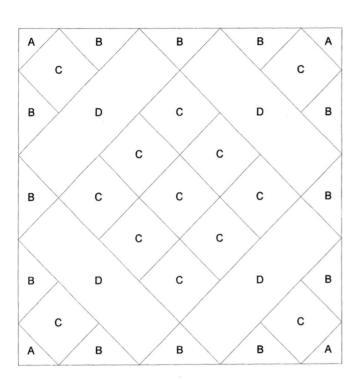

Rotary cutting instructions for each 10" Washington Pavement block

- For piece A, cut 2 squares color 3 (medium value), 2⅛" × 2⅛", and cut on the diagonal once.
- For piece B, cut 3 squares color 3 (medium value), 3¾" × 3¾", and cut on the diagonal twice.
- For piece C, cut 4 squares color 3 (medium value) and 8 squares color 2 (dark value), 2¼" × 2¼".
- For piece D, cut 4 rectangles color 2 (dark value), 2¼" × 5¾".

Decide first where you will inscribe this block, then choose your solid light value for that piece or pieces.

Rotary cutting instructions for each 10" Square in a Square with Sashing block

- For piece A, cut 2 squares, 5⅞" × 5⅞", and cut on the diagonal once.
- For piece B, cut 2 rectangles 1¾" × 7½".
- For piece C, cut 2 rectangles 1¾" × 5¼".
- For piece D, cut 2 squares, 3¼" × 3¼", and cut on the diagonal once.
- For piece E, cut one square 3⅞" × 3⅞".

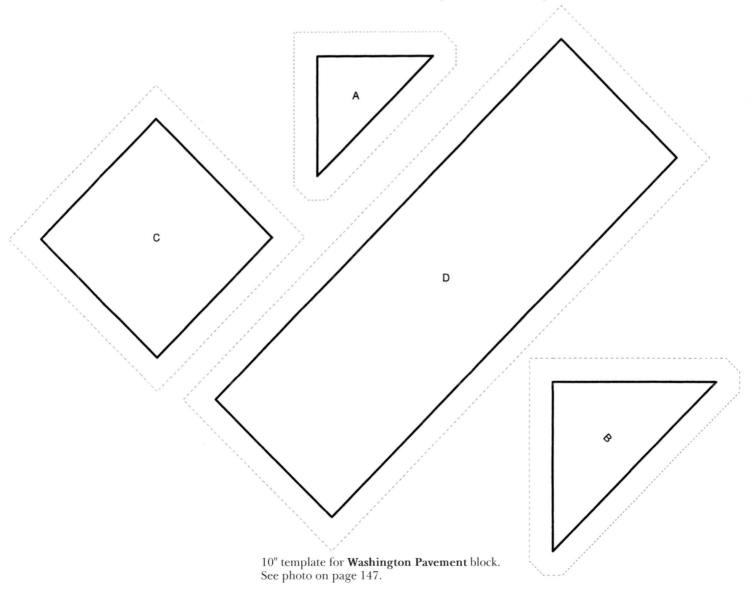

10" template for **Washington Pavement** block.
See photo on page 147.

Square in Square with Sashing

A   A

D

B   C

D   E   D

C   D   B

A   A

D

E

C

B

A

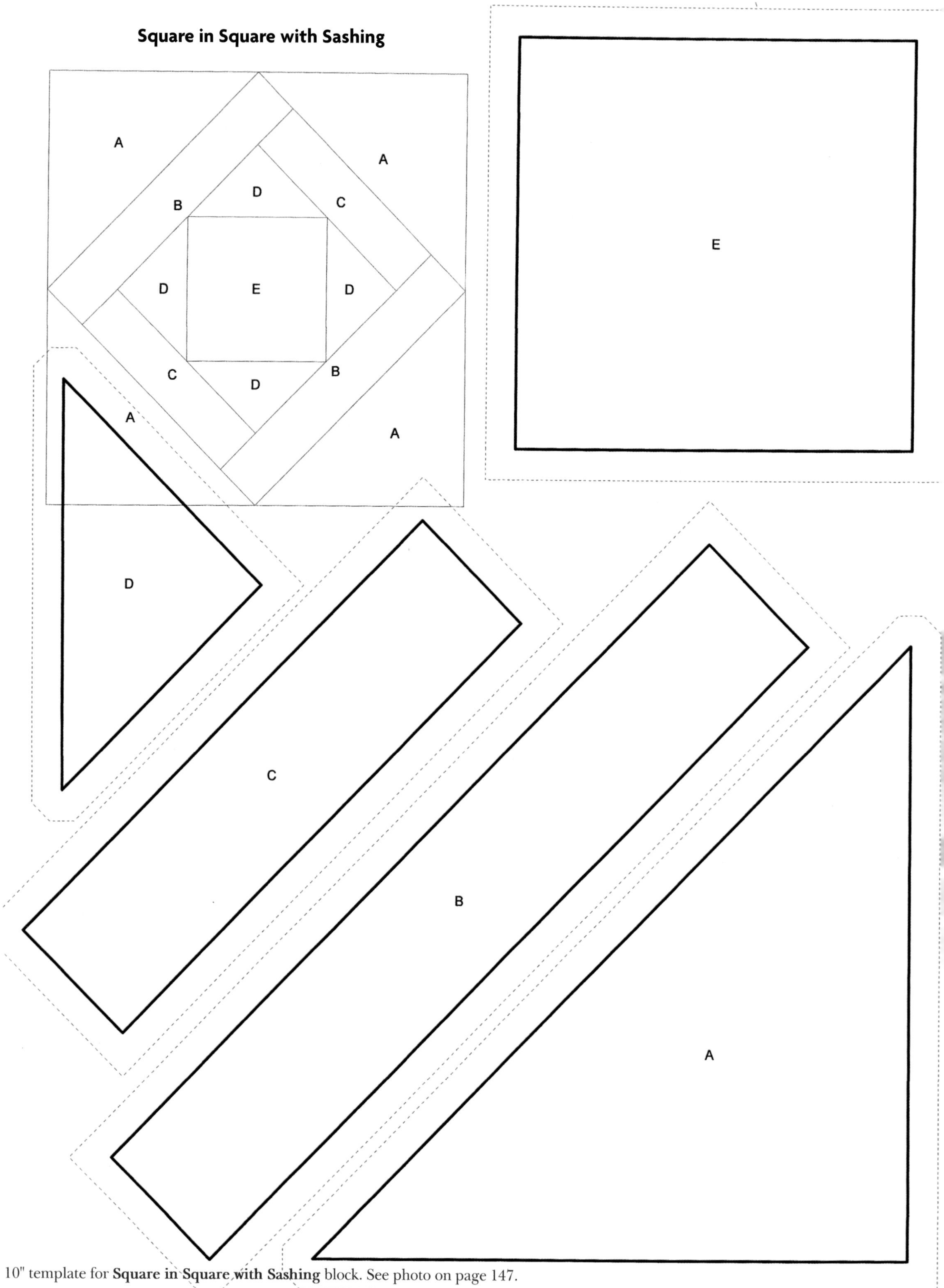

10" template for **Square in Square with Sashing** block. See photo on page 147.

Fractured Star

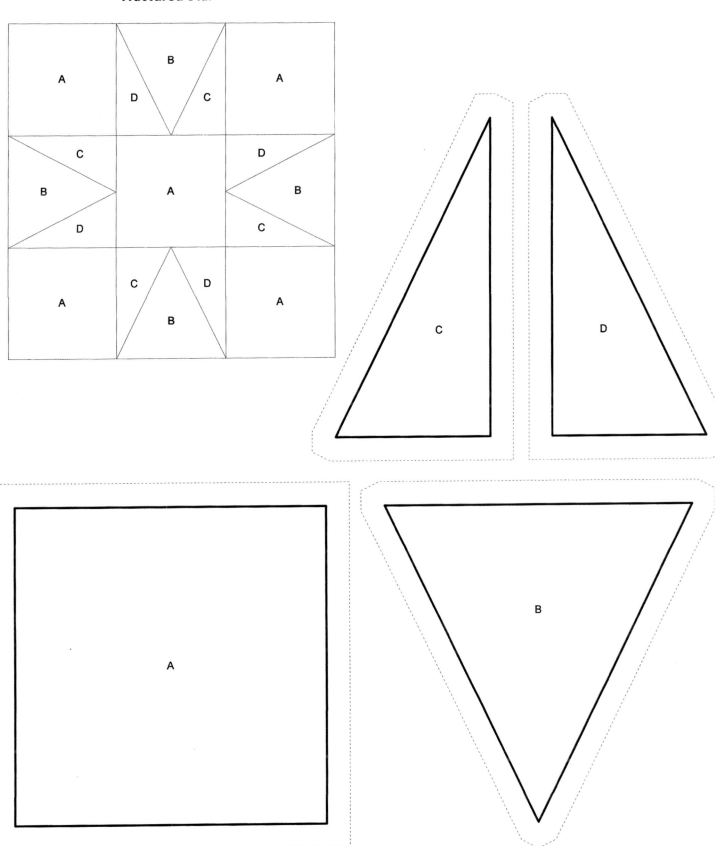

10" template for **Fractured Star** block.
See photo on page 147.

Eight-Pointed Star on point

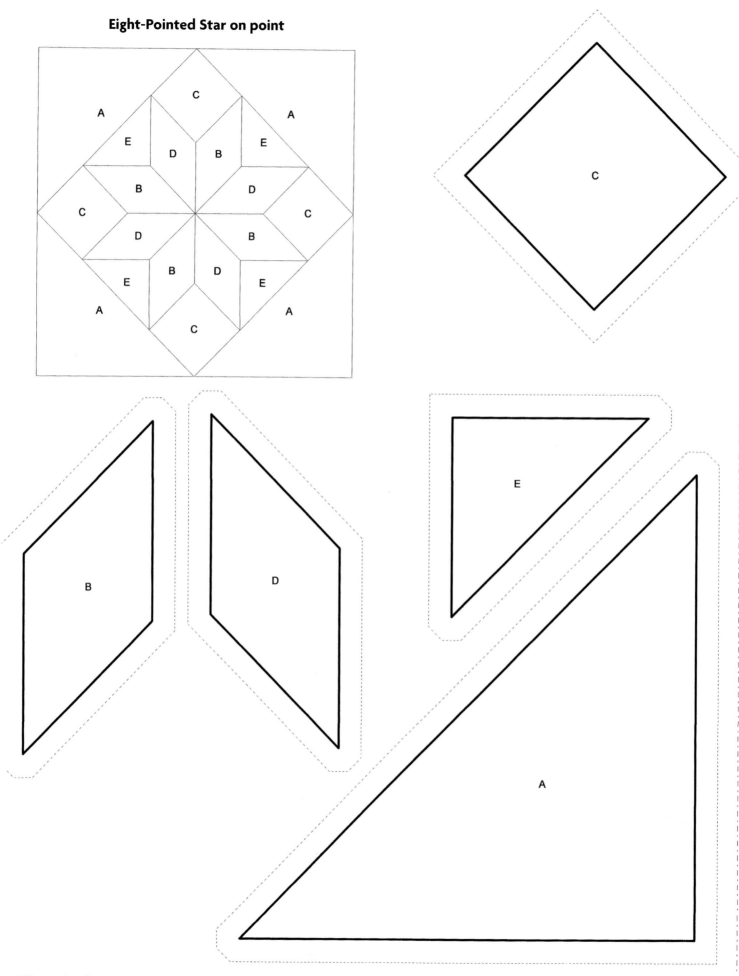

10" template for **Eight-Pointed Star on Point** block. See photo on page 147.

Uneven Nine Patch

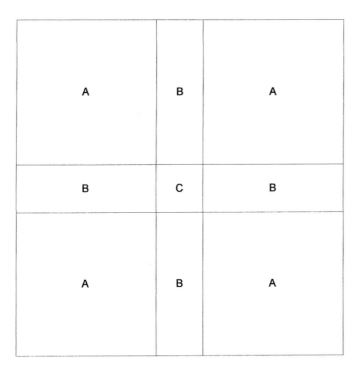

Decide first where you will inscribe this block, then choose your solid light value for that piece or pieces.

Rotary cutting instructions for each 10" Uneven Nine Patch block

- For piece A, cut 4 squares 4¾" × 4¾".
- For piece B, cut 4 rectangles 2" × 4¾".
- For piece C, cut 1 square 2" × 2".

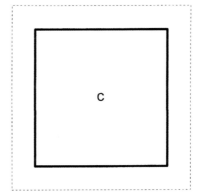

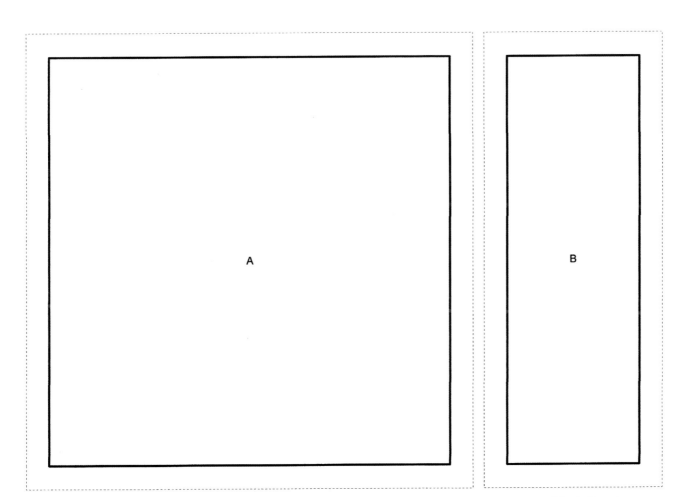

10" template for **Uneven Nine Patch** cross block. See photo on page 147.

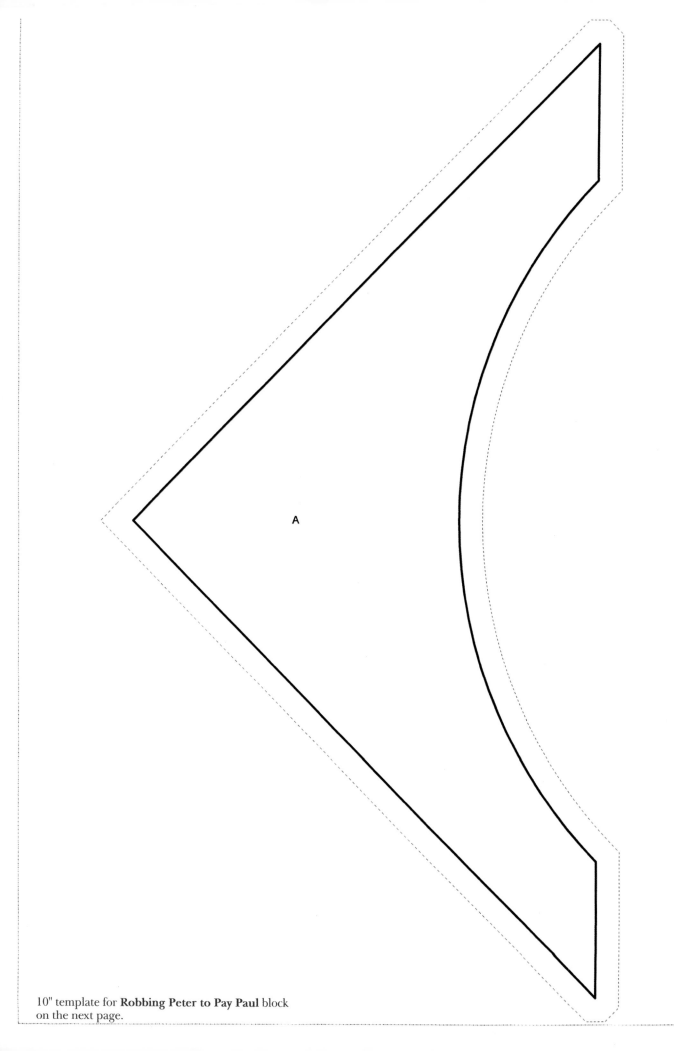

A

10" template for **Robbing Peter to Pay Paul** block
on the next page.

Robbing Peter to Pay Paul

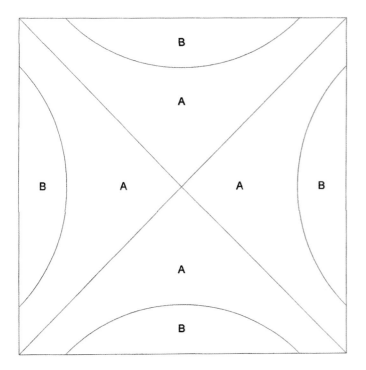

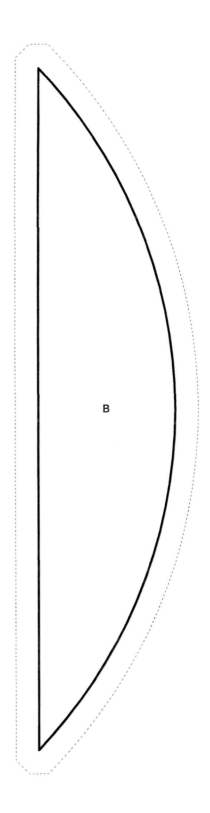

10" template for Robbing Peter to Pay Paul block.
See photo on page 148.

Flag

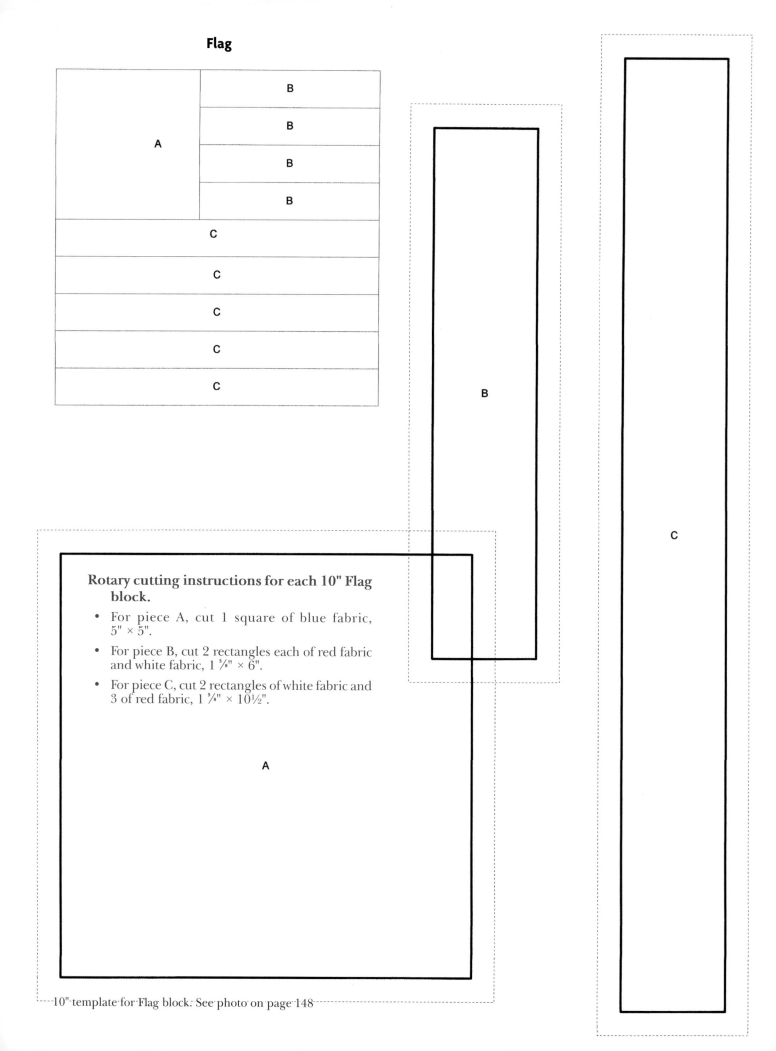

A	B
	B
	B
	B
C	
C	
C	
C	
C	

Rotary cutting instructions for each 10" Flag block.

- For piece A, cut 1 square of blue fabric, 5" × 5".
- For piece B, cut 2 rectangles each of red fabric and white fabric, 1 ⅝" × 6".
- For piece C, cut 2 rectangles of white fabric and 3 of red fabric, 1 ⅝" × 10½".

A

B

C

10" template for Flag block. See photo on page 148

Nine Patch on Point

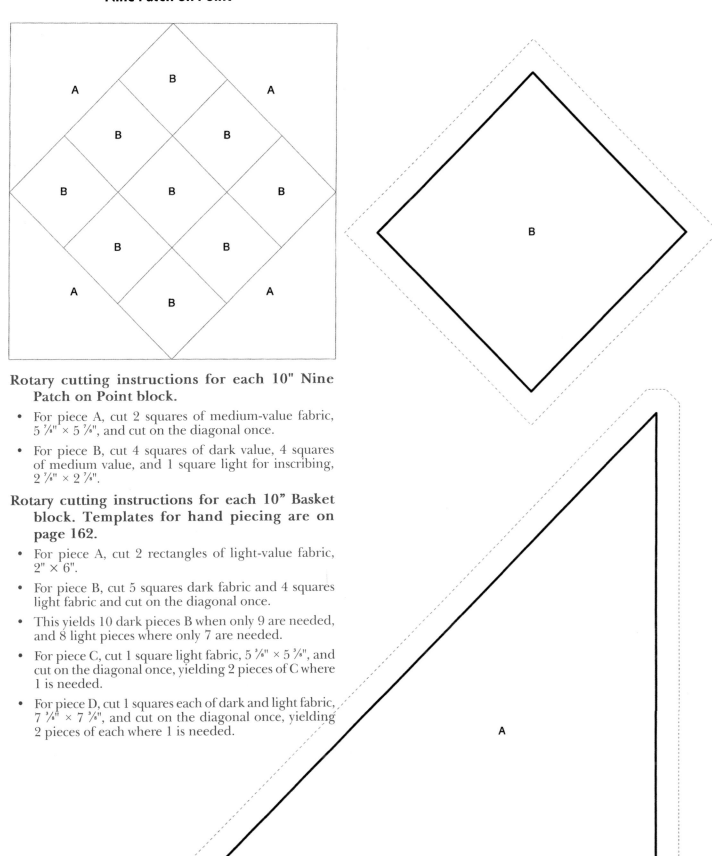

Rotary cutting instructions for each 10" Nine Patch on Point block.

- For piece A, cut 2 squares of medium-value fabric, 5 ⅞" × 5 ⅞", and cut on the diagonal once.

- For piece B, cut 4 squares of dark value, 4 squares of medium value, and 1 square light for inscribing, 2 ⅞" × 2 ⅞".

Rotary cutting instructions for each 10" Basket block. Templates for hand piecing are on page 162.

- For piece A, cut 2 rectangles of light-value fabric, 2" × 6".

- For piece B, cut 5 squares dark fabric and 4 squares light fabric and cut on the diagonal once.

- This yields 10 dark pieces B when only 9 are needed, and 8 light pieces where only 7 are needed.

- For piece C, cut 1 square light fabric, 5 ⅜" × 5 ⅜", and cut on the diagonal once, yielding 2 pieces of C where 1 is needed.

- For piece D, cut 1 squares each of dark and light fabric, 7 ⅞" × 7 ⅞", and cut on the diagonal once, yielding 2 pieces of each where 1 is needed.

10" template for Nine Patch on Point block. See photo on page 148.

Basket

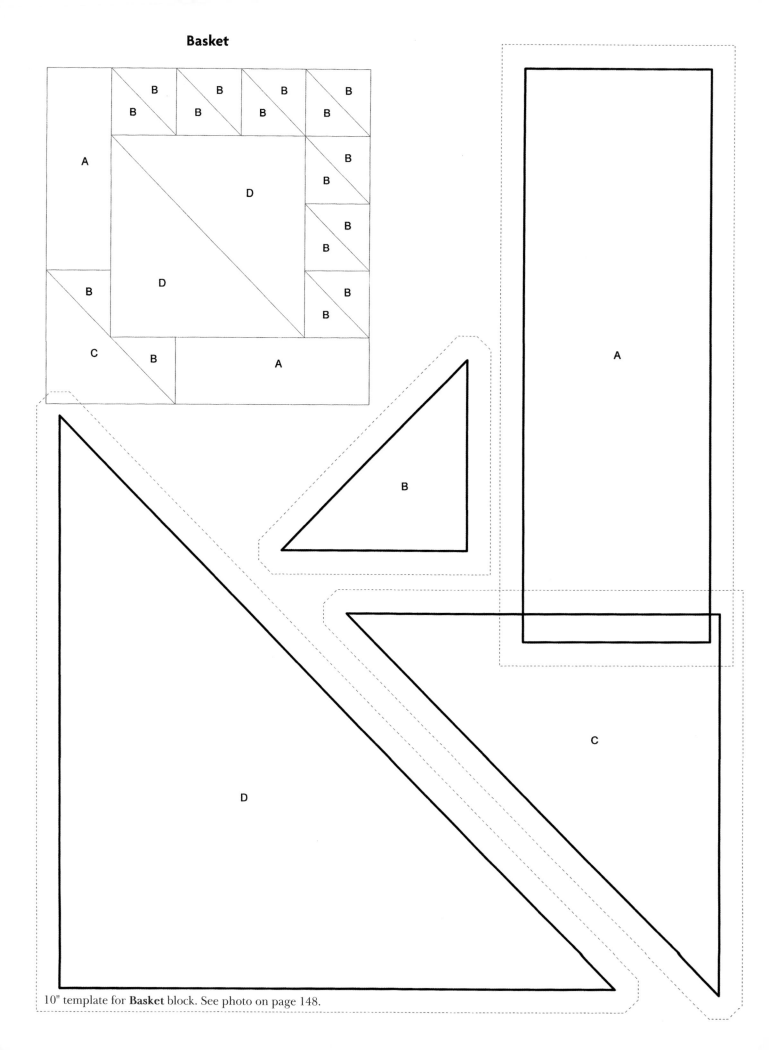

10" template for **Basket** block. See photo on page 148.

Unknown 2

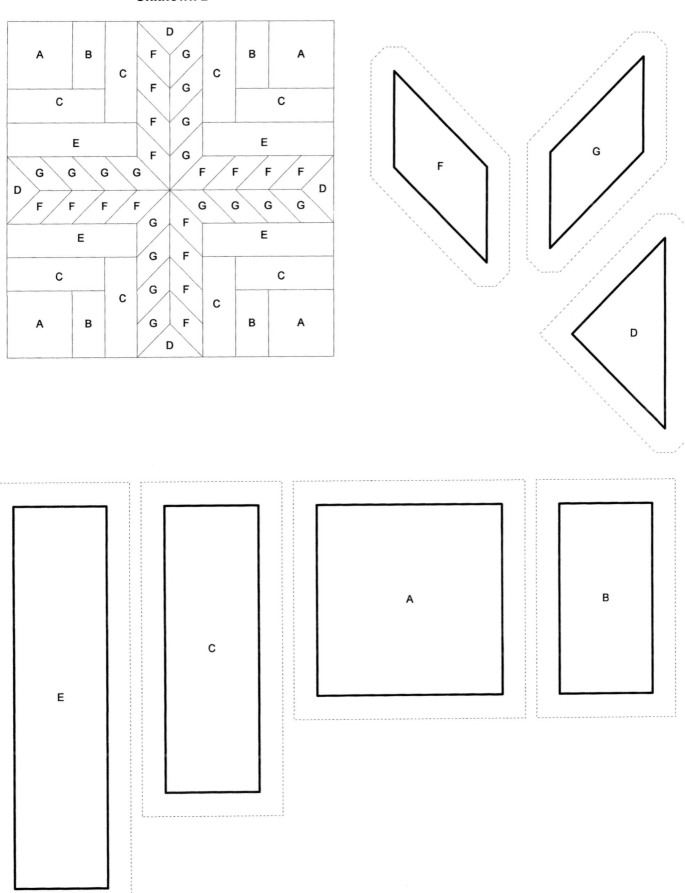

10" template for **Unknown 2** block. See photo on page 148.

Pratt Family Quilt

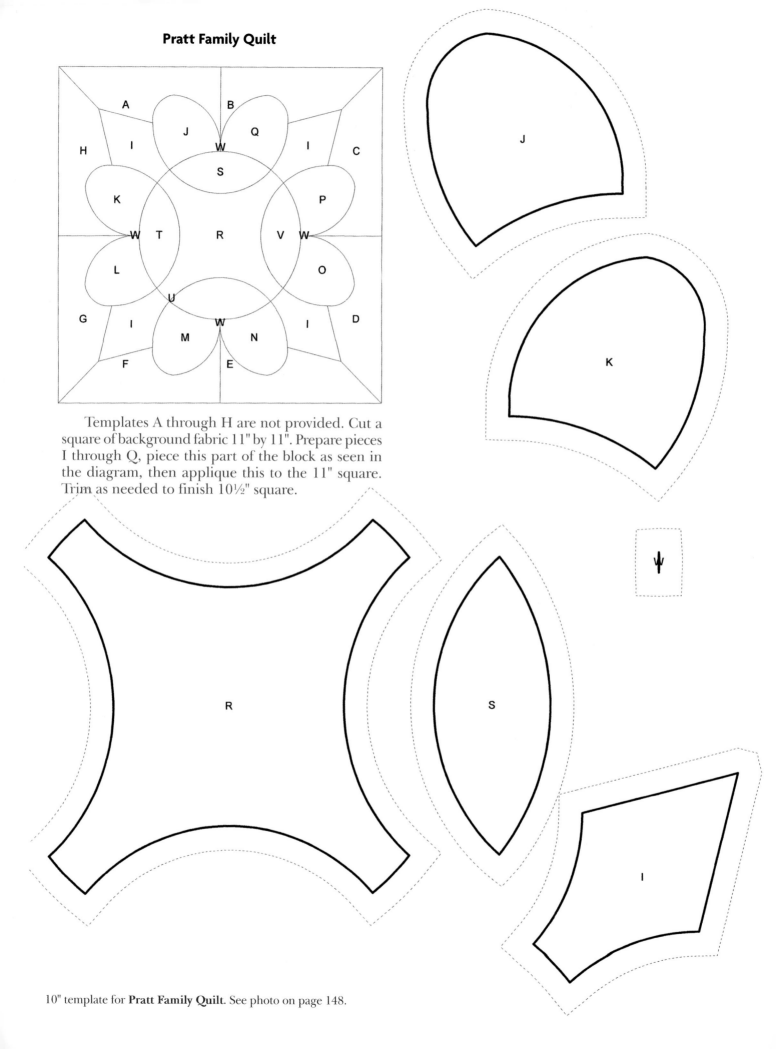

Templates A through H are not provided. Cut a square of background fabric 11" by 11". Prepare pieces I through Q, piece this part of the block as seen in the diagram, then applique this to the 11" square. Trim as needed to finish 10½" square.

10" template for **Pratt Family Quilt**. See photo on page 148.

Hourglass Variation 2

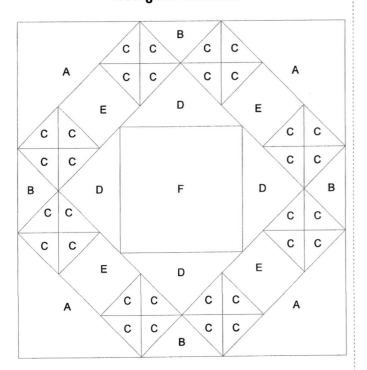

Rotary cutting instructions for each 10" Unnamed block

- For piece A, cut 2 squares dark value, 5 ⅛" × 5 ⅛", and cut on the diagonal once, yielding 4.
- For piece B, cut 1 square light value print, 3¾" × 3¾", and cut on the diagonal twice.
- For piece C, cut 8 squares light print and 8 squares color medium value, 2 ⅝" × 2 ⅝", and cut on the diagonal once, yielding 16 pieces of each color.
- For piece D, cut 2 squares medium value, 4 ⅜" × 4 ⅜", and cut on the diagonal once for 4 pieces.
- For piece E, cut 4 squares light print, 2¼" × 2¼".
- For piece F, cut 1 square light value for inscribing, 4¼" × 4 ¼".

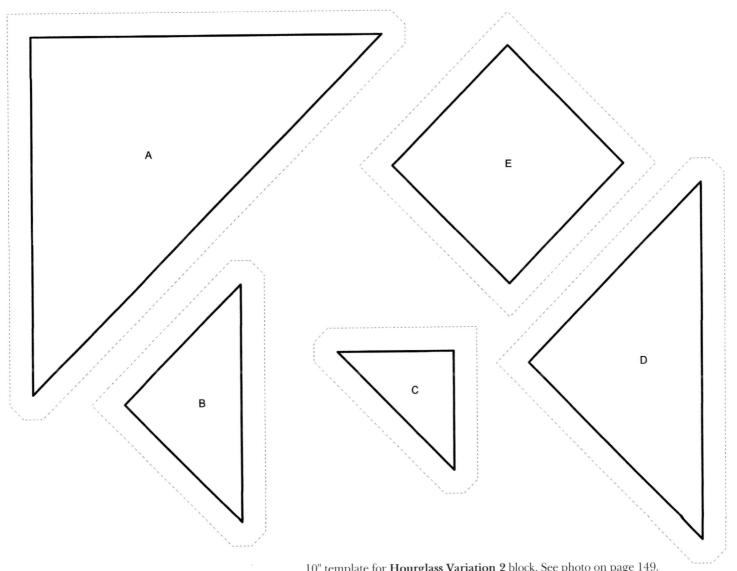

10" template for **Hourglass Variation 2** block. See photo on page 149.

Fly Away

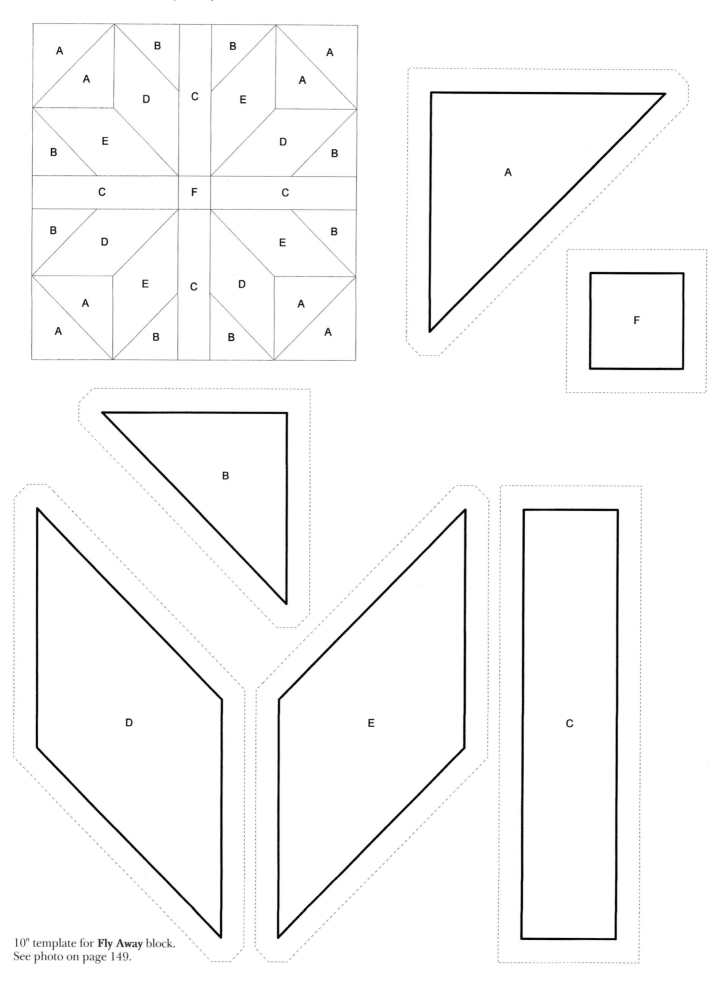

10" template for **Fly Away** block.
See photo on page 149.

Hourglass variation

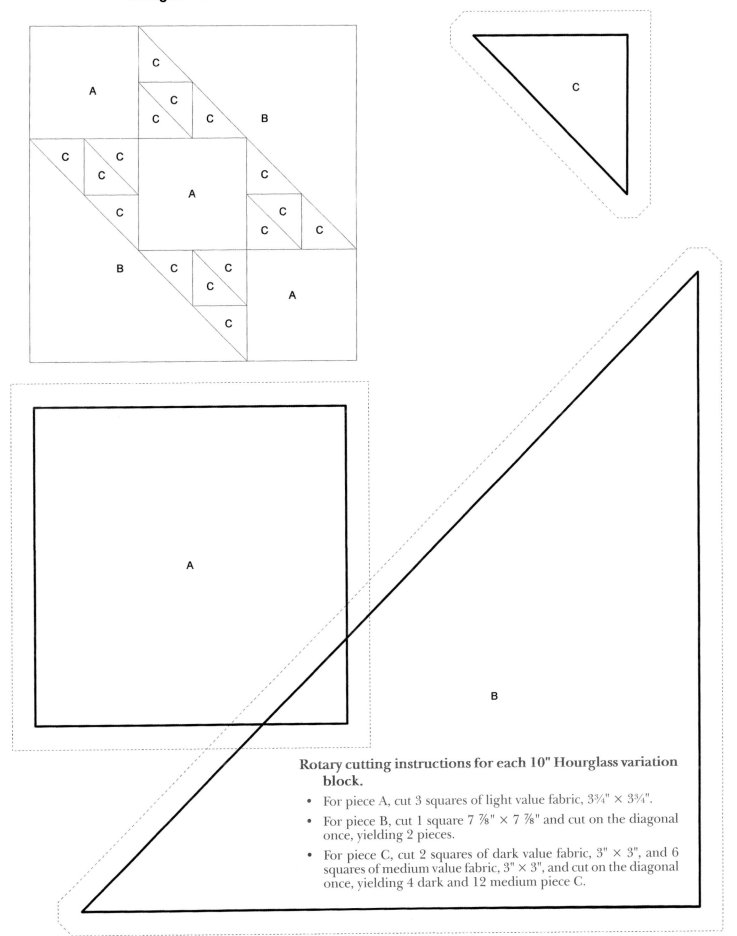

Rotary cutting instructions for each 10" Hourglass variation block.

- For piece A, cut 3 squares of light value fabric, 3¾" × 3¾".
- For piece B, cut 1 square 7 ⅞" × 7 ⅞" and cut on the diagonal once, yielding 2 pieces.
- For piece C, cut 2 squares of dark value fabric, 3" × 3", and 6 squares of medium value fabric, 3" × 3", and cut on the diagonal once, yielding 4 dark and 12 medium piece C.

10" template for **Hourglass variation** block. See photo on page 149.

Citrus Belt Quilters Guild, of Redlands, California, decided at its July 2004 guild meeting to make replica Civil War Union soldiers' quilts for the families of fallen heroes from the Iraq and Afghanistan conflicts who listed the Inland Empire of Southern California as their homes of record. The guild wanted to continue the great tradition of giving that quilters have demonstrated throughout the long history of quiltmaking in America. They named it the Home of the Brave (HOTB) Project.

The idea to make commemorative quilts as replicas of Civil War Union soldiers' quilts was suggested by Don Beld, who volunteered to lead the effort. It was inspired by the fact that the local library, the A. K. Smiley Public Library and Lincoln Memorial Shrine, was the owner of one of two US Sanitary Commission quilts owned by public institutions. A third has since been discovered. Don thought that giving replicas of a quilt from the Civil War would link the sacrifices of these brave men and women in today's conflicts with the historical sacrifices Americans have made in previous struggles.

When Citrus Belt Quilters began their effort, the Inland Empire had only sixteen casualties. Don wasn't sure if guild members would respond well to the idea, but he felt that he and a few other guild members could make the sixteen quilts if that proved necessary. Patterns were distributed and guidelines were given (i.e., use reproduction fabrics or military-appropriate fabrics and have friends and families sign the center squares with names, home towns, and messages of comfort and

Home of the Brave Quilt Project Fallen Heroes quilt, based on a US Sanitary Commission quilt.
Courtesy of the National Home of the Brave Quilt Project; photograph: Jonathan Strait

support for the grieving families).

At the next meeting in August 2004, the guild was surprised when an elderly lady named Theresa Law came to the meeting with two completed quilts. She said she made one in remembrance of her first husband, who had died in World War II, and the other in remembrance of her second husband, who had served in the same war.

The project was designed to be a true grassroots quilting movement. In its early stages, no contributions were accepted, no advertising was done, only simple rules were followed, and no nonprofit status was requested. It was decided that every quilt presented would be from the heart(s) of the quiltmaker(s) to the hearts of the family who received the quilt in honor of their fallen hero.

Don Beld designed and printed on his home computer a certificate that was presented with each quilt, which tells the story of the US Sanitary Commission Civil War Union soldiers' quilts and links the recipient's loss to the great losses over the years that the United States has suffered in its numerous conflicts. A label was designed for the back of each quilt that individualizes the quilt to its fallen hero, and another Citrus Belt Quilters Guild member, Cathy Kreter, faithfully made these labels not only for the fallen heroes of the Inland Empire, but for many states across the nation. Cathy also longarm machine-quilted almost all of the Home of the Brave (HOTB) quilts for the guild.

Within a year, this movement had spread to many states across the nation. Quilters such as Linda Heminway in New Hampshire; Robin Armstead in Texas; Bev MacBeth in Ohio; Janet Curtis in Ventura County, California; Barbara Shillinger in Washington; Carol Smith in North Carolina; Sandi Carstensen in Iowa; and too many others to single out had joined as regional or state coordinators. In fact, there was a joke among the early coordinators who called for information that Don tricked them into becoming state coordinators when all they had intended to do was make a few blocks. Such is the giving nature of quilters. Sandi Carstensen took over from Don as the national coordinator in 2011 and initiated the project's website.

One exceptional American mother in Tehachapi, California, Terisa Edwards, personally made all the quilts for her son's group under Command Sergeant Major Brian D. Edwards, USA, 7th Special Forces Group at Ft. Bragg, North Carolina—as well as coordinating the effort to make quilts for Orange County, California. There were groups and coordinators for all states as well as a group of American service personnel dependents in Great Britain and a group of French quilters in France who also are making quilts.

Because there were few rules, each area decided what quilt pattern to use and who should receive a quilt. In some areas, families received numerous quilts: one for the grieving spouse, one for the parents, one each for a divorced mother and father, and one each for the fallen hero's children. A number of states presented at least one quilt to every fallen hero's family in their state. California, which had the majority of fallen heroes, has presented over 650 quilts to the families. That initial group of sixteen fallen heroes in the Inland Empire of Southern California reached over

Home of the Brave Quilt Project Fallen Heroes quilt, based on a US Sanitary Commission quilt. *Courtesy of the National Home of the Brave Quilt Project; photograph: Jonathan Strait*

ninety, and each family received at least one quilt; over 3,800 quilts were distributed nationally as of the date of publication of this book.

The efforts of this grassroots movement were recognized by generals, governors, senators, and congresspersons, but most importantly by the families of the fallen. Hundreds of heartfelt letters, emails, and telephone calls told HOTB contributors how much their efforts meant to the grieving families. Often, mothers talked about wrapping themselves in their quilts and feeling a closeness to their lost loved one. As one mother said, "It's as if his arms were wrapped around me and he was saying, "It's okay, Mom." One wife reported that her children could not sleep unless they were wearing a piece of their daddy's clothes, but when the quilts were on their beds, they snuggled under them with Daddy's name next to their hearts. Many families report that the fallen hero was a Civil War buff and that the quilt's connection to the Civil War made the gift even more precious.

In 2014 the Home of the Brave Project slowly began to wind down under the able leadership of Cathy Kreter, another friend of founder Don Beld and a member of the Citrus Belt Quilters Guild. In a phone interview in December 2018, she stated that by 2013, many coordinators were having difficulty finding the families of the service members who died on active duty. Several state coordinators continued limited involvement, but the project was officially disbanded on the national level in 2015, having delivered more than 7,000 quilts in the United States and its territories. ❧

HOTBQP block inscribed "Rosemary LaSalle, Army Nurse, WWII." *Photograph: Jonathan Strait*

HOTBQP block inscribed "Cowboy" top dog, Vietnam, Ralph Haskins." *Photograph: Jonathan Strait*

National Iraq-Afghanistan Fallen Heroes Memorial Quilt #1.
Collection of the New England Quilt Museum, 2012.26; photograph: Jonathan Strait

Because of the success of the Home of the Brave Project (chapter 18), Donald Beld launched the National Iraq & Afghanistan Fallen Heroes Memorial Quilt Project in 2010, and quilters around the country were engaged by Don to participate. United States military personnel who were killed in these conflicts are memorialized with a quilt block made in potholder style from Civil War reproduction fabric, using block patterns appropriate to the Civil War era. These quilts replicate those made for Civil War soldiers by Ladies' Aid Societies and other women's groups.

National Iraq & Afghanistan Memorial Quilt Project

PFC Caesar S. Viglienzone, USA, memorial block in National Iraq & Afghanistan Fallen Heroes Memorial Quilt #1. *Courtesy of the National Home of the Brave Quilt Project; photograph: Jonathan Strait*

When talking to Dennis and Norma Viglienzone about their son and only child, Caesar, I was taken by their strength and by their pride in all that he had accomplished in his young life.

I explained that I wanted to send them a quilt from our HOTB quilt project. Norma shared that she is a quilter and that she wanted to volunteer to help make quilts for other families.

Four men were lost that day, February 1, 2006, in that 101st Airborne unit. Two died in the same IED explosion with their son, Caesar. They were LT Garrison Avery and Specialist Marlon Bustamante. Also lost in a separate accident was their brother-in-arms, Specialist Anthony Owens.

Norma worked over the following months in a labor of love to make quilts for the other 3 families. This has made a special bond for the 3 families whose sons lived, served and died together with Caesar.

Janet Benson Curtis, coordinator, Camarillo, CA March 2010

Back of PFC Viglienzone's memorial block. Block maker: Janet Benson Curtis, Ventura County Coordinator, HOTBQP. *Courtesy of the National Home of the Brave Quilt Project; photograph: Jonathan Strait*

Spc. Marlon A. Bustamonte, USA, and L.Cpl. Brad S. Shuder, USMC, memorial blocks in National Iraq & Afghanistan Fallen Heroes Memorial Quilt #1. *Courtesy of the National Home of the Brave Quilt Project; photograph: Jonathan Strait*

Each block contains the name of the soldier on the front of the block, and, on the back, their branch of service, death date, home city, and sometimes a short vignette of their personal life. The blocks are then joined into quilts, and during the duration of the project, eleven quilts were made. Quilt #2 honors the seven deceased Medal of Honor recipients. Some Fallen Heroes Quilts are regional—there are three for Los Angeles County, California, alone; one was made for Nebraska, another for Nevada and North Dakota, and one for three New England states.

The New England Quilt Museum has the eleven quilts in their collection, and they are often displayed on Memorial Day and Veteran's Day at the Museum.

Spc. Marion A. Bustamonte, USA, and L.Cpl. Brad S. Shuder, USMC, memorial blocks in National Iraq & Afghanistan Fallen Heroes Memorial Quilt #1. *Courtesy of the National Home of the Brave Quilt Project; photograph: Jonathan Strait*

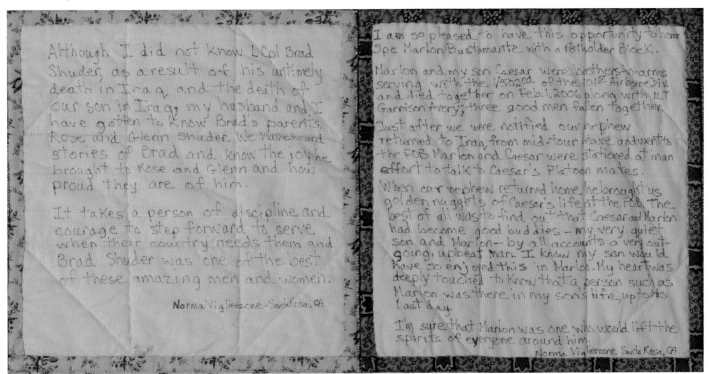

Center Medal of Honor block for National
Iraq & Afghanistan Fallen Heroes Memorial
Quilt #2. Block maker: Bernice Foster.
*Collection of the New England Quilt Museum,
2012.27; photograph: Jonathan Strait*

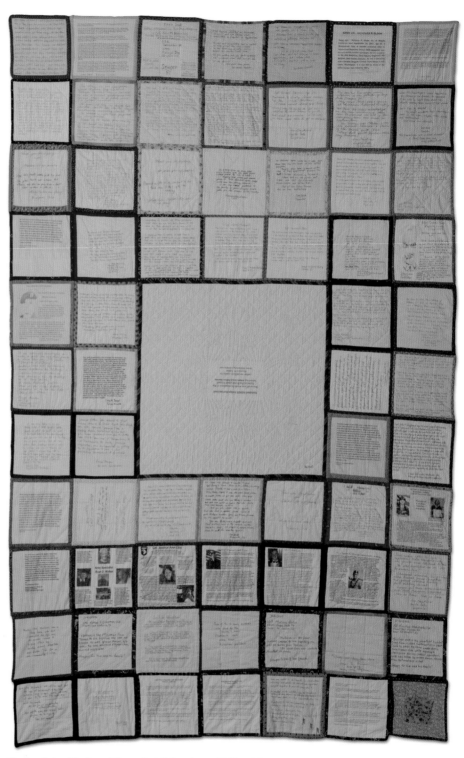

Back of the National Iraq & Afghanistan Fallen Heroes
Memorial Quilt #1. *Collection of the New England Quilt
Museum; photograph: Jonathan Strait*

Center medallion Eagle block for National Iraq & Afghanistan Fallen Heroes Memorial Quilt #1. Block maker: Bernice Foster.
Collection of the New England Quilt Museum, 2012.26; photograph: Jonathan Strait

THE EAGLE MEDALLION

Quilt #1 has a center Eagle medallion, reflecting the eagle symbol that is on the Medal of Honor. Quilts #1 through #11 are complete, and these quilts were seen in major exhibits beginning in 2011 and are now in the collection of the New England Quilt Museum.

The eagle motif used as the center medallion comes from a Civil War–era folk art quilt with a similar eagle used in the four corners, with their wing tips touching. In the center of that quilt is a medallion star. This is a pattern from the Civil War era and is referred to as the Union Eagle.

The pattern to make the Eagle Medallion is on page 180 so you may design your own eagle quilt. An example of a post–Civil War popular eagle quilt is also included.

Eagle patterns in quilts and fabrics have been around for almost as long as the United States. After the

Mid-nineteenth-century Eagle quilt.
Courtesy of Sue Wildemuth

bald eagle's selection as the official bird of the United States in 1782, it began appearing in fabric patterns, and by the beginning of the nineteenth century, it was appearing in quilts and coverlets. Its popularity increased after the War of 1812 and continued through the golden anniversary of the Declaration of Independence in 1826 and the golden anniversary of the passing of the Constitution and the election of George Washington in 1839. It has remained, in many forms, a popular embroidery, appliqué, and fabric pattern. ❦

Detail, mid-nineteenth-century Eagle quilt. *Courtesy of Sue Wildemuth*

The Medal of Honor was *the* medal of the Civil War; in fact, it was the only medal. In the nineteenth century, military medals were considered to be elitist, Old World decorations. No medals had been given out by the United States since the Badge of Military Merit (commonly called the Purple Heart) had been authorized by General Washington during the Revolutionary War, on August 7, 1782. Only three Continental army soldiers received the Badge of Military Merit. In 1932, the current Purple Heart Medal was created, as we know it today. It was retroactive to World War I.

The Medal of Honor is now our nation's highest military honor, but during the Civil War it was the only medal given, and the criteria were different than today's medal. It was given "to such noncommissioned officers and privates as shall "distinguish themselves by their gallantry in action, and other soldier-like qualities, during the present insurrection." This may explain why 1,522 Medals of Honor were given to both military and civilians during the Civil War.

The Medal of Honor continued to be awarded throughout the last half of the nineteenth century, with 426 given during the Indian Wars, 110 during the Philippine (Spanish-American) War, and another 145 in other nineteenth-century and early-twentieth-century military engagements in other nations.

One of the most common reasons for giving the Medal of Honor during the Civil War was for "saving the flag." When the flag bearer was shot or killed during battle, it was customary for another soldier to "save the flag" by grabbing it before it hit the ground and continuing to carry it in the battle. The flag bearers on both sides were frequent targets of sharp shooters, since it was considered a coup to have the battle flags fall. The flag was saved not just because of patriotism, but because the flag was a means for communication among units, positions, and headquarters.

The Medal of Honor was also awarded to civilians, including the only woman to receive a Medal of Honor— Dr. Mary Edwards Walker. The military pallbearers for President Lincoln's coffin were also awarded Medals of Honor. Some recipients have received two Medals of Honor for two different acts of gallantry and bravery. During the Civil War, the only two-time recipient of the Medal of Honor was (then) Lt. Thomas Custer.

As of December 2010, only eight Medals of Honor have been award for Operation Iraqi Freedom and Operation Enduring Freedom: seven posthumously and one to a living recipient: SSGT Salvatore A. Giunta, USA, Iowa.

Benjamin Hilliker's GAR ceremonial drum with drumsticks.
Courtesy of the Lincoln Memorial Shrine, Redlands, California; photograph: Jonathan Strait.

THE DRUMMER BOY

One of the Medals of Honor was awarded to a member of the 8th Wisconsin Volunteer Infantry and it was awarded to a drummer, Benjamin F. Hilliker.

Born in New York in 1843, but with his family having moved to Wisconsin in 1857, Benjamin Hilliker enlisted in the 8th Wisconsin in 1861. He became the drummer for Company C of the 8th Wisconsin. He saw battle at the terrible fight at Corinth, Mississippi, where the 8th Wisconsin lost half its troops, and it was during the siege of Vicksburg that he earned his Medal of Honor.

On June 4, 1863, while on a reconnaissance mission to locate the Confederate forces of General Joseph Johnson, Hilliker and his company mounted a ridge and came face to face (40 yards) with the Confederate troops. Both sides immediately began firing at each other.

Hilliker's Medal of Honor citation tells the rest of the story: "For extraordinary heroism on 4 June 1863, while serving with Company A, 8th Wisconsin Infantry, in action at Mechanicsburg, Mississippi. When men were needed to oppose a superior Confederate force, Musician Hilliker laid down his drum for a rifle and proceeded to the front of the skirmish line which was about 120 feet from the enemy. While on his volunteer mission and firing at the enemy, he was hit in the head with a minie-ball which passed through him. An order was given to 'lay him in the shade; he won't last long.' He recovered from this wound being left with an ugly scar."

Hilliker went on after the war to live until 1916 and died in Los Angeles, California, where he is buried at Hollywood Forever Cemetery, along with early movie notables such as Cecil B. DeMille, Douglas Fairbanks Sr., Rudolph Valentino, and Tyrone Power.

After the war, as many Union troops did, he joined the Grand Army of the Republic and carried his drum at meetings of his detachment unit.

Benjamin Hilliker's Civil War Medal of Honor. *Courtesy of the Lincoln Memorial Shrine, Redlands, California; photograph: Jonathan Strait*

MARY EDWARDS WALKER

Mary Edwards Walker was an early women's-movement proponent. Born in upstate New York to an abolitionist family, she graduated from the country's first medical school, Syracuse Medical College, in 1855 as the only woman member of her class; she became one of the United States' first woman physicians.

When she married in 1856, she further exhibited her independence and belief in women's rights by wearing men's trousers and a man's coat to her wedding and by refusing to take her husband's name at the ceremony.

As soon as the Civil War broke out in 1861, Walker immediately went to Washington, DC, to enlist as an Army medical officer. But denied a commission, she volunteered to be an "acting assistant surgeon." She served in the field at Fredericksburg and at the Battle Chickamauga. In September 1863, because of her proven service and abilities, she was finally appointed to the Army as an assistant surgeon, thus becoming one of the first women to serve in the military. She was allowed to design and wear a modified officer's uniform, as would be more suitable for a woman in the field.

Assigned to the 52nd Ohio Infantry, Walker served both as an assistant surgeon and, probably, as a Northern spy. On one of her excursions behind enemy lines, she was captured by Confederate troops and sent to a prison. In 1864, along with twenty-four other Union surgeons, Walker was swapped for seventeen Confederate surgeons.

On November 11, 1865, President Andrew Johnson awarded Mary Edwards Walker the Medal of Honor for rendering valuable services in her contributions to the war effort. She is the only woman ever to receive a Medal of Honor.

However, when Congress changed the criteria for awarding the Medal of Honor in 1917 to include only "actual combat with the enemy," the Congress asked the 910 Medal of Honor recipients, including Walker, who did not meet the new criteria to return their medals.

Mary Edwards Walker refused and continued to proudly display it on her bosom for the remainder of her life. In 1977, by a special act of Congress signed by President Jimmy Carter, Mary Edwards Walker's Medal of Honor was officially restored to her.

Dr. Mary Edwards Walker, ca. 1866, wearing the Medal of Honor. Dr. Walker is the only woman recipient of the Medal of Honor. *Courtesy of the Library of Congress*

After the war and throughout the rest of her life, Walker continued her crusade for women's rights and spoke at public meetings about women's rights, dress reform, temperance, and tobacco usage. She even published her own magazine. Elected president of the National Dress Reform Association in 1866, she was one of the first to advocate women wearing what later became known as "bloomers" in public. Walker herself frequently lectured in public wearing men's evening clothes, complete with wing collar, bow tie, and top hat.

Mary Edwards Walker died in 1919, just months before the ratification of the Nineteenth Amendment to the Constitution, which gave women the right to vote.

Dr. Mary Edwards Walker, ca. 1890s, dressed in men's evening clothes, wearing her Medal of Honor. *Courtesy of the Library of Congress*

EAGLE WITH SHIELD

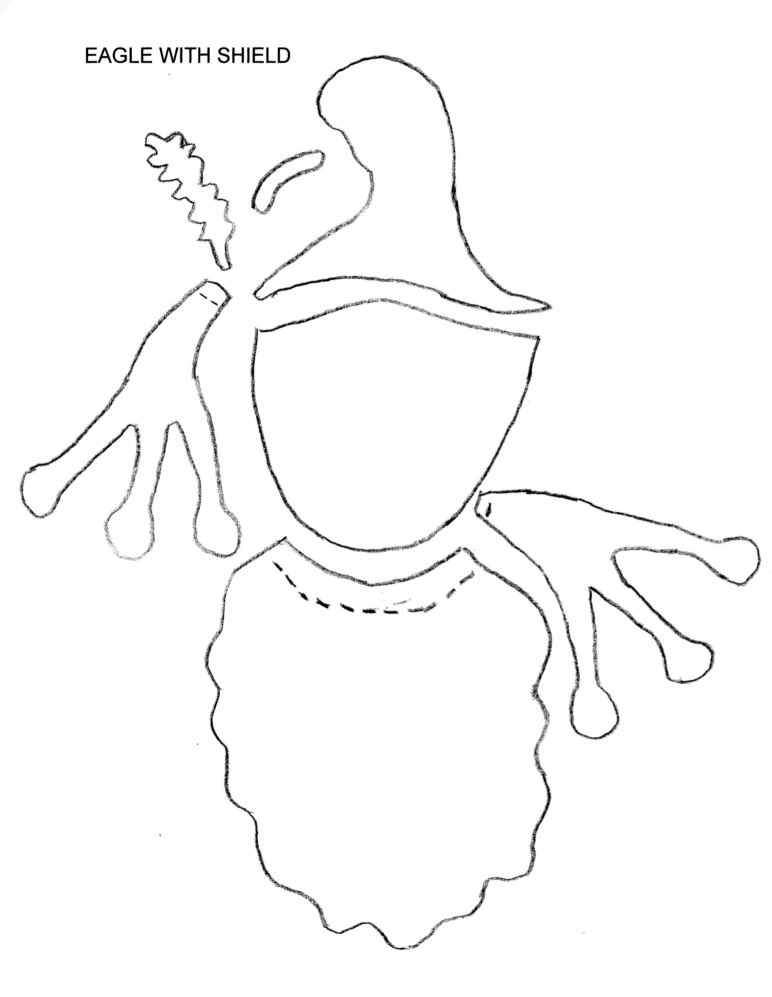

Pattern for Eagle appliqué, part 1. *Courtesy of Bernice Foster*

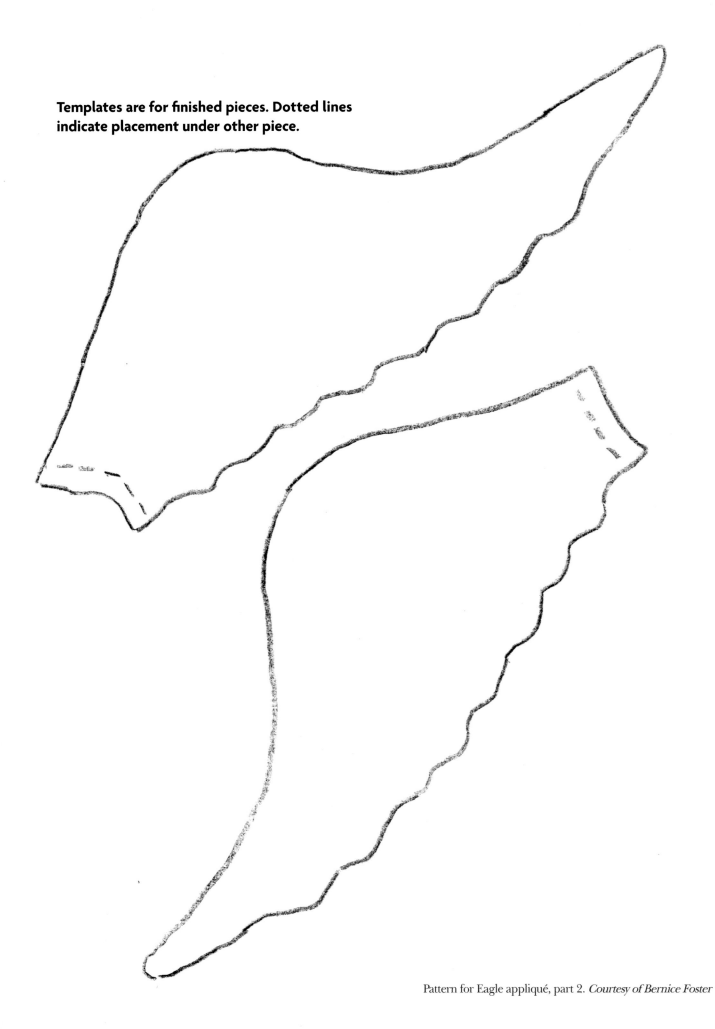

Templates are for finished pieces. Dotted lines indicate placement under other piece.

Pattern for Eagle appliqué, part 2. *Courtesy of Bernice Foster*

APP

Appendix

Quilt Name	Town/State	Date
Hussey-Fitzgerald	Detroit, MI	1864
Cornelia Davis/Dow	Portland, ME	1864
Ladies' Industrial Union	Florence, MA	1863
Rebecca A. Sibley	Boston, MA	1865
Sunday School Scholars	Augusta, ME	1863
Fort Hill Sewing Circle	Hingham, MA	1864
Norridgewock Album	Norridgewock, ME	1863
Beverly Farms Album	Beverly Farms, MA	1865
Granville Album	Granville/Cambridge, NY	?
Ladies' Aid Society Munjoy Hill	Portland, ME	1864
Ladies' Aid Society II Munjoy Hill	Portland, ME	
Ladies' Volunteer Aid Society	Belfast, ME	1864
Vernon Album	Vernon, CT	1864
Carolyn Fairbanks	Brandon, VT	ca. 1863
Ladies' Soldiers' Aid Society	Dublin, NH	1864

USSC Stamp	Construction	Collection
no	potholder	International Quilt Museum
no	potholder	Maine State Museum
no	potholder	private collection
no	potholder	NEQM
no	potholder	Smithsonian
yes	potholder	International Quilt Museum
yes	potholder	unknown
no	potholder	Rochester Historical Society
yes	potholder	Wadsworth Atheneum
no	potholder	Brick Store Museum
no	potholder	Mystic Seaport Museum
no	standard	Belfast Historical Society
yes	standard	Lincoln Memorial Shrine
yes	standard	Vermont Historical Society
yes	standard	private collection

Introduction

1. Thomas R. Kemp, "Community and War: The Civil War Experience of Two New Hampshire Towns," in *Toward a Social History of the American Civil War*, ed. Maris A. Vinosvskis (Cambridge, UK: Cambridge University Press, 1990), 37.

2. Charles Stille, *History of the United States Sanitary Commission: Being the General Report of Its Works during the War of the Rebellion* (Philadelphia: J. B. Lippincott, 1866).

3. Virginia Gunn, "Quilts for Union Soldiers in the Civil War," *Uncoverings 1985*, vol. 6 (Mill Valley, CA: American Quilt Study Group, 1986), 113.

4. Judith Ann Giesberg, *Civil War Sisterhood: The U.S. Sanitary Commission and Women's Politics in Transition* (Boston: Northeastern University Press).

5. Except from a notice generated by the US Sanitary Commission on October 1, 1861, and printed in many northern newspapers.

6. Frank Goodrich, *The Tribute Book: A Record of the Munificence, Self-Sacrifice and Patriotism of the American People during the War for the Union* (New York: Derby & Miller, 1865), 112.

7. Mary Clark Brayton and Ellen F. Terry, *Our Acre and Its Harvest: Historical Sketch of the Soldiers Aid Society of Northern Ohio* (Cleveland, OH: Fairbanks, Benedict & Col, 1869), 62.

8. Unpublished minutes of the Bethel, Maine, Soldiers' Aid Society, in the collection of the Maine Historical Society, Portland, ME.

9. Barbara Brackman, "Signature Quilts: Nineteenth-Century Trends," in *Quiltmaking in America: Beyond the Myths*, ed. Laurel Horton (Nashville: Rutledge Hill, 1994), 22.

10. Jessica F. Nicoll, *Quilted for Friends: Delaware Valley Signature Quilts, 1840–1855* (Winterthur, DE: Winterthur Museum, 1986), 17.

11. Two other quilts are documented as Civil War fundraiser quilts. See Jacqueline Marx Atkins, *Shared Threads: Quilting Together—Past and Present* (New York: Viking Studio Books, 1994), 39; and Sue Reich et al., *Quilts and Quiltmakers Covering Connecticut* (Atglen, PA: Schiffer, 2002), 76–77.

CHAPTER 1
Inscribed Quilts

1. Brackman, "Signature Quilts: Nineteenth-Century Trends," 23.

2. Vivian L. Sayer and Anita B. Loscalzo, "Andersonville Prisoner of War Quilt," in *Massachusetts Quilts: Our Common Wealth*, ed. Lynne Zacek Bassett (Hanover, NH: University Press of New England, 2009), 252–56.

3. William Addison Benedict and Hiram Averill Tracy, *History of Sutton, Massachusetts*, vol. 1, *From 1704 to 1876* (Worcester, MA: Sanford, 1878).

4. United States Census, 1850, 1860, 1870, and 1880; available at www.ancestry.com; accessed May and November 2010.

CHAPTER 2
Potholder Quilts

1. Pamela Weeks, "'One Foot Square, Quilted and Bound': A Study of Potholder Quilts," in *Uncoverings 2010*, vol. 31, ed. Laurel Horton (Lincoln, NE: American Quilt Study Group, 2010), 131–60.

2. Hussey-Fitzgerald, Civil War Quilt, collection of the International Quilt Museum, accession number 1997.007.0569.

3. "Rally round the flag, boys!" is a phrase taken from the chorus of "The Battle Cry of Freedom," composed by George Root in 1862. It was one of the most popular songs of the period, and 700,000 copies of the sheet music were sold.

4. Jonathan Gregory, genealogical narrative, September 7, 2010, International Quilt Museum, Lincoln, NE, 1997.007.0569 genealogical file. (Rechecked by the author by using Ancestry. com, with access to the United States Census, December 15, 2010).

5. George H. Turner, *Record of Service of Michigan Volunteers in the Civil War 1861–1865, vol. 24* (Kalamazoo, MI: Ihling Brothers & Everard, 1903).

6. Examination of the Beverly Farms Civil War Album Quilt in the collection of the Rochester (New York) Historical Society, 2004.511.

7. Massachusetts Historical Society, Loring-Jackson-Noble papers, accessed November 12, 2018, www.masshist.org/collection-guides/view/fa0421.

8. Charles Henry Pope, Loring genealogy, www. archive.org, New York Public Library, pp. 264–66, accessed November 12, 2018.

9. Ibid.

10. Massachusetts Soldiers, Sailors, and Marines in the Civil War, compiled and published by the adjutant general of Massachusetts, 1931, p. 492.

11. Genealogical extract prepared by Stephen P. Hall, interim executive director, Beverly Historical Society & Museum, November 27, 2004.

CHAPTER 3
Ladies' Aid Societies

1. Unpublished minutes of the Bethel, Maine, Soldiers' Aid Society, in the collection of the Maine Historical Society, Portland, ME.

2. Giesberg, *Civil War Sisterhood*.

3. Minutes, Bethel Soldiers' Aid Society.

4. Email correspondence between Donald Beld and Cindy Brick, July 2010.

5. United States Census, 1860; available at www. ancestry.com; accessed November 2010.

6. Tomas Tracy Bouve, Edward Tracy Bouve, and John Davis Long, *History of the Town of Hingham* (Cambridge, UK: Cambridge University Press, 1893), 361.

7. Email correspondence between Donald Beld and Debbie Knapp, which included photographs and transcription of information inscribed in the quilt.

8. United States Census, 1860; available at www. ancestry.com; accessed November 2010.

9. Bouve et al., *History of the Town of Hingham*, 362–63.

10. Fearing Burr and George Lincoln, *The Town of Hingham in the Late Civil War* (Cambridge, UK: Cambridge University Press, 1876), 379.

11. Burr and Lincoln, Town of *Hingham in the Late Civil War*, 335.

12. "Local Intelligence," *Hingham Journal and Advertiser*, Friday, January 1, 1864.

CHAPTER 4
A Vermont Quilt

1. Examination of the Fairbanks/Brandon, Vermont, US Sanitary Commission quilt in the collection of the Vermont Historical Society, accession number 1897.38.1, December 7, 2010, and January 20, 2011.

2. Grant Fairbanks, great-grandson of Luke and Caroline Fairbanks, researched and wrote voluminous notes on the Civil War history of the male members of the Fairbanks family, which the authors use with his permission and for which we are grateful.

3. United States Census, 1850, 1860, and 1870; available at www.ancestry.com; accessed June 2010.

4. William Samuel Harris, *The Harris Family: Thomas Harris in Ipswich, Massachusetts in 1636* (Nashua, NH: Barker and Bean, 1883), 86.

5. Author's interview with Grant Fairbanks, July 10, 2010.

6. Vermont Historical Society file for accession number 1897.38.1.

CHAPTER 5
Patriotic Quilts

1. Ethel Alice Hurn, *Wisconsin Women in the War between the States* (Madison: Wisconsin History Commission, 1911), 9.

2. "Evolution of the United States Flag," www.usflag. org/history/flagevolution.html. It wasn't until 1912 that an executive order by President Taft established proportions of the flag and proscribed the arrangement of the stars in six horizontal rows of eight each, with a single point of each star to be upward.

3. *Sheboygan Telegram*, December 2, 1909, as quoted in Hurn, *Wisconsin Women in the War between the States.*

4. As transcribed from a photograph of the quilt.

5. Henry Augustin Beers, ed., *A Century of American Literature, 1776–1876* (New York: Henry Holt, 1878), 150.

6. The other quilts containing quotes from "The Battle Cry of Freedom" are the Portland, Maine, quilt attributed to Cornelia Dow, and the Hussey-Fitzgerald Quilt, Detroit, Michigan; International Quilt Study Center, Lincoln, NE, 1997.007.0569.

7. www.nps.gov/archive/gett/gettkidz/gkmusic/ cwsong1.htm

8. Free Congregational Society of Florence, *The Free Congregational Society of Florence, Mass., with Its Platform, By-Laws, Roll of Members, for 1887–88* (Northampton, MA: Wade, Warner, 1888), 13.

9. "Florence: Its Past, Present, and Future," *Northampton Free Press*, Friday, August 31, 1866, as quoted in https://davidrugglescenter.org/?page_id=352. The Rally Round the Flag quilt was also published in Atkins, *Shared Threads*; Robert Bishop and Carter Houck, *All Flags Flying: American Patriotic Quilts as Expressions of Liberty* (New York: E. P. Dutton, 1986); Jennifer Regan, *American Quilts: A Sampler of Quilts and Their Stories* (New York: Gallery Books, 1989); Robert Shaw, *American Quilts: The Democratic Art, 1780–2007* (New York: Sterling, 2009); and Robert Shaw, *Quilts: A Living Tradition* (New York: Hugh Lauter Levin, 1995).

10. "Flag Quilts," *Sanitary Commission Bulletin* 3, no. 39 (July 1, 1865): 1224–25.

CHAPTER 6
Local Stories from Portland, Maine

1. Examination of the Munjoy Hill Album Quilt in the collection of the Brick Store Museum, accession number 2453, June 6, 2010.

2. Jack Coggins, *Arms and Equipment of the Civil War* (Garden City, NY: Doubleday, 1962), 132.

3. Ibid.

4. John K. Moulton, *Captain Moody and His Observatory* (Falmouth, ME: Mount Joy, 2000), 32.

5. Moulton, *Captain Moody*, 63–64; and Sue Bailey, "June 27, 1863, Confederates Raid Portland, Maine!!," *Camp Griffin Gazette* 17, no. 4 (April 2009): 5.

6. The Dow Patriotic Quilt is published in Atkins, *Shared Threads*, 88, 92–93; Jeanette Lasansky, *In the Heart of Pennsylvania: Symposium Papers* (Lewisburg, PA: Union County Historical Society, 1986), 68–71; Jane Benson and Nancy Olsen, *The Power of Cloth: Political Quilts, 1845–1986* (Cupertino, CA: Board of Trustees of the Foothill–De Anza Community College District, 1987), catalog from Euphrat Gallery, De Anza College; and Elaine Hedges, Pat Ferrero, and Julie Silber, *Hearts and Hands: Women, Quilts, and American Society* (Nashville: Rutledge Hill, 1987), 75. In each of these books, some description of the variety and kind of verses is given. While these authors attribute the quilt to the wife of Neal Dow of Portland, Maine, whom he names in his memoir (*Reminiscences of Neal Dow: Recollections of Eighty Years* [Portland, ME: Evening Express, 1898], 83–87) as Maria Cornelia Maynard Dow, the maker is more likely his daughter, Cornelia Maria Dow (the quilt is signed C. M. Dow, and Cornelia Dow). She was active in the temperance movement after the Civil War and was elected as national treasurer for the trust fund for payment of debt of the WCTU in 1897 (*New York Times*, November 1, 1897).

CHAPTER 7
"Wanted—Correspondence"

1. Nancy L. Rhodes and Lucy E. Bailey, eds., *Wanted— Correspondence: Women's Letters to a Union Soldier* (Athens, OH: Ohio University Press, 2009), 28.

2. Examination of the Vernon, Connecticut, Album Quilt in the collection of the Lincoln Memorial Shrine, January 2010.

3. Rex C. Myers, ed., *Lizzie: The Letters of Elizabeth Chester Fisk, 1864–1893* (Missoula, MT: Mountain Press, 1989).

4. Florence Fisk White, "The Autograph Quilt," unpublished manuscript, MC 31, Box 4, Folder 2, Fisk Family Papers, Montana Historical Society Archives.

5. Letter, Elizabeth Chester to Robert Fisk, November 15, 1864.

6. Myers, *Lizzie*, 9.

7. Inscriptions from the quilts, as quoted in Virginia Eisemon, "Sunday School Scholars Quilt: Civil War Textile Document," in *Uncoverings 2004*, vol. 25, ed. Virginia Gunn (Lincoln, NE: American Quilt Study Group, 2004), 57.

8. Ibid., 46.

9. Eisemon, "Sunday School Scholars Quilt," 78.

10. Smithsonian Institution, National Museum of American History, Behring Center, "Collections," http://americanhistory.si.edu/collections/object.cfm?key=35&gkey=169&objkey=7218.

CHAPTER 8
Stars and Stripes, the Teter Quilt

1. *Peterson's Magazine* 40, no. 1 (July 1861), color plate frontispiece.

2. Other Stars and Stripes are in the collection of the Museum of the Daughters of the American Revolution as well as several other museum collections, and references are found on the Quilt Index.

3. Smithsonian Institution, "Life & Culture: Union Quilt," www.civilwar.si.edu/life_unionquilt.html.

4. Florence Wilson Houston, *Maxwell History and Genealogy* (Indianapolis: C. E. Pauley, 1916), 362–65.

5. The obituary as quoted in Doris Bowman, *The Smithsonian Treasury of American Quilts* (Washington, DC: Smithsonian Institution Press, 1991), 57.

6. http://ahnenwald.net/Ahnenwald_T-D_civilwar.html=Teter's in Civil War.

7. Houston, *Maxwell History*, 364.

8. United States Census, 1850 through 1930; available at www.ancestry.com; accessed July 2010.

9. Smithsonian Institution, "Life & Culture: Union Quilt," www.civilwar.si.edu/life_unionquilt.html.

CHAPTER 11
In War Time: The Jane A. Blakely Stickle Quilt

1. Barbara Brackman, "Signature Quilts, Nineteenth-Century Trends," 27–30.

2. Examination of the Bennington Museum catalog records, accession number 2064, March 15, 2013.

3. Donna Bister and Richard Cleveland, *Plain and Fancy: Vermont's People and Their Quilts as a Reflection of America* (Gualala, CA: Quilt Digest Press, 1991), 60–61.

4. Brenda Manges Papadakis, *Dear Jane: The Two Hundred Twenty-Five Patterns from the 1863 Jane A. Stickle Quilt* (West Warren, MA: Wrights, 1996).

5. Pamela Weeks, "The Jane Stickle Quilt: 'In War Time, 1863,'" *Walloomsack Review* 11 (Spring 2013): 25–32.

6. Examination of the Jane Stickle Quilt, collection of the Bennington Museum, accession number 2064, March 15, 2013. Thanks to Callie Stewart, collections manager, for her assistance with all available resources.

7. "Vermont, Bennington County, Manchester District Estate Files 1779–1935" images, FamilySearch (http://Familysearch.org), accessed 2013. Citing Probate Court, Supreme Court of Vermont, Montpelier: Box 3, images 692 to 742, Last Will and Testament of Erastus Blakely. The records include the probate inventory of his estate.

8. By a Lady, *The Workwoman's Guide* (London: Simpkin, Marshall, 1838), 181. Reprinted by Piper, 2002.

9. "Jane (Blakely) Stickle, Quilter," http://kduncanquilts.blogspot.com/2015/07/jane-blakely-stickle-quilter.html, accessed in September and November 2018.

10. United States Census, 1830 through 1940, index and images accessed through Ancestry.com.

11. Shaftsbury, Bennington County, Vermont. Deed book 25, page 140. Charles Thatcher and Charles Welling, administrators of the estate of Erastus Blakely, v. Walter P. Stickle and Jane A. Stickle, June 10, 1878.

12. "Annual Reports of the Town Officers of Shaftsbury, Vermont"; for the years 1880 to 1896, located at the Office of the Town Clerk.

BIBLIOGRAPHY

General Quilt History:

Kiracofe, Roderick. *The American Quilt: A History of Cloth and Comfort, 1750–1950.* New York: Clarkson Potter, 1993.

Orlofsy, Myron, and Patsy Orlofsy. *Quilts in America.* New York: McGraw Hill, 1974.

Inscribed Quilts:

Atkins, Jacqueline Marx. *Shared Threads: Quilting Together—Past and Present.* New York: Viking Studio Books, 1994.

Brackman, Barbara. *Clues in the Calico: A Guide to Identifying and Dating Antique Quilts.* McLean, VA: EPM, 1989.

Brackman, Barbara. "Signature Quilts; Nineteenth-Century Trends." In *Quiltmaking in America: Beyond the Myths.* Edited by Laurel Horton, 20–29. Nashville: Rutledge Hill, 1994.

Clark, Ricky. "Mid-19th-Century Album and Friendship Quilts, 1860–1920." In *Pieced by Mother: Symposium Papers.* Edited by Jeannette Lasansky, 76–85. Lewisburg, PA: Oral Traditions Project of the Union County Historical Society, 1988.

Quilt As You Go:

Fanning, Robbie, and Tony Fanning. *The Complete Book of Machine Quilting.* Radnor, PA: Chilton, 1980.

Civil War Era Quilt History:

Beaver-Buffington, Karen. "A Quilt for General Grant." In *Uncoverings 2004.* Vol. 25. Edited by Kathlyn Sullivan, 109–28. Lincoln, NE: American Quilt Study Group, 2004.

Bonfield, Lynn A. "Quilts for Civil War Soldiers from Peacham, Vermont." In *Uncoverings 2001.* Vol. 22. Edited by Virginia Gunn, 37–64. Lincoln, NE: American Quilt Study Group, 2001.

Chase, Loretta B., and Nan Coor-Pender Dodge. "The Dublin Quilt: A Civil War Textile Document." In *Uncoverings 2011.* Vol. 32. Edited by Laurel Horton, 129–55. Lincoln, NE: American Quilt Study Group, 2011.

Gunn, Virginia. "Quilts for Union Soldiers in the Civil War." In *Uncoverings 1985.* Vol. 6. Edited by Sally Garoutte, 95–122. Mill Valley, CA: American Quilt Study Group, 1986.

Henley, Bryding Adams. "Alabama Gunboat Quilts." In *Uncoverings 1987.* Vol. 8. Edited by Laurel Horton and Sally Garoutte, 11–24. San Francisco: American Quilt Study Group, 1989.

Horton, Laurel. "South Carolina Quilts for Civil War Soldiers." In *Uncoverings 1985.* Vol. 6. Edited by Sally Garoutte, 53–70. Mill Valley, CA: American Quilt Study Group, 1986.

Papadakis, Brenda Manges. Dear Jane: The Two Hundred Twenty-Five Patterns from the 1863 Jane A. Stickle Quilt. West Warren, MA: Wrights, 1996.

Ramsey, Bets, and Merikay Waldvogel. Southern Quilts: Surviving Relics of the Civil War. Nashville: Rutledge Hill, 1998.

Shaw, Madelyn, and Lynne Zacek Bassett. Homefront and Battlefield: Quilts and Context in the Civil War. Lowell, MA: American Textile History Museum, 2013.

Weeks, Pamela. "'One Foot Square, Quilted and Bound': A Study of Potholder Quilts." In *Uncoverings 2010.* Vol. 31. Edited by Laurel Horton, 131–60. Lincoln, NE: American Quilt Study Group, 2010.

INDEX *Index*